REVIEWS FOR OTHER GHOST BOOKS BY TROY TAYLOR

Troy Taylor has done it yet again. In HAUNTED ILLINOIS, the author has hit that rare (and delightful) middle ground between fascinating paranormal research and compelling storytelling. His stories will put you on the edge of your seat and his insights into the supernatural will keep you there. A rare and delightful find and a must-read from one of the best ghost authors writing today.
MARK MARIMEN, author of the **HAUNTED INDIANA** Series

Troy Taylor's HAUNTED ILLINOIS manages to capture the spookiest aspects of life on the prairie in a way that no other book has done. For those who believe that Illinois is merely corn fields and forests, he only needs to read this book to realize that strange things are lurking on the midwestern plains.
DAVE GOODWIN, author of **MILITARY GHOSTS** & Others

If you are looking for the real history, hauntings and weird stuff of Illinois, then look no further than Troy Taylor's HAUNTED ILLINOIS titles!
You won't find anything else like them on the market!
KEITH AGE, President of the **LGHS** & Host of Sci-Fi Channel's **SPOOKED**

Troy Taylor works hard to unearth new hauntings and to keep the old lore alive. In spite of this, many of the stories which shaded our cemeteries and lingered over our abandoned buildings are lost. So while some of us wonder about the light burning in the old warehouse, or quicken our step in the dusky graveyard, or pause to make sure those are our own footsteps echoing off the attic wall, most of us won't. Yesterday's stories, like yesterday's spirits, draw their power from being remembered. In the absence of memory, legends die, and like forgotten ghosts are left to fade away.
JOE RICHARDSON --- ILLINOIS COUNTRY LIVING Magazine

GHOST BOOKS BY TROY TAYLOR

HAUNTED ILLINOIS BOOKS
HAUNTED ILLINOIS (1999 / 2001 / 2004)
HAUNTED DECATUR (1995)
MORE HAUNTED DECATUR (1996)
GHOSTS OF MILLIKIN (1996 / 2001)
WHERE THE DEAD WALK (1997 / 2002)
DARK HARVEST (1997)
HAUNTED DECATUR REVISITED (2000)
FLICKERING IMAGES (2001)
HAUNTED DECATUR: 13TH ANNIVERSARY EDITION (2006)
HAUNTED ALTON (2000 / 2003)
HAUNTED CHICAGO (2003)
THE HAUNTED PRESIDENT (2005)
MYSTERIOUS ILLINOIS (2005)
DEAD MEN DO TELL TALES: BLOODY CHICAGO (2006)

HAUNTED FIELD GUIDE BOOKS
THE GHOST HUNTER'S GUIDEBOOK (1997/ 1999 / 2001/ 2004)
CONFESSIONS OF A GHOST HUNTER (2002)
FIELD GUIDE TO HAUNTED GRAVEYARDS (2003)
GHOSTS ON FILM (2005)
SO, THERE I WAS (With Len Adams) (2006)

HISTORY & HAUNTINGS SERIES
THE HAUNTING OF AMERICA (2001)
INTO THE SHADOWS (2002)
DOWN IN THE DARKNESS (2003)
OUT PAST THE CAMPFIRE LIGHT (2004)
GHOSTS BY GASLIGHT (2007)

OTHER GHOSTLY TITLES
SPIRITS OF THE CIVIL WAR (1999)
SEASON OF THE WITCH (1999/ 2002)
HAUNTED NEW ORLEANS (2000)
BEYOND THE GRAVE (2001)
NO REST FOR THE WICKED (2001)
HAUNTED ST. LOUIS (2002)
THE DEVIL CAME TO ST. LOUIS (2006)

BARNES & NOBLE PRESS TITLES
WEIRD U.S. (Co-Author with Mark Moran & Mark Scuerman) (2004)
WEIRD ILLINOIS (Barnes & Noble Press) (2005)
HAUNTING OF AMERICA (2006)
INTO THE SHADOWS (2007)
SPIRITS OF THE CIVIL WAR (2007)

-The Haunted Field Guide Series -

SO, THERE I WAS.....

MORE CONFESSIONS OF GHOST HUNTERS

BY TROY TAYLOR & LEN ADAMS

- A Whitechapel Productions Press Publication -

Troy: *I'll save most of the room here for Len but, of course, I want to thank Len for all of his help, hard work and support over the years. He is one of my favorite people in the world and it was my pleasure ---- and honor --- to do this book with him. I had hoped to follow my earlier "Confessions" book with an update at some point but the chance to do it with Len moved the book to the top of the schedule.*
Thanks also to all of my friends in the American Ghost Society and the paranormal field for the great times that we have had over the years --- with many more to come!

Len: *There are so many people to thank for bringing this book to fruition. First of all, my good buddy and mentor, Troy Taylor. Your friendship means more than you know. Also ---- AGS reps, authors, tour guides and good friends, Ursula Bielski and John Winterbauer. Have we ever not had a good time when we've been together? My wonderful team of Luke Naliborski, Julie Warren, Bill and Louise Alsing, and Matt and Kelly Blunt. You nut-cases keep me young. My family who've supported me and most of the strange ideas I've had over these many years. Thank-you Megan, Josh, Andrea, and, of course, the light of my life, Kim. I love you all. My mom and dad for keeping me around, even when their better judgment told them to run! And last, but not least, a special thank-you to the major influence for me in this field of the strange and weird. Yes, Virginia, there is a Santa Claus and his name is John Brill. God bless you all.*

Original Cover Artwork Designed by
© Copyright 2006 by Michael Schwab &Troy Taylor
Visit M & S Graphics at www.manyhorses.com

This Book is Published by:
Whitechapel Productions Press
15 Forest Knolls Est. - Decatur, Illinois - 62521
(217) 422-1002 / 1-888-GHOSTLY
Visit us on the Internet at http://www.prairieghosts.com

First Edition - April 2006
ISBN: 1-892523-44-2

Printed in the United States of America

- THE HAUNTED FIELD GUIDE SERIES -

Welcome to the new book in a continuing series from Whitechapel Productions Press that will be dedicated to providing the readers with "field guides" to not only haunted places, but to ghost research as well. In the books to come, we will continue to take you beyond the edge of the unknown and provide detailed listings, maps and directions to haunted places all over the Midwest and America, plus additional books on ghost research and more!

We hope that you continue to enjoy the series and that you will journey with us in the future as we take you past the limits of hauntings in America and beyond the furthest reaches of your imagination!

Happy Hauntings!

TABLE oF CoNTENTS

SO, THERE I WAS...

FOREWORD

He nodded to himself, like a man who feels secure in the conclusion that he has just reached. "I guess this is the point in the conversation where you tell me that you don't scare easy," he said.
"Being scared isn't the problem," I replied. "It's not running away that's the hard part."
John Connolly

Come with me on these exciting explorations and judge for yourself. I have not colored the accounts in any way; they happened exactly as I describe, and it is possible that you can suggest a cause or solution. If so, I would like to hear from you, as I would if you know of a haunting that cries out for personal and private investigation. I have long been of the opinion that 98 percent of reported hauntings have a natural and mundane solution but it is the other 2 percent that have interested me for more than 40 years.
Peter Underwood

It is this question as to the truth or falsity of intercommunication between the dead and the living, more than anything else, that has claimed my attention and to which I have devoted years of research and study. Sir Arthur Conan Doyle says in one of his lectures: 'When one has a knock at the door, one does not pause, but goes further to see what causes it and investigates, and sooner or later one discovers that a message is being delivered...' So, I have gone on to investigate the knocks.....
Harry Houdini

Welcome to another journey into the weird world of ghost hunters.

That's the most fitting opening line that I could find for this book of strange stories, amazing tales and just plain goofy happenings from the adventures --- and frequent misadventures --- of investigators for the American Ghost Society. In the pages that follow, you'll find a number of odd tales of ghost hunts, paranormal investigations, spirited tours, haunted overnights and more. You'll also find two voices within these pages, that of myself (Troy Taylor) and my friend, Len Adams, who helped to compile this book of some of our strangest cases --- and most entertaining outings. For the most part, we'll alternate the chapters that follow, providing a look at different stories (and occasionally, different viewpoints of the same one) and chronicling a number of years of haunting research.

In addition to Len and I, you may also hear from a few American Ghost Society members and be introduced to many others. Some of the names within the text have been changed to not only protect the innocent, but the unwitting and the inebriated as well.

However, if we did change a name or two here and there, or left out an embarrassing moment that happened to someone other than ourselves (we've got plenty to be embarrassed about!), we can promise that what you are about to read is "real". In other words, these are "real" stories that, for the most part, "really" happened to us. The reader may judge the truth of each tale for himself but keep in mind that usually when I write about a haunted location, I can't really vouch for the veracity of the tale. In the stories and accounts that follow though, I can --- and so can Len.

Where to begin? That's an easy one.

So, there I was.....

Troy Taylor & Len Adams
Spring 2006

TRoY) INTRoDJCTIoN

Sometimes when you write about the things that I do, I wrote in an earlier book called *Confessions of a Ghost Hunter*, you become a part of the story, whether you want to become part of it or not. That's what that particular book was about and that's what this book is about as well --- becoming a part of the story. In this case though, I'm joined in my adventures, and often misadventures, by my friend, Len Adams, who is not only the Chief Operations Officer for the American Ghost Society, but he is also the head guide for the Alton Hauntings Ghost Tours that we started in Alton, Illinois. Together, Len and I have had more fun chasing down ghosts --- and occasional wayward tourists --- during our ghost tours and paranormal investigations than either of us can even remember.

And it's funny that Len ended up working with me on the Alton Hauntings Tours. It was because of that tour that we met in the first place. Len and his wife, Kim, came on one of the tours that I was hosting back around 2000 or so. I vaguely remember this guy (who would not go away!) who told me about how his relatives used to be gangsters in southwest Illinois back in the 1920's and 1930's. I heard from him again a short time later (and yes, he was still telling the same story) and we became fast friends soon after. Len remains one of my closest friends, and "haunted staffers", to this day. In fact, I think it's fair to say that the Alton Hauntings Tours couldn't run without him!

In addition, Len and I also spend much of our time in pursuit of the ghosts that inspire the tours and the books like the one that you are now holding in your hands. It's all of the research that has gone into the books and tours that has made them successful. Over the past several years, Len has made a name for himself in the field of ghost research and over the past 10 years or so, since the founding of the American Ghost Society in 1996, I've managed to (reluctantly) become known as one of the leading authorities on ghosts in the country. Thanks to some of the books that I have written, namely the *Ghost Hunter's Guidebook* and a few others, people have come to me looking for standards, ideas and (God forbid) rules for ghost hunting. For the most part, I have been happy to accept the role as someone to come to for help. I have been involved in this field for nearly two decades and I have done a lot of research into ghosts and hauntings, which is what I base all of those ideas and standards on.

With that in mind, I have often recounted anecdotes about my ghostly outings in lectures and books, offering my past experiences as a way that other people can learn about investigations and paranormal research. But ghost hunting isn't always pretty and to be honest, I have never been much good at following rules ---- even my own. Much of the ghost hunting that I have done (and I'm sure that Len can agree) has not exactly been "according to standards" and in fact, has often not been anything that I would offer as a "how-to" for other ghost hunters. I've done a lot of things over the years that I specifically tell other people not to do --- go on an investigation alone for one thing ---- but I swear that I have done all of them for the benefit of the field.

And for a little excitement too, I have to confess.

But isn't that why you bought this book? To hear some of the "confessions" of ghost hunters who don't always do things by the book? Isn't it so you can read about some of the uncensored, behind the scenes misadventures that plague the so-called "authorities" in the field? I thought so ---- and well, you won't be disappointed.

In addition to our ghost investigations, you'll also find a lot of about the strange things that sometimes occur during the ghost tours and haunted overnight excursions that both Len and I host in Illinois and beyond. We always insist to everyone who comes along on our tours that we can never guarantee that anything paranormal will happen in the course of a tour but, we always tell them, be warned that some very bizarre things have happened in the past.

What kinds of things? How about.....

Closet doors that open and close by themselves?

Ghost lights that appear and disappear?

Automobiles that move by themselves over haunted railroad crossings?

Objects that move around purportedly haunted houses?

Full-figured apparitions?

And you can bet there is even more than that within these pages!

But why ghost tours and how did I get started in such a weird business? As it turned out, the tours were really an offshoot from the books. I had wanted to be a writer my entire life and, at about age 12, discovered the world of true ghost stories. After finding out that someone could actually make a living by traveling around the country and writing about ghosts and hauntings, I was hooked. Around 1993, I started a small publishing company and a year later, started work on what would turn out to be my first book, *Haunted Decatur*, which chronicled the ghost stories and haunted places of Central Illinois, where I had grown up.

It would be the publicity that was garnered by the book project that led to the founding of the Haunted Decatur Tours. The publicity started with a small newspaper article that talked about my plans for the book and mentioned that I was looking for additional stories and material. The article led to television interviews from all over Central Illinois, which led to a flood of stories from all over the region. I was also contacted by a number of local radio stations and many of them began expressing an interest in having me do shows on local haunts for the coming Halloween season.

Around this same time, I was at the home of my friend Skip Huston and he and I began talking about the idea of putting together a tour of some of the haunted places in Decatur. The possibility of the book had gotten such a great response, so why not give people the chance to actually experience the places that they could read

Although a caption like "The Three Stooges" is tempting... This is actually the cast of the Alton Hauntings Ghost Tours. (Left to Right) Luke Naliborski, Troy Taylor & Len Adams

about?

At that time, Skip was hosting a popular radio show for a local radio station and he took the idea of a "Haunted Decatur Tour" to the station manager ---- who quickly dismissed the whole thing as being ridiculous. No one, he insisted, would want to buy tickets to drive around town on a tour to look at places that were supposed to be haunted. Skip persisted and spent the next couple of weeks begging for a shot at it. Finally, mostly because of the popularity of the show that Skip was doing, the manager agreed that the station would sponsor the tour but since he was convinced that no one would buy the tickets, we would have to give them away for free on the air.

While we were a little disheartened by the lack of support for the tour, we figured that it would get the word out for the upcoming book --- even if the word only got out to the people who called in for the free tickets. When the morning came for the tickets to be given away, we expected the worst. Even though a full-page article had appeared in the newspaper touting the tour and giving me a huge space to promote the book, the station manager continued to insist that we would be lucky to get the 50 people that we needed to fill the bus. The on-air people announced the tickets and we waited for something to happen.....

The first call came in to claim tickets, followed by another, and another ---- ending with over 600 calls on the first morning! We stopped counting how many people called later on in the day and in the week to follow before Halloween. The bus was filled in a matter of a few minutes and so the on-air personality suggested that those who were unable to get on the bus should come down to the pick-up spot in case something opened up. Again, we were assured that the interest in the tickets was a fluke and that no one would show up to be put on the waiting list. As it happened though, another 400 people showed up on the night of the tour! And the Haunted Decatur Tours were born!

That was the first year and we were assured that it would never last. Sure, lots of people came for free tickets but wait until we tried to sell them the next year ----

the tour would never happen. For those who don't know, the Haunted Decatur Tour is still going as of this writing, now solely hosted by Skip, although I do occasionally return for guest tours. Skip took over the tours when I moved to Alton, Illinois in 1998 ----- and started a whole new set of tours.

In 1999, we launched the History & Hauntings Tours of Alton (now known as the Alton Hauntings Tours) and also began offering tours in nearby Grafton, St. Charles and St. Louis, Missouri. These new tours shifted from outings aboard a trolley to walking tours, which made them even more successful than we could have imagined. In a short time, Len Adams began helping out with the tours and we have since been joined by Luke Naliborski as another guide, as well as Julie Warren, Steve Mangin, Kim Adams, Len's daughter Megan, and a few others as our assorted assistants or, as we call them, our "cabooses". The walking tours now visit many of the most haunted places in Alton, a town that has gained a reputation for being "one of the most haunted small towns in America." As you will see in the pages to come, many of the locations on the tour will make an appearance in this book. As we always say ---- we never guarantee anything supernatural will happen on the tour but .... well, you get the idea.

In 2000, the tour business took another turn with the founding of the American Hauntings Tours, which began offering haunted overnights and excursions to spots in Illinois and Missouri. Eventually, we expanded to include sites all over the country. In past years, I had host-ed an annual Halloween event where people had the chance to spend the night at a haunted place. With the American Hauntings Tours, we decided to offer such a chance on a regular basis and began setting up locations all over America. These tours, like the others tour we were already doing, were not with incident --- as you'll see in the pages to come.

The Weird Chicago Bus

We continued to grow and things changed again. In 2006, I took back over the tours from my friend, Skip Huston, in Decatur and in the fall of that year, started the Weird Chicago Tours with my friends Ken Berg and Adam Selzer. These new tours were based on my book *Weird Illinois*, as well as on the experience that all three of us had with hauntings (and strange stuff) in the Windy City. With those guys, along with assistance from Len, Luke, John Winterbauer and Haven Starrett (Taylor), what were once several different tour companies were placed beneath one banner ---the Illinois Hauntings Tours, which now offered tours in Alton, Chicago, Decatur and Springfield, Illinois. These tours, along with the American Hauntings Tours, have certainly made us busy but they have also provided great material for the book that you are about to read. If you think that ghost tours are nothing more than entertainment for the general public, and don't offer anything for the diehard ghost enthusiast, think again!

Between the weird happenings, strange stories and mysterious events from ghost tours and ghost hunts, this book is jammed full of "confessions" that are sure to both educate and entertain... well, entertain anyway. The education may come from knowing "what not to do" in the future, but I think you will have as much fun as Len and I did when we were looking back and recounting these stories.

LENS INTRODUCTION

If anyone had told me that, at the ripe old age of 50, I would be a paranormal investigator, I would have told them they were batty!

Growing up, I had a love of horror flicks, not the garbage they spew out today, but the classics; *The Wolfman; Dracula; Frankenstein;* the Hammer films and Vincent Prices' Edgar Allan Poe flicks were my bill of fare. Unfortunately, they had repercussions. On many nights I lay in bed, covers wrapped tightly around my body so the monsters couldn't get me. I was so afraid of the dark that when I had to go down the hallway to my room, I would carry my sister, Robin, who was three years younger, under my arm to feed her to the evil that I knew was waiting for me. My mother said I could turn the switch in the back of the house and be in the living room before the light went out. These were my early years.

Halloween, which is still my favorite holiday, held no terror for me, only candy! As a teenager I still loved horror films. Because I was older, they could be explained away as only something Hollywood created, but then came *The Exorcist*! Being raised Catholic and attending Catholic grade school in the 60's I was fed a steady steam of God's wrath and the evil all around us. Possession was a result of being bad, a punishment. I attended *The Exorcist* with a group of 20 of my friends. I didn't sleep for the next 3 nights! That demonic face still haunts me, as do my years of grade school. I've been able to overcome Catholic school, but not the face of evil.

A 1961 photo of Len and his sister, Robin --- often referred to as "monster bait" for whatever was hiding in the shadows of their house.

I met my current wife, and she'll kill me if I don't say my only wife, two years after high school. Neither one of us had any money. We did have something more important though. We had a love of the horror classics. There was a program in the mid 70's on WSIU Carbondale, channel 9 on the old black and white TV. It was called Monster Horror Theatre, hosted by Irv Coppi, and it was on every Friday night at 10 p.m. Kim and I, popcorn and soda at the ready, would lose ourselves in the classics. This passion, and our two children have kept us together for more than 29 years.

Despite this love of horror films, I still denied the possibility of something out there that was real; something legitimate.

Kim and I married on October 16th, 1976. On April 15th, 1979, our daughter, Megan, was born. At this time my father-in-law, Bob, and his second wife, Doris, lived in a farmhouse in Okawville, Illinois. This house, and the property around it, had been in Doris' family for many generations. On many a Saturday, Kim and I would load up Megan in the car to travel the 25 miles to the old farmhouse. The days were spent working around the farm and the nights were spent at Original Springs Hotel. Dinner at the hotel always consisted of fried chicken with all the fixings. Of course, an ample amount of beer was needed to wash everything down. You don't grow up half-Irish and half-German and not drink beer. After dinner at the hotel, we would sit on the porch at the farmhouse and tell stories. On many nights, the stories would take a ghostly turn. Bob, Doris, and Doris' brother, Richard, who lived next door, would tell us tales of the hauntings in the house and on the property. Bob, whose stock and trade is being a draftsman, had fixed up one of the downstairs bedrooms for his office. Because he was his own employer, he could work whenever he wanted. On more than one occasion, Bob would be at the drafting table well Into the night.

One night, around midnight, Bob told us that he was working at the drafting table and a shadow moved across him and his work station. For this to happen, someone, or something, would have had to move behind him and in front of the ceiling light. Of course, when he turned around, no one was there.

Richard Baer, Doris' brother, had lived in the house until Bob and Doris moved in. Richard is a very down to earth, quiet individual. He'll speak up when he has something to say. If he doesn't, he's as quiet as a church mouse. During one of our ghost story sessions on the back porch, we were all stunned when Richard smiled and said that he had a few strange experiences in the house. Now, we were the quiet ones.

Richard said that while living alone in the house, he would hear footsteps upstairs, see doors opening and closing, and see shadows moving from room to room. He laughed when describing how the kitchen faucets seemed to have a life of their own.

Richard worked the many acres of the family farm. That's why, when Bob and Doris moved into the farmhouse, Richard bought a mobile home and moved it next door.

One evening, while walking towards the farmhouse, Richard saw a young girl sitting on the back porch steps. As he entered the yard through the back gate, he saw that the girl appeared to be in her late teens. She was clad in an old fashioned white dress and had long curls in her hair. The young lady was sitting on the steps crying. As Richard approached her, he asked if she was okay and whether she needed help. He said the young girl lifted her face out of her hands, looked him in the eyes, and simply vanished. When questioned by Doris why he never shared this story before now, Richard simply stated, " I didn't think anyone would believe me."

Doris was the kindest, sweetest person you could ever meet. The sharpest criticism I can ever remember her saying of someone was that a particular person was not very nice. Although sharing many of the same experiences as Bob and Richard,

A cracked old Polaroid photo of Bob & Doris' farm house near Okawville. Even this old photo doesn't accurately portray how creepy this house could be.

Doris tended not to share them as readily. She preferred a quieter approach to the problem. Doris had religious items spread throughout the house. The items didn't slow down the paranormal activity, but they made her feel better and more protected.

I, of course, never believed any of it. You need to know that I was born in Missouri, and the saying is true, "You have to show me for me to believe."

One Saturday in November 1979, after dinner and tall tales, we all retired for the night. Kim and I would sleep in the living room on the hide-a-bed sofa. Megan would be in a bassinette next to us. What makes this night so frightening for me was what happened earlier that day.

During the mid-afternoon, I was helping Bob move some bedding and frames up to the second story. The second story consisted of 2 bedrooms on opposite sides of a long hallway. The end of the hallway had a door that opened onto a balcony. Doris' daughters were coming for a visit so the bedrooms, which were normally empty, needed to be fixed up. Around 2:00 p.m., as I was assembling a bed frame in the hallway, I noticed Bob standing next to me. I thought it was him because I could see his legs. I kept rambling on about all we had to do, not letting it sink in that he wasn't responding to any of my questions. After a few minutes, I heard footsteps coming up the winding staircase that led to the second floor. This was to my left as I knelt on the floor. As the foot falls reached halfway up the staircase, I noticed that they were coming from my father-in-law. Turning to my right, I saw that the person I had been talking to wasn't Bob, but a tall, well-proportioned man in overalls and a dark shirt. He had a small beard, Amish in appearance, and graying hair. The look on his face was one of anger. He had evidently been standing and staring at me the whole time. I turned back a second time to glance at Bob on the steps. When I turned back to my right the figure had vanished. My only thoughts and emotions were, what the hell was that!? Not once was I scared. I didn't tell anyone what I had seen because I didn't want to appear as nutty as they were. Over dinner, this episode was forgotten.

Around midnight, as I lay in the hide-a-bed, I felt nature's call. Yes, I had had some beer at dinner, but not the usual gallon and a half that I normally had. Nature's call was soon answered and, as I was washing my hands at the bathroom vanity, I looked into the medicine cabinet mirror. Standing behind me was the farmer I had seen earlier in the day! I spun around and there was no one there. Turning back to the mirror he was still there. Spinning around again, there was no one. Looking into the mirror a third time, he was gone.

Now he had my attention and now I was scared! I raced into the living room and jumped into bed right up against Kim. Her response to my terror and need to be close was to inform me that it was too late and she wasn't in the mood.

This was the first, but far from the last, episode in this house. Over the next two years, we would be witness to shadows moving across walls, disembodied voices, footsteps in empty rooms, and of course, the apparition of the farmer.

One Saturday night, after our trip to the Original Springs Hotel for dinner, someone produced a Ouija Board. I had never used one before and thought they were just a stupid game. When Bob suggested we use the board to try to contact the spirits in the house, I was all for it. I didn't believe that anything would actually happen, but what the heck --- I was willing to give it a shot.

Bob and I sat down at the kitchen table with the planchette under our fingertips. After making each other swear that we wouldn't move it, we were ready to begin. Kim and Richard were seated on the other side of the table, pen and paper in hand, ready to record any answers we might get from the spirits. Doris was holding Megan and standing off to the side.

We started with the usual questions, such as, is anybody here, how many, etc. The planchette was going wild, spelling out answers to our questions. At one point, Bob and I were staring at each other, positive the other was moving the thing. As we did that, it still kept answering our questions. It wasn't us moving it around. After 30 minutes of this, Bob asked if we could help the spirit in some way. That's when Doris grabbed the board off the table, ran out onto the porch and flung it into the yard. "You never ask something like that," she screamed at us. "You're just inviting trouble!"

Whether we were or not, I didn't know. A name we did pick up that night was Adam. On researching former owners of the property, we did find a family that had a son by the name of Adam. Was it he that was haunting the property? What about the Amish- looking man and his wife? Yes, she started to appear also. Mostly they were now seen in the detached summer kitchen. That's where Bob kept his tools for home repairs and projects. When he would ask me to go and get a wrench or hammer, I would tell him to get it himself. I was staying inside with everyone else.

Days and nights at the farmhouse were now taking a comical twist. No one wanted to be in the house by themselves. A trip to the bathroom brought a look of relief (literally) or one of, I can't believe what just happened! Even after the two upstairs bedrooms were finished, they were still used primarily for storage. Between Bob and Doris, they had kept a multitude of old books and magazines, along with quite a few antiques. Kim is an antique nut and I will read anything I can get my hands on. We would often go upstairs to wade amongst the treasures of the past, but never alone.

One spring day, Doris decided to organize the upstairs by putting the extra antiques in one bedroom and all the books and magazines in the other bedroom, which was directly across the hall. That weekend during our normal visit , Kim and I decided to venture upstairs. It was 2:00 p.m. on a bright and beautiful day. What could happen?

Sunshine, warmth, and the sweet smell of honeysuckle greeted us on the upstairs landing. We smiled, as surely nothing could ruin this wonderful day. It didn't take long to realize the changes that Doris had made. It wouldn't be a problem. The bedroom doors faced each other across the hall. We would leave the doors open so we could see one another. Nothing would ruin this adventure.

After about 10 minutes, I yelled across to the other room to see how Kim was doing. On receiving no reply, I turned to leave the room I was in and make my way across the hall. From the open doorway of my room, I could see Kim standing, transfixed and in horror, as the door to her room was slowly closing under its own power. I would love to say that I made a mad dash for the closing door to save my wife. I would love to say that but ---- it didn't happen that way. I casually walked over to the door , opened it, and then surveyed the room. The only thing out of place was Kim. She was pale as a sheet and frozen to a spot in front of the window.

On questioning her, she said that she had a distinct feeling of being watched. On turning around, she saw the door, though propped open, start to close on its own. I know what you're thinking...... old house, old door, things settle and move on their own. I will agree with that , but this door was propped open. When it started to move, the doorstop that held it open was now five feet away. The door came to a complete stop halfway through, then started to move again before closing completely.

I opened the door without a problem and, on further examination, could find no reason for it to move on its own. It was hinged and weighted properly. It only opened and closed under someone else's power.

We decided that this was a good time for a break. Surely someone would need our assistance downstairs.

About an hour later, I got the urge to return to the bedroom that held the treasure trove of books. Kim said that she would go also, if I would stay close. We wandered around the antiques in the one bedroom, until the pull of the bookroom cast it's spell on me. I slipped across the hall and into the other bedroom. Both doors were propped open to prevent their closing. Kim could see me, no problem.

After 20 or 30 minutes had elapsed, I was sitting on the bedroom floor, lost in a book on ancient history. Surely, by now, Kim realized that I was across the hall. As I exited the room to check on her, I saw that the other bedroom door was closed again. I turned the knob and the door opened without a problem. Standing just on the other side of the door was Kim, tears in her eyes. "Where were you?" she screamed. I had to take her downstairs before she would calm down.

I asked her what had happened. Kim said that when she realized that I had left, the entire room changed. Although it was warm outside, the bedroom had become icy cold. She knew it was time to leave. When she got five feet from the door, it slammed shut! She pounded on the door and screamed for me. To her, it seemed like an eternity before I showed up. All I can say is, that the entire time I was in the other room, I heard nothing. The only reason that I ventured back across the hall was because I saw that the door was closed.

From that time on, any trips that I made upstairs were made alone.

Whatever, or whoever, was haunting the upstairs bedrooms was not content to stay there. One night, after our ritualistic dinner of chicken and beer at the Original Springs Hotel, Kim and I were hunkered down in the living room of the house in the hide-a-bed.

What was unique about this room was that in the old days, before the funeral homes were in full use, people used to lay out their deceased loved ones in the living rooms or parlors of their homes for viewing. The living room where we were sleeping was used many times in this capacity. On this particular night, I slept (ironically) like a dead man. I don't think a stick of dynamite could've woken me.

Around 1:00 a.m., Kim awoke with a start. The sound of footsteps marching through the rooms upstairs had gotten her attention. As this had been heard upstairs on a regular basis, this was nothing new. To Kim though, these were different. The footfalls weren't of someone casually walking around as they usually were. These were louder and more purposeful. Kim tried to wake me up to listen to the commotion upstairs. I was literally out cold. What happened next terrified her beyond imagination.

As the footsteps grew louder, Kim said that they left the upstairs bedrooms and made their way down the hall. From there, they grew louder and louder, as they then descended the winding staircase into the parlor below. From the parlor to the living room that held our bed was a total of 12 steps. The footsteps continued until they stopped at the foot of our bed! As if on cue, I immediately woke up. As I rolled over, I saw Kim sitting upright in the bed, eyes as big as fifty-cent pieces. It was becoming a habit in the old farmhouse for me to ask Kim what had happened. After telling me about the footsteps, I bravely decided that we should take Megan out of the crib next to our bed and let her sleep with us.

I eventually fell back to sleep, but by the look of Kim's eyes the next morning, she never did. That was one of the last nights we spent in the house. We had originally gone out on weekends to relax and unwind. We were now going home totally stressed out. Weekends in Okawville were now spent looking over your shoulder, waiting for something to happen.

In 1981, Bob & Doris moved to Phoenix and they told us that the window fan they had left at the farmhouse could be mine if I wanted it. All I had to do was go and get it. It was a warm and pleasant summer day. The house was vacant and I was told where to find the hidden key. I had to work that day, which meant that I wouldn't get to the farmhouse until early evening. Because it was summer, with plenty of daylight, this wouldn't be a problem.

Now, I've always been a fan of vampire films but there is one thing in almost every one of them that drives me crazy. Why, when the hero wants to kill the vampire, and he knows where it is, does he wait until its almost sundown to go and do it? How stupid can he be? Why would you go and do something so terrifying when it's almost dark?

Instead of arriving at the farmhouse around 5:30 p.m., I met some friends at the hotel for a couple of beers, and then went to my destination. I wasn't killing vampires, but I was going alone into a haunted house. The house had electricity, but no permanent light fixtures. It was now 7:30 p.m. and the sun would be gone by 8:00.

So there I was.....

And yes, I was now the stupid hero of my own ghost story. I entered through the rear of the house by way of the porch. From the porch, I would have to enter the kitchen, then the parlor, then up the stairs to the second floor bedroom, which held my window fan in its clutches. Yes, this was the same bedroom with the cold spots and the magical door but I knew I could do this and announced to the house my intentions.

Just in case I needed to make a quick getaway, I left the kitchen and porch doors open. I made my way up the stairs and into the east bedroom. I now had 15 minutes of daylight left. No problem, I thought, the fan was propped in the window just waiting for me. I opened the window and grabbed the fan to sit it on the floor. I soon realized, when the fan wouldn't budge, that it was screwed into the windowsill. Now what?

Luckily, I had a pocketknife with a screwdriver attachment and set to work on freeing my fan. Of course, I didn't realize that the four screws holding my prize were three inches long! Halfway through the second screw, I realized that the room was now in the shadows.

Sweat rolled down my forehead and my arms ached as I hurriedly kept working at the screws. Then a feeling came over me that I was no longer alone. At one point, as I felt someone directly behind me. I spun around and saw that the bedroom door was closed. This was the same door that I had propped open to get some light from the west side of the house. I screamed, "I'm only here for the fan. Bob and Doris said I could have it!"

I don't remember if I removed the last two screws or ripped the fan from the sill. I only remember slamming the window and running for the stairs. As anyone who's been on a ghost hunt with me will attest, I have no night vision. It hasn't gotten worse as I've aged. I never had it at all! This didn't stop me from hitting the stairs, fan in my arms, at full speed! Miraculously, I made it down the steps and into the kitchen. I made a sharp 90 degree turn to the right and ran smack dab into the now closed kitchen door. As I got to my feet and picked up the fan, the water in the sink somehow came on full blast!

I threw open the kitchen door and ran across the porch to my car. My heart was racing and I was drenched in sweat. I survived! I made it! Ummm, I forgot to lock up the house! As much as I wanted to leave, I promised Bob I would make sure that everything was locked up good and tight. I usually have a pretty long stride when I walk, but now I was tip-toeing. I made it through the porch to the kitchen door. As I stepped in, I noticed the kitchen faucets weren't running anymore. I did remember to close the bedroom window, so I didn't have to go any further. As I stepped from the kitchen to the porch every water fixture in the house seemed to come alive. From the bathroom, which was next to the kitchen, I could hear the toilet flush and the shower running. The kitchen faucets came back to life as I slammed the door and locked the deadbolt. As I turned to escape the porch, I almost fell into the cellar whose doors were now wide open! I leapt over the opening and ran to my car. As I sped away, I cursed my cheapness for wanting a free fan so desperately.

What makes a location become haunted? Is it due to a tragic death or other occurrence? Or can it be due to an imprint woven into the fabric of time? The farmhouse in Okawville seems to be in the perfect location for a residual, as well as an intelligent haunting.

If a residual haunting is an imprint of the past that replays itself over and over, then this particular area is ideal for this to happen. The age of the farmhouse means that many have lived and died there. But the ground that the house sits on may have a tale or two of its' own. During our walks across the fields, we would often come across Indian arrowheads and shards of pottery. Quite a community must have thrived there at one time. Also, the house is only a half-mile from the Kaskaskia River. The old homes, with their wells supplied by underground sources, and the river so close, would make the area a logical spot for paranormal activity. Steams and underground waterways act as paranormal highways. Locations atop these "highways" are usually teeming with things that go bump in the night.

The house also seems to have its share of intelligent hauntings. From the Ouija Board episode to the encounters with the bearded man and his wife, the spirits of the past interact with the living.

During the mid 80's, a new family moved into the farmhouse. The summer kitchen and back porch were torn down. I've talked to others that know the new owners. Not one word has been said about ghosts. Possibly, by altering the houses' configuration, all paranormal activity stopped. Another possibility is that the activity was connected to Doris, Richard and their family because they were there for so long.

Whatever the answers are, I'll never forget the farmhouse as being my springboard into a life-long quest for the answers that lie just beyond our reach.

In the years to come, my interest in the paranormal took a backseat to the trials of everyday life. From the early 80's to the late 90's, Kim and I were occupied with two children, four residences, several jobs and quite a few pets.

One October in the late 1990's, Kim told me about a haunted tour in Alton, Illinois, hosted by Troy Taylor. I had been a reader of Troy's books for about a year and enjoyed them immensely. His *Haunted St. Louis* book really held my interest. When he explained how violence often spawns a haunting, and then used the old St. Louis gangs as an example, I was hooked. One of the gangs he wrote about was the Hogan gang, run by Edward "Jellyroll" Hogan and his brother, James. They just happen to be my great-great uncles. The more I read, the more I realized that Troy knew as much about my family's past as I did. I had to meet this guy!

Not knowing how fast the tours sold out, I called for a reservation --- and learned that they had been sold out for quite some time. Fortunately for me, two people had to cancel their Saturday reservations. When the night of the tour came, I was really excited. I could actually go into some haunted locations with a lot of people. I would be scared, but thankfully, not alone. As Kim and I entered the History & Hauntings bookstore, I was awestruck by the amount of books dealing with the paranormal. This was a ghost enthusiast's paradise.

Before the tour, I got to meet the great man himself. Kim and I checked in with Troy as he stood behind the counter. Not being able to control myself, I immediately started telling Troy about my connection to *Haunted St. Louis*. The look on his face was one of mild concern. He probably thought, just great, another dingbat on the tour.

The tours at that time were on board a trolley. As much as I wanted to discuss all aspects of hauntings with Troy, I soon realized that so did everyone else. When the tour was over we were told about the American Ghost Society. The next day I spent some time going over the website. I decided that this is what I had been looking for. My quest would be to help unravel the mysteries of the paranormal ---- the game was afoot!

I became a member of the American Ghost Society. I eventually became an area rep. I honestly can't say if the promotion was because of all the reading and studying of the paranormal that I did --- or the countless phone calls and e-mails to Troy that followed me joining the group.

Whichever it was, I can honestly say that it was one of the best happenings in my life. Troy is one of my best friends, ghosts or no ghosts. Through Troy and the AGS, I've met so many wonderful people, and yes, some unique people. I'm still an area rep, but also, the Chief of Operations and Investigations Coordinator for the organization. I'm working with fellow paranormal enthusiasts in England and Wales to set up a paranormal investigation exchange program. I belong to the best investigative team in the world and I'd match them against anyone. The team consists of myself and Kim; then fellow area rep, Luke Naliborski; History & Hauntings bookstore and national headquarters owners, Bill & Louise Alsing; investigators, Julie Warren, Matt Blunt, my daughter, Megan Stroot, and son, Josh Adams and his girlfriend, Andrea Easlick. I would march through the gates of hell with these people but of course ---- we would make Luke go first. Our group enjoys each other's company. We know when to be serious and when to start cracking the jokes. We also don't agree on everything that happens, but, being friends and family, we can debate the pros and cons of each issue that arises.

As the old saying goes, most people can count their true friends on one hand.

Using my hands and my feet wouldn't be enough to count the friends I've made in this field. I'm truly blessed in that respect.

I've even been able to turn an unforeseen disaster in my life into a positive thing in the field of the paranormal. In October 2004, I was having a really rough go at work. I worked heavy construction for a local utility company. By the end of each day, I could hardly move and the pain throughout my body was intense. By the end of the month, I couldn't even stand erect. After a multitude of doctors and tests, it was determined that I had degenerative arthritis (osteoarthritis) brought on by my many years of heavy labor.

By June of 2005, having just turned 50, I was starting to fight depression. The arthritis was throughout my spine. Everything hurt, even parts of my body that had nothing wrong with them. The neurosurgeon suggested physical therapy at St. Elizabeth's Hospital in Belleville, Illinois. On my first day of therapy, I saw men and women much younger than I dealing with tragedies much greater than mine. There were folks suddenly missing limbs, trying to learn how to deal with the little every-day things in life. Although every move is painful, how could I complain when I could still open my eyes and get out of bed in the morning? My whole attitude changed. The pain, and its side-effects, is now just another part of my life. I've accepted the cards I've been dealt and decided to play out the hand.

This negative has now become a real asset when doing paranormal investigations. Because I've been slowed , I now can be a better observer of all the things around me. As my body has been slowed down, my mind has picked up the pace. Slow and steady does win the race. Of course, the team immediately jumped in to help. Without hesitation, they grabbed the gear and help me set things up. Luke ---- who was always the "bait" anyway ---- goes into the little nooks and crannies that I can't anymore. And, because I no longer have a real job, I have more time to collect stories and do initial interviews.

Helping Troy with the Alton tours has also been a plus. I'm supposed to walk, walk, walk and walk some more and what better place to do all that walking than in Alton, where everything seems to be haunted.

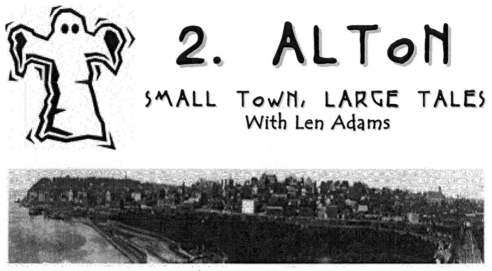

2. ALTON
SMALL TOWN, LARGE TALES
With Len Adams

Alton, Illinois --- One of the Most Haunted Small Towns in America

Alton, Illinois is a hotbed of cold spots.

From the time that I attended my first History & Hauntings Tour on a trolley to the present day, when I am the main guide for the tours, I can honestly say that something very strange is going on here.

For those that attend our tours, the first thing you'll hear us say is that we won't guarantee that anything supernatural will happen. Every place that we go to has been investigated by us. We use the history of the locations to explain the hauntings. We don't tell you what you should see or feel, only what has happened at the location in the past or has happened to us, and others, on the tours or during the investigations. You make up your mind whether it's real or not.

You can find out about the history of the locations I'm going to talk about by reading Troy Taylor's book, *Haunted Alton*. In these pages, we want to tell you about some of the wild and crazy things that have happened to us during the tours.

THE MERIDIAN COFFEEHOUSE

In my opinion, the Meridian Coffeehouse building is one of the two most actively haunted locations in Alton. It was a fixture on our tours for years but it had changed hands a lot and not all the owners had been enthusiastic about us being there. I'll let Troy interrupt here for a moment:

Troy: I first started investigating the coffeehouse back in 1998, shortly after moving to Alton. Some readers will remember the investigation that I did (alone, of course) in the building one winter's night that had me calling things off early and going home. I never had any doubt that this was a haunted place.

I had talked to a lot of people about the hauntings here, many of who claimed to have their own personal encounters. However, it was not until I started bringing tour groups to the coffeehouse, that I started to witness these happenings --- and the guest's reaction them ---- with my own eyes.

One night, during a History & Hauntings Tour, I brought a group to the building and we went up to the second floor to talk about the ghosts and strange sightings. Just as I was beginning to talk about the place, one of the attendees suddenly ran out of the side room where he had been standing and hurried down the stairs. I was a little startled but continued the story. When it was over, I gave the group some time to look around on their own and went downstairs to see if I could ask the man who had run through the tour group what was wrong. I found him standing outside on the sidewalk but he refused to talk to me about it. His face was quite flushed and he acted very nervous. I was acquainted with his wife and she assured me that she would see what she could find out from him and would let me know after the tour was over. At the end of the night, she took me aside and explained to me what had happened.

After coming upstairs, the gentleman had entered a dark side room and was looking around while the group assembled to hear about the haunting. Just as I started to speak, he told his wife that an icy cold hand had taken hold of the back of his neck and had shaken him. He was so frightened that he took off running through the group and had hurried downstairs. He refused to go back into the coffee house. Did it really happen or was it his imagination? I can't say for sure but I will tell you that he was quite upset about whatever did happen in that room and certainly had no reason to lie about it.

We continued coming to the Meridian for several years and our connection to it only ended when a "storefront" church of some sort took over the building and the owner, pastor or whatever he was, told me that he had chased all of the ghosts out of the building. The "church" didn't last long and we soon found out that his claim of having "busted" the resident ghosts was not even close to being true.

Len: In August of 2004, Nicki Dodson and Lori Mitchell opened Piece of Cake Theme Parties at the building where the Meridian had been located. Thankfully, they enjoyed us being there. We've done, and continue to do, tours and overnights at this wonderfully haunted location. Although I've seen and experienced many things at this old coffeehouse, the summer and fall of 2005 were especially active.

We bring the tours into the main level of the building to start our tales. Then, we move upstairs. Because the upstairs has changed, with smaller rooms rather than a large open area, people now stand in open doorways and dark corners with us in the middle of the room telling the stories. You would think that having more people in the room would make it less frightening. Oh, no! Having folks standing in the locations where activity has reportedly occurred, causes many sideways glances and more than a few shuffling feet. However, not all scary happenings can be attributed to the paranormal.

In the summer of 2005, on an otherwise beautiful evening, I was checking in our tour guests, as usual. Five minutes before the tour was to start, two ladies staggered into the bookstore. I won't tell you where they were from, but... okay, it was Chicago. As they gave me their names, I almost keeled over from the whiskey fumes emanating from them. Apparently, they had taken a side trip to a distillery before coming to the tour!

I had a feeling that I needed to keep an eye on them and I was right. By the time we made it to the Meridian, I was ready to strangle both of them. They either had alcohol with them, or were being supplied by every bar we passed.

The upstairs stories became a train wreck. As one of the ladies sat passed out in a booth downstairs, the other kept interrupting the tour with such comments as, "Will you hold me if I'm scared?" I managed to get through the stories, and to my delight, the woman had disappeared. Not hearing anyone tumbling down the steps, I assumed she found her friend without too much difficulty. After apologizing to the sober tour guests, I repeated any stories that had been interrupted. Everyone then got to walk around and take photos.

As the group went downstairs to gather for the trek to the next location, I did my usual sweep of the upstairs to make sure we left nothing behind. I noticed a light on in one of the bathrooms that had not been on before. When I opened the door, I received a shock! Sitting on the toilet, pants around her ankles, and passed out, was the offending story interrupter. Before I could react, (honestly, I didn't know how to respond to this) the drunken woman awoke and let out a hair-raising scream. I screamed, not expecting anyone to be in there. Averting my eyes, I asked what she was doing in there. Her response was, "What the **** do you think I'm doing in here?"

My patience had now reached its limit. Through the closed door, (yes, I am a gentleman) I informed the drunken patron that she had 30 seconds to come out or I was leaving her behind. It only took 10. Out the door she came, hopping along while pulling her pants up. After she made it downstairs, I stood in the darkness of the upper floor and began to laugh. To any ghost that was unseen but around me, I exclaimed, "And they're afraid of you!?"

During the spring and summer, I also tried experimenting with dividing up the tour and taking a smaller group upstairs and then switching them off. One tour in May was just such a night. The group was so large, that I broke them into thirds. The first third came and went without a hitch. The second group would be different.

My second group consisted of about 20 patrons. I seated them in a semi-circle in the main room so that I could see all of them. We did this because, on an average of every other tour, somebody thinks it's humorous to scare their wife or girl-friend ---- or the tour host. I warn you now! Jumping out of the dark at us will only result in you getting a flashlight, and a large one at that, smacked across your head. If you come out of the dark, we don't know if you're friend or foe, real or ethereal. We will defend ourselves, so be warned!

In this second group was a young lady in her late teens or early 20's. She sat at the end of the semi-circle with her boyfriend. She was a cute gal, who was thoroughly enjoying the tour. At this time, while talking about one of the ghosts that has been sighted in the red room (it's called that because of the horrible paint job) I stepped out further into the room than normal. No more than four feet from me, in the shadows of the room, stood a man with a plaid shirt, dark pants and nothing from the knees down. I don't mean shoes and socks ---- I mean from the knees down, there was nothing to see!

On our tours, we see things move around the group all the time. Usually it's a shadow or a door moving. We're used to it and keep moving along but this time, I was definitely stopped in my tracks. I don't remember if I blinked, or shook my head, or what but in an instant, he was gone. My reaction was to just keep going and keep the tour moving.

As I turned around and started to speak again, the young lady I just mentioned, started to scream, "Did you see him, did you see him?" I asked her what she saw. She said she turned to follow me into the room and, as she did, she saw the same man I did. She described him exactly, without me telling her what I saw. Then she screamed, "He was there, then he was just f***ing gone!" My angelic-looking tour guest had the vocabulary of a sailor. Her words, rather than scaring everyone, broke us all up instead and everyone started laughing. The wild part was that I saw the ghost, she saw the ghost, but no one else saw him. I wouldn't have said anything to the tour if she hadn't. I don't believe you should bait your guests, or tell them what they should be seeing. Also, I can't blame her for swearing. Having worked construction, I know all the words. When I get scared, I have no problem using them, either.

October seems to have more sustained activity at the Meridian than any other month. I believe it's because of all the tours. Throughout the entire month we're taking large tours, (thank-you to everyone) one after the other, into the place. I do believe that all that energy helps keep the place stirred up. There's nothing stronger than human emotion! By the end of the month tour patrons were getting more than they bargained for.

By October, we had gone back to taking everyone up at once. It just seemed to work better. On one particular tour, as I was talking in the middle of the group, I turned to see a young lady just before she screamed. She was terrified because her ponytail was standing straight up in the air! She jumped up, clawing at the air, as if she was covered with a spider web. She was terrified but I thought it was great!

No more than five days later, as I was upstairs amidst another group, I turned towards the red room. Two young ladies were standing in the doorway of the room. Behind them was a white face, but no body. Before I could react, they both screamed and ran out of the doorway. I immediately went into the room with my flashlight. No one was there! After the girls calmed down, I asked them what had happened. Both said that they felt breathing on their necks and a hand on their shoulders. Having seen a face floating behind them, I didn't feel that it was only their imaginations.

Filming with Channel 4 at the Piece of Cake Bakery. (Left to Right) Luke Naliborski, Virginia Kerr from Channel 4, Len Adams & Nikki Dodson

When November rolled around, I thought that I would get some rest. The fall tour season was over and we don't do many tours during the winter due to the hills of Alton, mixed with the bad weather.

One morning though, I got a call from Nikki at Piece of Cake and she told me that the CBS affiliate's (Channel 4) morning program in St. Louis wanted to feature the Meridian on a morning broadcast. The reporter for the assignment was Virginia Kerr and she wanted to have a paranormal investigator on site to explain why the Meridian was so haunted. I couldn't pass up this opportunity to promote the American Ghost Society.

Because it was a weekday that we would be doing this, it was a little hard to assemble the team. Remember, the rest of the team have real jobs, I don't. I was able to get Luke, it was his day off, and Julie, because her husband could watch the new baby during the early morning hours that we would be doing the ghost hunt.

At midnight, Luke, Julie and I met Nikki at the Piece of Cake Theme Party building (old Meridian). A few moments later, Virginia Kerr and her cameraman arrived. Introductions were made and our quest for positive publicity began. I gave Virginia all the historical background on the building that Troy had so painstakingly researched. Next, Luke, Julie, and I filled her in on the hauntings. We then taped some footage at the front of the building to have on file. Next, we went upstairs. For anyone who's ever been to the old Meridian Coffeehouse, you know that even though the entire building is haunted, more things happen upstairs.

Luke, Julie and I set up our equipment. As we set up, we explained what we were doing and why we were doing it. Then by the light of a lone candle, I started asking questions of the entities that might be present. During this time, several large orbs were filmed. One spectacular shot was of an orb moving behind Julie as she was filming. It moved around her and into the next room.

After about an hour, we decided to move around a little bit. Julie and Luke were standing out in the large room talking as I sat in the infamous red room with Virginia. Just as Virginia's cameraman came into the room, Virginia screamed as the hair on the right side of her head flipped out to the side as if pulled by an unseen hand. Not being ready for this, she screamed quite loudly, while jumping out of the chair. I was no more than four feet from her and saw the entire episode. The cameraman saw it, but his camera didn't have a night-shot mode, so he missed it. My video camera was pointed into the room, but blocked by the cameraman.

Later on, we had a door slam next to us while upstairs. That was all for this night.

Though not ghostly, the next couple of hours were exciting for me. I got to edit all of our footage with Julie and Luke. Julie had to leave, motherhood was calling, which meant time to feed the baby. As Luke slept in one of the downstairs booths, I worked our footage with their editing guy, who had just arrived in the Channel 4 news van. I learned quite a lot about the whole process of putting on a good report. Virginia went over a few notes to make sure she had the facts straight. Then, it was show time! From 6:15 a.m., until 7:45 a.m., we were featured with Nikki and the Meridian at least five or six times. Some friends taped the program for me, and I must say, Virginia and the Channel 4 team were great. While having fun, they treated us with respect. In this field, that's very hard to get.

To me, the old Meridian just seems to sit and wait for us. Whether we're bringing a tour through, or just visiting Lori and Nikki, the place does not disappoint.

After a tour, the last thing I do is make a sweep of the upstairs to make sure we have everybody. In May 2005, my daughter Megan was the "caboose" for one of the tours. We made a sweep of the upstairs and decided that we had everything and everyone. Meg and I chatted for a couple of minutes in the red room and then we figured it was time to leave. As we walked across the large open part of the room that leads to the landing, we heard footsteps behind us. The footsteps were of a hard-soled shoe on a hardwood floor. The room we were in was carpeted and we had on tennis shoes --- it wasn't us! Even though I was a little scared, I went back and recreated the walk through the room. The only sound was a slight shuffling of my feet. I even tried to make the floor creak with added pressure. The sounds hadn't come from us.

Two weeks later, my caboose for the night was Luke Naliborski. The tour was peaceful, paranormal-wise, even by the Meridian standards. Luke and I did a sweep of the upstairs as the tour guests got ready for our next location.

As we exited the room, I heard the same footsteps as before, hard-soled shoes on a hardwood floor. Before I could say anything Luke whispered, "Did you hear that?" This was very exciting because nothing ever happens to Luke --- ever. Because of this, we use him for "bait" in many of our investigations.

The fact that Luke heard something was verification for me that I was not imagining things. I told Luke that I had also heard the footsteps. We made our way to the middle of the room, where we encountered an intense cold spot. It was like a funnel of frigid air in the center of the room. When I am in the midst of a paranormal occurrence, I usually get goose bumps and the hair on my neck, arms and legs stands up. Before I could look, Luke was showing me that the exact thing was happening to him. It was verification number two. Although we wanted to stay and investigate, we had a tour to do. The intensity of this event hasn't happened since, but we are always holding out hope.

Last, but certainly not least, my good buddy and AGS rep from Springfield, Illinois, John Winterbauer (who started hosting the Springfield Hauntings Tours in 2006) came down in October of that same year to go on a tour. Of course, I made him the "caboose".

When we arrived at the Meridian, I had all the tour guests get comfortable downstairs. While they were doing this, I took John upstairs to tell him about the things that had been happening lately. In addition to everything else I've written about, we now had furniture that was moving through the room. I would go upstairs before bringing the tour patrons up and put tape around the chairs and tables. Then, when I took everyone upstairs, I could see if something moved. We even had a chair move while we were all in the room!

As I was telling John the stories, he yelled, that he saw a figure move in another room. This was the blue room, so named because of its (also bad) paint job. The blue room has a large five-foot by five-foot glass block window along the back wall. The window was slightly illuminated by a street light and John had seen a figure walk past the window! After a thorough investigation, we found out what we already knew ---- no one was upstairs with us, that is, no one with a human body.

John's ghostly experiences for the night were far from over. On this tour, I was able to fit the entire group upstairs. John, as the "caboose", stayed at the top of the landing with another friend of ours who had come on the tour. As I entertained our patrons with supernatural tales, John and our friend sat on the landing listening to footsteps walk up and down the stairs for 10 straight minutes.

The stairs seem to be particularly haunted, but then, don't many staircases seem to be? What other location in a house or large building sees as much activity as the stairs? Forget someone dying. Human emotion and energy expelled on a staircase can't help but leave an impression behind.

I highly recommend a trip to the old Meridian Coffeehouse, a.k.a., Piece of Cake- Theme Parties. Remember, we never promise that anything will happen, but be warned --- it often does!

THE FIRST UNITARIAN CHURCH

During the Alton Hauntings Tours, the "cherry on the milkshake" is our last stop of the night ---- the First Unitarian Church. The building, or should I say the foundation, has been around since 1830. Two different fires have destroyed two previous churches on this site. The second fire was the original Unitarian Church, but unlike the Catholic Church that was there before it, the Unitarians stayed and rebuilt. The current church has been there since 1905, built on the 1830 foundation.

A few years ago Troy Taylor, and the American Ghost Society, was featured on The Learning Channel (TLC) around Halloween in a show about paranormal investigations. Troy, along with assistance from Luke Naliborski, told the story of the First Unitarian Church. (An account of this, from Luke, is featured later in this chapter)

Several hauntings in the church are discussed during the Alton Hauntings Tours. The most prominent would be the haunting by Reverend Phillip Mercer, a former minister of the church who committed suicide in the building. Over the years, there have been many people who have had strange encounters with his ghost on the main floor of the church. The sanctuary, and the large room beyond it, has such an atmosphere that whenever anyone enters it, they get the distinct impression that it is someplace special.

During the storytelling in the upstairs (where the Reverend Mercer haunting is centered), we have had doors in the sanctuary open and close, gusts of cold air blow by, and shadows move across the walls. Behind the altar, in the gathering area, is the spot where Reverend Mercer was found, hung by the neck in the doorway of a hall leading down to the basement. Access is from either side of the altar through some pocket doors. One set of the pocket doors is left open for our access into the back room. On an average of every third tour, we have had a tour guest gasp or scream as they see someone walk past the opening in the doors, which are behind me as I speak. Of course, every time we look for someone, no one can be found.

I mentioned earlier that during our tours, we see things move around and behind our guests all the time. This church is the most active for this kind of movement. As I speak, I often see shadows move across the back wall, entry doors open and close and silhouettes on the inside of the stained glass windows. These were nothing compared to my first experience with Phillip Mercer. About three years ago, in August, Troy was giving the tour on a Saturday night. I was the "caboose" that night and stayed in the back to make sure we didn't lose any stragglers. My wife,

Kim, was helping me that night.

As the group got comfortable in the sanctuary, Kim and I stayed to the rear. Kim sat in the last pew by the door to listen to the story of Phillip Mercer. I had heard it (and told it on numerous occasions) so I just paced across the back of the church. The real reason I was pacing was that I was so miserable because it was very hot in the church that night. It was sticky and stuffy since they obviously can't turn the air conditioning on just for us.

I soon realized that I might be distracting someone by my pacing, so I stood behind the last pew that Kim was seated in. I can only describe what happened next by saying that it was as if I had just stepped into a meat locker. It was freezing! Then, I felt someone brush across my back. It was like being on a crowded bus at rush hour. I spun around to see who had gotten behind me because I had always prided myself on never losing anyone on a tour but there was no one to be seen. As I turned back around, the cold sensation had left. Kim though, had definitely picked up on something. Although still seated, she was staring around the back of the church. After several seconds, she went back to listening to Troy.

It's about a 45 minute drive home for us from Alton. On the way, we decided to talk about the tour. I asked her how she enjoyed it and if anything had happened during the evening. Kim said everything was fine, except for one crazy occurrence at the church. During Troy's story in the sanctuary, she closed her eyes and lowered her head and just listened. That's when she felt the cold creep in around her. Upon opening her eyes, she now realized that she could see her breath. She turned around to ask me if I felt the intense cold and she saw a man in a white shirt, gray pants and black tie walk right behind me. She thought this was strange and turned again to tell me about it --- but the man had vanished. While this was happening, she missed the description of Phillip Mercer that Troy was giving. Kim turned pale on the way home when I told her the part of the story that she had missed. We were convinced that it was Reverend Mercer that we had seen. We had both had our first experience with Phillip Mercer. This would not be Kim's last.

On the night of October 30, we had our last tour of the Halloween 2005 season. It was a pretty large group for a Sunday night and assisting me that night was my good friend and AGS investigator, Steve Mangin. Steve was the tour "caboose" for the evening. The "caboose" is best compared to a cattle prod and he makes sure that everyone stays together and that no one is left behind. Our last stop of the tour that night was the Unitarian Church. As I completed my sanctuary portion of the tour, I then moved the group into the back gathering area. Steve, while making sure that everyone moved into the next room, said that he felt the sensation of being watched. Steve spun around and took some photos. When the film was developed, you could see a three-dimensional shadow that had been moving across the back of the sanctuary.

The gathering room, behind the sanctuary, has also had its share of ghostly experiences, some of which have been chronicled in Troy's book about Alton. Just for giggles and grins, we sometimes ask the tour guests to see if they can figure out where Phillip Mercer hanged himself. Everyone is reminded that the large room is much different than it was in 1936, when he committed suicide. Most of the people get a kick out of this morbid little game. When Troy would give the tours, and I was the "caboose",, I would stand in the spot of the hanging. Troy would then give me the nod and I would turn on my flashlight to reveal the correct location. Also, for added flair, I would yell, "TA-DAA!" Troy endured this with the patience of a saint.

Despite her first run-in with Reverend Mercer, Kim still went along on several more tours with me. About 10 months after her initial encounter, she helped me again. With nothing happening this time in the sanctuary, Kim felt safe. The feeling wouldn't last for long! As I stood in the dim light of the back room, waiting to turn on the flashlight and yell my famous line, Kim stood next to me. The moment came and the light went on, "TA-DAA!" I turned to Kim with a smile on my face, but she wasn't there. She was sitting on a bench, about 10 feet away, with her face buried in her hands. I sat next to her and asked her what had happened. As she lifted her head, her face was as white as a sheet. She was gasping for air and she said that she had to get out of the building. I took her out the side entrance and sat her on the steps. After a couple of minutes had gone by, she regained her composure. Kim told me that she had a bad feeling on entering the back room. That's why she stuck so close to me. As we were standing in the dark, waiting for the rest of the story where I turn the flashlight on, she started to feel a tightening around her throat. She felt herself gasping for air, so she sat down. Relief only came from me taking her out of the church. To this day, she has not returned to the First Unitarian Church and has no desire to ever go inside again.

During our expanded "ghost hunter's tours" with Alton Hauntings, we also go into the basement of the church. These tours have become so popular that we are doing more and more of them since the attendees get to see more of the buildings, and hear more stories, than they get to experience on a regular tour. From the basement area, we move into the original 1830 foundation of the church. This is a very haunted area, but I don't feel it's haunted by Reverend Mercer.

The original stones sit in silent testament to the history of this location. They have witnessed two major fires and three churches, along with countless people moving in and around over 175 years. By the time you also add on the fact that this was alleged to be a station on the Underground Railroad, you find the church's foundation has quite a sorted history.

Some of my favorite programs on The Travel Channel are the ones about haunted castles. Be they in England, Scotland, Wales, Ireland or France, many of them have one thing in common ---- the stones of which they are made. For a reason we can't explain, these stones seem to suck up psychic activity like a sponge, then hold onto it like a battery. What sets it off, we don't know. The foundation of the First Unitarian Church is just like one of these castles. This foundation has been there all this time and has soaked up the history around it. Time is something that constantly replays itself in the church. Believe me, I know .....

We had a problem, about a year ago, with someone locking the door into the back part of the basement. For awhile, as the tour patrons would seat themselves, I would have to go downstairs and make sure everything was unlocked. This journey would take me from the sanctuary to the back gathering room. From there, I took a short walk down the hallway to the basement steps. That led to another hallway with classrooms and offices. At the end of all of these halls were the doors into the original foundation.

Believe me, no matter how long you have been a ghost hunter, being by yourself in a scary location is not the most wonderful thing in the world. I would check the doors as quickly as I could, then go back to the tour as fast as I could. But after October 2005, I stopped doing this by myself.

During one venture, early in the month, I checked that all the doors were unlocked. As I turned to make my way back down the hall, all the lights went out, even the exit signs. I always carry two flashlights on me (because I can't see a thing in the dark) but neither one of them worked! I called out in the total darkness, addressing whoever --- or whatever ---- was down there with me. "I don't care", I said, "I'm still bringing everybody down here!"

After what seemed like an eternity, I found my way back upstairs. Julie Warren was my "caboose" that night and she wanted to know who I was yelling at down there. I told her what happened and she assured me that no one had left the group.

Two tours later, I returned to the basement to check on the doors. As I walked down the last hallway, flashlights and now, a non-battery operated glow stick in hand (just in case), I noticed that all the office and classroom doors were closed. I checked that the door into the church foundation was unlocked and then turned to make my way back. Every door in that hallway was now wide open! I mentioned earlier that I can't run due to physical limitations ---- but I sure have learned to walk very fast.

Because the church is our last stop of the night, I usually have to use the bathroom by the time we arrive there. So, I started using the upstairs church bathroom as the tour guests enter the building. I wasn't even safe going to the bathroom! Twice, I've had doors open and slam shut next to me as I made my way down the hall to the toilets. Hall lights have turned on, then off. Fear can be a very strong emotion, but nature's call will beat it every time. When I've gotta go, I'm like a bull in a china shop and nothing's going to stop me --- not even ghosts!

Some of the things that have happened to us in the church can be quite puzzling, and quite frightening. During a tour near the end of October 2005, I took the group into the basement. Despite all that had happened to me in that area, I felt no fear being with a large group of people.

After I finished the stories down there, most of the guests made their way back upstairs for the final goodnight speech. A young couple had held back to talk to me about something that had happened to them while we were there. As I chatted with them at the base of the steps, Julie Warren, who was the "caboose" again that night, came running down the stairs with two other ladies in tow. Wide-eyed and pale, Julie wanted to know if we were okay. Were we safe? We told her we were fine and wanted to know what had happened. Julie and the other two ladies said that while they were talking at the top of the stairs, they heard a woman scream as if in agony. The scream came from our location.

We had heard nothing.

It always amazes me how people in the same location can have different experiences. Can the ghosts show themselves to one person and not another, although they're standing side by side? Can this also happen with sound? As I've always stated, the deeper we go, the more questions we come up with.

The last incident that I experienced in the Unitarian Church during the Halloween 2005 tours was on Saturday, October 29. I was more than a little tired after almost nightly tours throughout October. Luke Naliborski and Matt Blunt (no, not the governor of Missouri, but a nice guy and friend of ours) worked the back of the tour to help me out. Luke also gives tours when we double up in October, or when I'm on vacation. By the time we were in the church, he and Matt could tell that I was exhausted. So, when it was time to go downstairs, Luke said they would do that part for me. This was perfect because Luke was the one who assisted Troy on the TLC special several years before. I helped them march everybody downstairs and then I turned to go back and make sure that nothing, or no one, was left behind.

Halfway down the lower hallway, I felt as if a wall of energy was coming right up behind me. There's no other way to explain it. I spun around to see and feel nothing though. As soon as I turned around to walk to the stairs however, I felt a hand shove me in the middle of my back. It almost knocked me down. My first reaction was "feet don't fail me now", and I made my way quickly back upstairs. We had all our belongings and people, so I went back downstairs. Thankfully, Luke and Matt were done by then and we all made our way back to the bookstore, none the worse for wear.

People often wonder if the First Unitarian Church can be as haunted as we maintain that it is with our tours and Troy's books. I can offer you this as further evidence....

One night in October 2005, I did a private bus tour for the Argosy Casino company, which owns the riverboat in Alton. There were about 35 patrons on the tour and only about a third of them had a clue about what was going on. The other two-thirds were either intoxicated or kept wondering aloud why we weren't still gambling on the riverboat.

Our first off-the-bus stop of the tour was the First Unitarian Church. We needed to go there first because they were having a large meeting later on that evening and we needed to leave before it started.

After we made our way into the back room, behind the sanctuary, and I finished with the stories, an older gentleman came out of the kitchen. Yes, he was real and yes, I knew he was there. His first words to the group were, "You know, I've been here for 30 years.....

I panicked. I was positive that he was going to say that nothing ever happened to him and that I was full of, well, you know what. What a disaster this would be for the tour! Thankfully though, he didn't say anything of the kind.

He continued, "....and in the 30 years I've been here, I've seen some strange things!" He then verified every story I told that night and added a few of his own. During the entire time he talked, I stood in the back and wondered if there was a way to hire this man!

SPIRITS oF ONE KIND --- OR ANoTHER

Saturday night seems to be the worst night for other kinds of spirits in Alton.

Our Alton Hauntings Tour is a walking tour of the downtown area, traveling near the Mississippi River and through our acclaimed antique district. Our path is a giant oval that takes us up and down the old streets and along the bluffs that the city is built upon. It's rare, but a few people do complain about the hills. My answer is always the same. Our tour guests only have to walk them once, I'm there almost every night. Troy has another reply --- in Alton, there are no right or left turns, just uphill and downhill turns. After awhile, those who spend much time here just have to get used to them.

Anyway, because we make our way through the downtown area, we pass quite a few bars and taverns that are open for business. On Saturday nights, especially in the warmer weather, we find these places of local spirits packed to the hilt.

One of our most popular stops is at the old Franklin House. Not only do our tour guests find the stories historically significant and entertaining, but so do many bar patrons. The Franklin House is in the center of about four taverns. On many a night, as I spin the tales of ghostly happenings at the location, I'll glance at the rear of the crowd and see three or four extras have joined our group. I can tell they were at a local drinking establishment because they have drinks in hand and are usually swaying back and forth. In their defense, I must say that I have never had a bar patron interrupt the stories, or cause a disturbance of any kind. I actually believe that they would go with us to the next stop if we served cocktails.

During the warmer weather, we do have a small problem with motorcycles and pick-up trucks. The riders and their machines are very loud and require me to stop speaking (even with a microphone and amplifier) until they pass. Also, especially on Saturday nights, we will have some folks hanging out of their pick-ups and scream-ing as they go by. If I had a dollar for every time I've heard, "Hey, ghostbuster!", I'd be rich.

I've done the tours for so long now that I've learned not to be annoyed by the commotion around me. Instead of being thrown off my game by the disturbances, I'll just yell back, "Love ya!", or something similar, and wait the two seconds for them to go on their merry way.

One of the stops on our walking tour is the alley where a police officer named August Mayford disappeared in 1946. I really enjoy this story and I believe the tour guests do also. This unsolved tale of murder is usually told at the alley opening. After that, we make our way to our last stop of the night, the First Unitarian Church.

One balmy summer night, I decided to actually take the tour group down the alley to the spot where August Mayford was last seen. The alley is dark and fore-boding and the perfect setting for the creepy story.

Some members of the group were scared and a bit tentative. If we only knew what lay ahead, we all would have been. As we made it to the end of the alley we came upon four individuals involved in a drug sale. Why this location, so near the police station, was chosen, I'll never know. I don't know which group had a bigger expression of surprise on their faces, them or us. Loudly, I yelled to the tour group, "Hey, let's go back!". Some members in the rear of the line wanted to know what was happening as the rest of us walked quickly past them. Always the proper tour host, I told them to move now --- or die.

At the top of the hill, we paused to catch our breath. That's when everyone was informed about our mad dash out of the alley. Rather than being upset and scared, these people got a rush out of being so close to future felons.

Since that time, I no longer take tours down the alley. The story is told from the safety of the lighted street at the top of the hill above the alley.

By the end of our tour, many of our guests feel safe and sound being back at the bookstore. If they wanted to be free of paranormal mischief, they couldn't have picked a worse spot however. The History & Hauntings Book Co. is one of the most actively haunted places in Alton. Before, during and after tours and conferences, we've had books disappear and reappear. Megan and I have stood talking before a tour and had a book fly by our heads and land on the floor 12 feet away! Footsteps have been heard throughout the store and many of the electrical fixtures seem to have a life of their own.

I do feel that many of our tour guests enjoy our little mishaps. As guides, we know the stories, but we don't have anything that is scripted. I've been on those kinds of tours and I find them extremely boring. We prefer to talk to you as if we were sitting around the fire and telling tales of the unknown. Our tours are interac-tive. We've been able to update many of our tales by patrons who give us little bits of information about locations and their owners.

Thanks to all of you for making our job so much fun and yes, a little bit scary!

HAUNTING ALToN WITH TLC
With Luke Naliborski

A few years back I had heard about this great store in Alton that sells books related to history and hauntings. I knew that I had to go there someday, but it was quite the drive from my home, so I didn't know if that day would come or not. That was until my wife, Heather, and I stayed in Grafton for our anniversary and I made the short drive to Alton. When I walked into the History and Hauntings Book Co., I was immediately captivated. I looked at everything I could get my grimy little fingers on. In matter of moments I selected two books (my first of many), *The Ghost Hunters Guidebook* and *Haunted Illinois*.

When I took them up to the counter, the gentleman told me about the Alton ghost tours, which I immediately signed up for. I remembered this guy from somewhere, but at the time, I couldn't place it. When I laid the books on the counter, he proceeded to open up each book and started writing on the first page. I was a little ticked off to say the least. What business does this guy have with writing in the books I just purchased?

When my wife and I left, I brought it up to her about how rude that was. As we drove away, she looked at what he wrote and she told me it was his autograph. Using my cunning and detective abilities and after seeing the photo on the back of the book, I realized that I had just come face to face with Troy Taylor. About a week after I went into the store, I realized where I had seen him before. It was in a classic movie called *The St. Francisville Experiment*. For those of you who have not seen this film, you are doing yourself an injustice. Not only did I have a brush with an author but also an actor! This turned out to be the start of my frequenting Troy's store. Even more importantly, throughout the past several years, we have built quite a wonderful relationship.

I guess Troy saw something special in me as we became friends. He must have had a keen eye for "up and coming" paranormal investigators because he was quick to take me under his wing and make me somewhat of an apprentice. One of our first investigations was in Salem at the McMackin House, a quaint little restaurant in Southern Illinois that had a deep history with the paranormal. To say I was excited that Troy would consider me for this task was an understatement. I had a head the size of the Waverly Hills Sanitarium as I pranced around my house gathering up my gear. It was a very "interesting" night for the two of us, and by all means, see Troy's section on it in the next chapter of the book.

Although this was a great time and I was very honored to have helped Troy with the investigation, it in no way, shape or form, compared to the next adventure in which I was about to partake.

In May 2003, Troy contacted me about doing another investigation with him. This time it was going to be in Alton at the First Unitarian Church. Before I could even say yes, he informed me that our investigation was going to be produced by The Learning Channel. For those of you who do not know me, I do like to entertain those around me. So with that said, the opportunity to appear on television, on a show that would air that Halloween, was a no-brainer!

I've acted before, so it wasn't something new for me. In 5th grade, I was a munchkin in a school play you may have heard of, *The Wizard of Oz*. In 6th grade, I took on a more demanding role as I played Ben Rogers. Ben Rogers was only one of the most important people who helped Tom Sawyer paint the fence. In high school I even had the lead in my school's musical, *Time and Time Again*. Basically this was the musical version of the movie *Back to the Future*. So in short, I was no stranger to acting and this was going to be my big break. All of these thoughts were going through my head as I muttered, "Three weeks from now? I'll have my people call your people". What Troy didn't realize was I was already doing the happy dance on the other end of the phone.

Brief History of the Church

The First Unitarian Church was built in the early 1830's. It was then called St. Matthews and was of the Catholic denomination when it first opened its doors. Unfortunately, a fire broke in 1855 and a new Catholic church was built across town. The only part of the original church that remained was the scorched foundation. The new Catholic Church was called Sts. Peter and Paul Catholic Church and was located on a hill deemed "Christian Hill". The previous property was then sold to the Unitarians and was renamed The First Unitarian Church. To show the feelings of the townspeople toward the Unitarian Faith, the location and hill that the Unitarian Church was located on was nicknamed "Heathen Hill".

The Unitarian Church and followers practiced their religion for many years at that location. That is, until tragedy struck as it nearly reached its 50 year anniversary. In 1904, another fire broke out in the building, and, once again, the church was destroyed leaving only the foundation. It was again rebuilt shortly after and finally, on the third attempt, the church has stayed erect and to this day, the entire original work from that church remains. Every time I think about this story, it reminds me of *Monty Python and the Holy Grail.* Each time the landowner built his castle on the swamp, it sank. That is until he built the third one, which was the strongest castle in the world.

Common knowledge in Alton is that a previous minister, Phillip Mercer of the First Unitarian Church, committed suicide inside the walls of the church in 1934. His body was found by one of his parishioners, James Makinney, on November 20th, 1934. His body was found hanging from the transom above a door. He was hanging there, with a broken neck, by a sash cord. There was no suicide note but no motive for him to have been murdered either. Reverend Mercer was loved by all those he came in contact with. He was a gentle, loving, and "high on life" kind of man and he was very well respected by his peers. With such a tragic thing as a man taking his own life, there certainly is the groundwork of a genuine haunting.

Reports of hearing music playing in the sanctuary run rampant. Visitors to the church have heard the sound of footsteps walking around with no one moving at all. Sometimes the smell of men's cologne fills the air as a cold draft blows past. There have been reports of shadows lurking around the Wuerker Room, just beyond the sanctuary. Not just any shadows either, these are shadows of a tall, slender person, much like the build of Reverend Mercer. Past ministers to the church have even reported seeing a man standing near a pew in the back of the church, only to see him disappear as they approached. All of these experiences make for great stories to tell, especially since we have experienced these things first-hand during our tours.

Here's where our plan for the investigation of the church comes into play. Proving the church to be haunted due to the minister committing suicide was not what Troy's intentions were for the television taping. Sure, a lot of the activity can be attributed to the minister's passing, but that activity is centralized around the sanctuary and the area where his office once stood. We already knew this to be true; we needed a challenge to push us to the limits of our intellect.

So, what about the basement? What could be causing the activities that are happening in that area of the church? One of the most common occurrences in the basement is that of different noises emanating throughout the building. Sounds of adults talking and singing are quite often heard, but also the sound of children. Sometimes happy, sometimes sad, either way a lot of emotion is still hanging around the basement of the church. The feeling that one gets while walking around in the basement seems to be more of an "uneasy" type of sensation. Perhaps fear, maybe desperation, either way we had our ideas of the cause to this phenomenon.

With that thought, we have finally reached the investigation part of this story. It was Troy's belief that this church was part of the Underground Railroad. Of course, there are no records stating that it was, but that's expected since no records were kept of anyone being involved with this service. So our plan for this show was to possibly use history to perhaps explain what was happening in the basement of the First Unitarian Church. See what you think.

Production Day

The show we were being taped for was called *Mysterious Worlds: America's Ghost Hunters* and it was going to be aired a couple days before Halloween in 2003. The show was set to showcase several paranormal investigative teams from all over the United States. Each team specialized in a different form of investigating the paranormal. There was Troy and myself, using history to help prove and explain why a place is haunted. Another team focused on Electronic Voice Phenomenon to record voices of the dead. A third team used a lot of high tech gadgets and a fourth team actually trained a dog to sniff out spirits. I can't help but think of the Sesame Street song, "One of These Things Is Not Like the Other" when I see this lineup. Well, three out of four isn't too bad, I suppose.

I had to leave work early that day to get to Alton in time for the investigation. Actually, I left a lot early, but I wanted to make sure that I didn't miss anything. Since I had some time to kill before the actual investigation was going to start, I spoke with the church secretary to hear some history and stories about the building. Although I had been to the building and I knew a lot of the history and stories from speaking with Troy and hearing his stories on the Alton Ghost Tours, it was still very interesting to get the opinion of someone who actually worked at the church. I must say I felt a little awkward at first. Most churches do not like to talk about their church being haunted. At least that's how it is in the states. Countries like England seem to be a little more open to discussing paranormal activities within a church's walls. The secretary began telling me stories of hearing noises coming from the sanctuary. Sounds of music playing, people singing, and other types of common noises would be heard at all times. When nighttime rolled around, it was very rare for anyone associated with the church to stay there after dark. If one person was to leave, everyone would leave because they wouldn't want to be left there alone. She expressed a sincere discomfort with some of the things going on around the church and oddly enough, it comforted me to have a chance to witness these things first hand. After speaking with the secretary for about 30 minutes, Troy and the production crew began showing up.

Now just to let you know, I was dressed for success. I had on my nicest pair of jeans, and a button-up dress shirt. I was having a good hair day, and my beard was nicely trimmed. Troy came wearing his usual jean shorts and denim shirt. For those of us who know Troy, I am convinced either he has his own denim clothing line, or he owns stock in Levi Strauss. Either way, I was about to be on TV!

We began the day with some shots of the outside of the church. The usual weird angles and close ups and zoom outs (if that's what they are called) that the production companies like to use as filler were filmed right away. I was getting concerned at this time because I hadn't really been on camera yet, but that was about to change. Well, kind of. We started to film some more filler material. A shot of Troy and I walking down the sidewalk in front of the church, a shot of us walking up the stairs followed, and finally through the front door. Although I was happy to be on camera at this point, I'm pretty sure my "behind" isn't my best profile.

Once inside the Church we met up with Peg Flach. She was a historian for the church who also experienced many strange happenings here. She too was to be used for the taping of this show. At first I saw her as competition for the camera, but that was short-lived once one of the production guys started filling me in on my role for the show.

My understanding of the investigation was that we were doing just that ---- investigating the church. What area or to what extent of investigating we were doing was beyond me. It wasn't until I was informed that I would be wearing a "hat camera" that I realized we may be investigating uncharted ground. The only uncharted ground I knew of in the church was the actual crawlspace. All of a sudden me dressing up for my "big break" was about to be a bad move because we were going to be getting dirty. But what the heck; the show must go on, right?

Once Troy got back from taping some segments with Peg, we started to gather our gear for the investigative part of the show. I was armed with a "hat camera" and a thermal scanner, Troy was armed merely with his digital camera and we both had flashlights. Not to sound too obvious, but a "hat camera" is a camera attached to the bill of a hat. It had a wire that came down behind my ear and ran under my shirt and into a hip pack. Inside the hip pack was a recording device that would tape the images captured by the camera. This camera had infrared so it would be able to record images in complete darkness. The thermal scanner is a device that can record temperatures in an area using infrared light. Above all the fancy tools we had, we were also armed with five other very important pieces to any paranormal investigation toolbox --- our senses.

As we approached the area where we were going to climb up into the crawlspace, I realized that we were about to crawl through dirt, rust, nails and most likely, asbestos. I felt pretty stupid at this point due to my choice of wardrobe. Those feelings were quickly remedied by Troy when I realized that he had his usual shorts on. Of course, Troy is the expert in this field and within minutes changed into a pair of pants at the bookstore, which was located only a few blocks away. That's Troy Taylor, always teaching me new things about the paranormal field. Lesson learned ---- always, always bring an extra pair of pants, not only in case of getting dirty, but also in case of soiling your pants out of pure fright.

Once we got into the crawlspace, it wasn't too bad. This may come to a surprise to some, but I think this area is called a crawlspace because we actually had to crawl to get through it.

There was an eerie feeling attached to this area and within seconds I already witnessed the largest orb I had ever seen in my life. I want to paint the picture for you as best I can. Imagine if you will, Troy crawling in front of me as we make our way under the church. I am crawling right behind Troy sticking close to him, not because I was scared, but just to make sure Troy was going to be okay in this scary setting. The camera on my hat was aiming straight ahead as I crawled through the rubble. The orb I captured was none other than Troy Taylor's backside. He must have been working out prior to the investigation because it was a perfectly-shaped orb. It was so bright, that while we crawled, I tried not to make eye contact as to protect myself from falling into its spell.

All joking aside, about halfway back through the crawlspace, Troy's digital camera went dead. The fully charged batteries were completely zapped of any life they had. I remember Troy's reaction to this was much like that of a kid who had his favorite toy broken in front of him by his old er brother. This wasn't the only thing to go wrong while were investigating the crawlspace. I'll get to that in a bit.

Digital camera or not, we had to press on. After crawling for what seemed like forever, we reached the back of the church. It was at this moment that we actually found something worthy of mention. In the far back corner of the church, we found an entrance to a little room. It would be my estimate that this room was approximately ten feet by ten feet with a height of around 48 inches. It seemed large enough for a person to crawl through the opening and sit comfortably in the room. It may have been bigger at one time. The debris under the church seemed pretty thick and it appeared to even clog up the doorway to the room. Once we found this room, we looked around, recorded some video and made our way back to the area where we entered the crawlspace. Oddly enough, although I was covered entirely in dirt and grime, a simple dusting off and my clothes became spotless. I wish I could say the same for my nose. I was still blowing dirt out of my nose when this show aired on TV in October, and we taped it in May.

If you have been reading my story word for word, (what do you mean you've been skimming?), you would have read where I mentioned something else happening after Troy's camera went dead. When we got our feet back on the basement floor and we were finally able to stand in the upright position, the production crew wanted to see the "hat camera" footage of the hidden room. Strangely, upon reviewing the tape, it actually stopped recording shortly after Troy's camera died. I was very upset at this because here we were, crawling through this rough terrain to find evidence that this was part of the Underground Railroad, and when we did find it, the camera didn't record the footage. Immediately, I told them to hook me up with another tape and batteries and we could crawl back in and try again. They actually said not to worry about it, they could make due with what footage we did have. I was surprised by this. What better way to prove our theory then to have a hidden room to justify the thought process. After a few minutes of going back and forth, they finally gave in and set me up for another go at recording the room. Bad move on my part.

Now ,when it comes to my investigative team, I am commonly known as "the bait" and/or "the meat" and sometimes just plain and simply known as "the rat". This is due to me always being the first to go into dark areas. Sometimes, I am the one who also gets shoved in to the small cramped doorways leading to who knows what. I am not really sure how I got this distinction because I am six feet tall and I weigh about 190, but that's part of the job. I don't mind doing it, because if there's treasure on the other side, I get first crack at it.

This time when they set me up with the new tape and batteries, I carried only the essentials. I had the "hat cam" on, along with the hip pack, and I had a little flashlight in my mouth. I climbed up into the crawlspace yet again. When I got everything in place to journey through the twists and turns, I asked if anyone was going to join me. The problem with that request was that no one answered me. Everyone had left and went back to the sanctuary to record more footage. So now I was in a dark, haunted basement, in an area where if I did get scared by a ghost, I couldn't even run away crying. My only chance would have been to either crawl away or lie there in the fetal position until help arrived. Unfortunately, I was about to partake in this task all by myself.

I will admit I was a little scared about this. I knew all the stories about the basement and I had seen enough scary movies to know that you never go into confined places alone. I can honestly say I had never crawled so fast in my life. If speed crawling were an art, my technique would have been considered masterful. I compare it to that of a cat in a litter box kind of movement. I was flinging dirt behind me as I made my way to the little room yet again. Once back there, I removed the camera from my hat, checked the recorder to make sure it was still recording and I actually put the camera into the room to better show the dimensions. Once I felt like I acquired enough footage to adequately prove our theory (about five or six seconds because I got scared), I made my way back into the basement. I dusted off, wiped off my scared expression and went back upstairs like it was nothing to be down there by myself. They had just finished filming and were getting ready to call it a day, thus ending my first televised investigation.

So, to answer the questions about the room and the possibility of the church being associated with the Underground Railroad. Here are a few things to take into consideration as you make your judgment. This room actually falls outside of the church's foundation. Not only does it fall outside of the original foundation, but it isn't even listed on the floor plans for the church. If you consider the difficulty required to get back to this room, it seems very strange that a church would require such a hidden location. Did I say hidden location? Also known as a location to hide things? Would the church need to hide Bibles, hymnals or candles? Perhaps, but most likely, it was probably used to hide more precious things --- like human lives. It would also explain why the sounds of people singing emanate from the basement. Escaped slaves would often find comfort by singing as it would give them hope for a better tomorrow.

The whole experience of this day will last me a lifetime. I told everyone I knew that I was going to be on TV, and if they didn't watch it, I disowned them. Now, Len has expressed some jealousy because of Troy selecting me over him, which is understandable. Len is much better looking than I am, and Troy wanted to be the center of attention for the program. The camera loves Len, as do the cold spots.

This day in my life was also the start of Troy following me wherever I went. When I went to Adams, Tennessee for the Bell Witch Festival, Troy followed me. When I went to Louisville, Kentucky to see Waverly Hills Sanitarium, Troy followed me. In fact, he also followed me the second time I went there just last year. When I went up to Decatur to the Lincoln Theater, Troy was right behind me. I've been teaching him everything I know, even when it comes to giving tours.

You have now entered my shameless plug section. Just recently, I have been honored with actually helping Troy Taylor and Len Adams conduct the Alton Hauntings Ghost Tours. Whether I am just helping out with keeping people in line, or when I am actually giving the tour, more things have happened at the First Unitarian Church than any other site. Well, actually, a lot has happened during our tours at Piece of Cake Theme Parties (formerly the Meridian Coffee House) as well, but we are talking about the First Unitarian Church, so I'll stick to the topic at hand. The church definitely has its share of activity. Both upstairs and downstairs seem to be inhabited by different spirits. The tours we do will actually take you inside the First Unitarian Church where you can listen to the stories in the same area the tragic events unfolded.

For those of you interested in coming on a tour, keep in mind that Troy's tours are an "Alton Original", my tours are the "Young and Hip" tour, and Len's tours are the "Old and Crusty" tours. Some of you may smirk at this remark, but don't be upset, I am sure Len made fun of me at some point in this book as well.

3. DINNER & SPIRITS AT THE MCMACKIN HOUSE
with Troy Taylor

Located a short distance from the downtown area of Salem, Illinois is a grand old mansion that was once home to the McMackin clan, known as Salem's "first family". The house has been the birthplace of leaders and over the years, has welcomed prominent visitors, celebrities, Illinois governors and an assortment of figures both famous and infamous. It continued its transition from family home to funeral parlor to a stylish restaurant and now, to an apartment building. Throughout all of this though, one thing about the house has never changed and this is the presence of the McMackin family themselves. Although none of the present members of the family reside within these walls today, it is said that past generations of the McMackin's have never left.

In November 2002, I had the chance to visit the McMackin House at the invitation of the owner at the time, who operated a restaurant in the old mansion. I was joined by Luke Naliborski, who I'm sure didn't have any idea as to what he had signed up for when I asked him to come along!

The McMackin Family

The McMackin family came to Salem back in 1850. The patriarch of the family, Warren E. McMackin, was born in Morganfield, Kentucky in 1817 and enlisted in the Third Illinois Volunteer Infantry during the Mexican War. After the fighting ended, Warren became the minister of the Cumberland Presbyterian Church and part of his duties included riding a circuit to surrounding areas for churches that had no pastors. His journey often took him from Fairfield to Salem and in 1850, he decided to make the small town his home. He settled down and became the minister of the Salem Presbyterian Church, marrying Delilah Jane Cruise a short time later. Together, the two of them raised seven children; May, Emma, Charles, Fred, Edwin, John and William.

Around this same time, Warren and his brother Thomas opened a tavern near the Old Park Hotel. This was their first business venture in the area and it became the foundation of the family's later political and business successes. The tavern became a stopping point for westward bound travelers and gained a reputation for its food, drink and warm beds. It also helped Warren to become more widely known in the area and his prominence soon got him appointed to the position of Marion County Justice of the Peace.

In 1860, the brothers expanded their holdings and Thomas began speculating in land while Warren opened a furniture store and a funeral home. This was a common combination in those days as the proprietors who made the furniture usually built the caskets for the local dead as well. This time period marked the early days of the embalming trade and "undertaking" was just coming into fashion.

When the Civil War broke out the following year, Warren left his growing business in the hands of his children and family members and enlisted in the 21st Regiment of the Illinois Volunteer Infantry under the command of Ulysses S. Grant. As the war continued on, Grant became President Lincoln's choice for the head of the entire Union army and so Warren McMackin was promoted to Lieutenant Colonel and replaced him as the commander of the regiment. He fought through one bloody battle after another for two years and then was wounded and captured at the Battle of Chickamauga. He was eventually released during a prisoner exchange near the end of the war.

Warren returned home to his family and to the gratitude of the people of Salem. In 1865, the same year that the city was officially chartered, they elected him the mayor of the city and in addition, he served as Salem's postmaster and as the region's Civil War Pension Disbursement Officer. He remained in these positions until 1870, when he also handed over the ownership of his furniture and funeral business to his son, Charles. Warren passed away in 1884, still suffering from complications from the wounds he had suffered in Tennessee during the war.

Charles Lincoln McMackin, Sr. carried on his father's business interests and followed in his footsteps by serving as the city's mayor and also as a four term state representative. In 1886, Charles married the refined and beautiful Eugenia Aline Drake, heiress to the prominent Merryfield Plantation in Virginia. Together, they had two children, Omar James (OJ) McMackin, born in 1888 and Helen May McMackin, who was born in 1895. During this period, the family hosted many elegant parties and gatherings for important guests from across the country.

The present-day mansion was constructed during this time, when Charles moved the family's existing home to erect the house that now stands in its place. The house was designed after the style of a southern mansion so that Charles could provide his bride, Eugenia, with all of the comforts that she was accustomed to. He had made a pledge to his wife's parents that in exchange for their permission to marry their daughter, he would build her a grand home that suited the heiress of the well-known Merryfield Plantation. So, in 1910, he had the family home moved to North College Street and the present mansion was built on the site.

Omar McMackin grew up working alongside his father in the family business. He married Mary Belle Wells in 1910 and they had two sons, Charles Lincoln McMackin II and Matthew Wells McMackin. They resided on North College Street, not far from the McMackin mansion, until tragedy struck in 1915. During that year, Matthew fell ill during a deadly influenza outbreak. Mary Belle, unsure of what else to do, brought the little boy to her in-law's home and everyone worked to nurse him back to health. Unfortunately, they did so without success and he died a short time later.

Mary Belle was distraught over the loss of her son and her depression may have contributed to her own death a short time later, when tragedy struck the McMackin's again. Just six months later, Mary Belle was at home and was attempting to adjust a kerosene stove when her hair caught fire. O.J. tried in vain to extinguish the flames, and to save his wife, and sustained serious burns in the process. Young Charles, only three years-old at the time, watched as his mother burned to death.

O.J. then returned to his family home to live and stayed there with his son, his parents and his sister Helen until the outbreak of World War I. Omar decided to enlist in the military and leaving his son in the care of his family, he left for Europe. Thankfully, he returned safely and in 1920, he was married again to a woman named Anna Bessie Cope. Together, they had two more children, Lorin and Martha Jean. In 1921, he organized Company I, 130th Infantry and 33rd Division of the Salem National Guard, of which he became a captain and later retired with the rank of Lieutenant Colonel.

In 1941, death came calling again for the McMackin family. Charles Sr. died in a fatal automobile crash on his way home from a furniture-buying trip to Chicago. Ironically, his funeral was the second to be held in the family's newly built funeral home, which still operates today in Salem as the Rankin Funeral Home.

After his father's death, O.J. took over the funeral business and Helen operated the furniture store. O.J. went on to serve four terms as the Salem Commissioner and played an important role in formulating the G.I. Bill of Rights. He served as the mayor of the city for three consecutive terms between 1935 and 1948 and was credited with the building of the Kaskaskia River Water Line in Salem. The city also enjoyed the prestige of being the only city in Illinois in those days to own, and operate at a profit, its own water, sewer, gas and electric utilities. O.J. and Anna divorced after his final term as mayor and he later married Ruth Allen in 1949 and remained with her until his death in 1963.

Helen McMackin never married, although she was engaged at one time. Her fiancée died during World War I and so she dedicated her life to the family business, along with many civic and patriotic organizations. She became the only occupant of the McMackin home after her mother Eugenia died from a heart attack in 1949 and

she became very passionate about preserving the place. She remained alone until 1950, when her close friend Beth Dunham was severely injured in a train wreck. Helen resolved to be her guardian and she added private living quarters to the home and employed nurses to care for her friend. She also made provisions in her will to insure that Beth would be cared for in her last days. She passed away just one year after Helen's death in 1965.

Charles Lincoln McMackin II became the last owner of the family funeral business after inheriting it from his father and his Aunt Helen. Like his ancestors, Charles always had an affinity for military service and as a boy attended the Western Military Academy in Alton, Illinois, where he joined the Western Military Drum and Bugle Corps. Charles' military academy roommate, Paul Tibbetts, later became the pilot of the "Enola Gay", the aircraft that dropped the

Aunt Helen McMackin

first atomic bomb on Japan.

After his graduation from the academy, Charles joined the Salem Fire Department and eventually served as the Fire Marshall and the Assistant Fire Chief. He also enlisted, in 1933, in the 113th Infantry of the Illinois National Guard and married Flora Jane Gibson of Sandoval in 1935. After the bombing of Pearl Harbor, Charles was called into active military duty and he served as the company commander of the 113th, 339th and 411th infantry regiments. He fought in the European Theater Campaign, in Germany and Northern France. He was decorated many times during the war and was awarded the Silver Star, the Bronze Star, three Oak Leaf Clusters, the Army Commendation Medal, the Purple Heart and the French Croix de Guerre. In 1948, he retired from the service as a Lieutenant Colonel.

After the death of Aunt Helen in 1965, Charles and Flora Jane became the last of the McMackin's to reside in the family home. In addition to all of his earlier accomplishments, Charles remained active in local politics as well. A great many social and political events were held in the family home and Charles chaired the Marion County Republican Party for years. He also served as the Mayor of Salem for three terms between 1975 and 1983.

Flora Jane was the last of the McMackin's to reside in the mansion. In her later years, she became the National Vice-President of the Am Vets Auxiliary and president of the 23rd District of the American Legion Auxiliary. In 1998, she was elected to a four-year term on the Salem City Council. She remained an active member of the community until she passed away in 1995 and according to reports, she remained active for a brief time after her death as well...

According to one of her daughters, no less than four members of the McMackin family were visited by Flora Jane shortly after she died. Around 4:00 a.m. on the night of her death, her daughter told me that she was awakened in the darkness by a figure standing next to her bed. She roused herself from her sleep and realized that it was her mother. Before she could speak, or even think about what was taking place, the figure turned and then vanished. The following morning, she learned that her mother had passed away at almost the exact same time that she had seen her in the bedroom. She was a little startled to hear that three other family members had experienced the same thing.

Despite this unnerving visitation though, Flora Jane is not believed to linger behind in the old family home. However, there is certainly no shortage of McMackin's here!

McMackin House Hauntings

Built in 1910, the McMackin House has managed to weather several generations of the family, use as a funeral home, service as a restaurant and finally, as an apartment building. Hal Harrison, and his son Justin, purchased the business in July 2002 but theirs was not the first eating establishment to be based in the house. The place had originally been converted into use as a restaurant not long after the death of Flora Jane. However, neither this business, nor the one that followed it, managed to last. Unfortunately, the Harrison's business did not last either, although it was certainly thriving at the time of our visit in 2002. According to the owner at the time, he credited the ghosts of the place with his success. He believed that they often offered subtle suggestions about doing things their way.

Not long after the Harrison's opened the place, members of the McMackin family gave him portraits of their Virginia ancestors to hang inside. Too busy with get-

The portraits of the McMackin relatives that Hal Harrison "just didn't get around to hanging". After the strange incidents occurred, he wasted no time in getting them onto the walls.

ting the restaurant open though, the portraits were placed aside and Hal didn't get around to hanging them. He was startled shortly after to discover that other pictures that were hanging on the walls had started falling down, crashing to the floor. Once the McMackin family portraits were hung though, nothing else out of the ordinary happened ----- until a similar event occurred a short time later. At that time, two more pictures were given to Hal by the family and once again, they were stored until time could be found to put them in place. This time, it was not just falling pictures that plagued the restaurant though. In the room where the earlier pictures had been placed (and where the new ones were supposed to be hung), two tables with glass tops mysteriously shattered without explanation. Hal quickly hung the new portraits and nothing else occurred.

"Now, whenever the family gives me anything to hang," Hal told me during an interview in November 2002, "I always hang it up right away."

Who the ghost might be that so bedeviled Hal over his failure to immediately hang the portraits is anybody's guess but family members believe that it might be that of Aunt Helen McMackin. She was fiercely devoted to the house during her life and she had other attributes that lead some to believe that it might be her ghost who lingers behind. "Aunt Helen was always mischievous," her great-niece informed me during our visit. "She was a prankster and loved practical jokes. That runs in the family too because we all love to play jokes on one another, but they're never malicious or mean."

And that seems to fit right along with some of the reported incidents in the house. During the renovations of the place, many of the workmen scoffed at the reputation the house had gained for being haunted. They laughed about it until their keys, tools and other items began disappearing and turning up again in various places. It's common for small items, especially keys, to vanish, as if someone is having a good laugh at the expense of the beleaguered property owner. And even the McMackin family members are not immune.

"Shortly after my mother died," Helen's niece recalled, "I came to clean her belongings out of the house and left a bag of things in the hallway outside of her room." After much of the work had been done, she returned to the hallway to retrieve the bag. To her surprise, it was missing. But rather than be upset or unnerved, she called out loud to her late aunt. "I yelled at Aunt Helen to bring the bag back and you know what, she did." She left and came back the next morning to discover that the bag was now back exactly where she had left it. There had been no one else in the house during the intervening hours and besides that, she knew that no earthly hands had replaced the parcel. It was simply Aunt Helen, playing another practical joke!

During the time the restaurant was in business, staff members and customers alike had odd encounters that were not easily explained. Many patrons came from out of town and were unaware of the reputation of the place, only to discover that they had experienced a ghost. Several customers also mentioned to me of feeling inexplicable cold chills throughout the restaurant, feeling as though they were being watched and catching glimpses of vanishing figures out of the corner of their eye.

One of the most reportedly haunted spots, at least for the customers, was the women's restroom. A number of ladies who had been in the bathroom stated that they were in the room alone when they were joined by another woman, who would come in the door, open the stall next door and then proceed to well, use the toilet. The toilet would then flush but the lady never left the stall. Curious, the original customer would check to see what happened to the other woman when she prepared to leave ---- only to discover that the other stall was empty! This happened numerous times to witnesses who had no idea that someone else had already reported the exact same thing!

And staff members had more encounters than they cared to admit as well. Manager Russ Dalton told me of an occasion when he was closing down the restaurant one night and was in the building alone. He was working in the bar area, counting down a cash drawer, and left to go take care of something else. When he returned, he found that someone had taken three pages of adhesive note paper and had stuck them on the bar in a straight line. Thinking that he must have done it himself, Russ dismissed the happening and placed all of the pages back on the pad they had come from. He then left to shut off some lights, preparing to leave the building, but when he returned to the bar to retrieve the cash bag and deposit, he found the sticky notes had again been placed in a line on the bar! He quickly left the building.

Another staff member told me about the strange happenings that had occurred in the basement. This area of the house, which was formerly the living quarters for the McMackin family servants, had been plagued with odd events. At one point, a security camera that was set up in the area spotted a dark figure as it moved across a lighted doorway. There was no one present in that part of the basement at that time. Another employee also spotted a man's face appearing in a window next to this doorway on another occasion.

Perhaps the strangest basement occurrence happened during the summer after the Harrison's took over the restaurant. At that time, the former coal room (which still had a sealed coal chute in it leading in from outside) was being converted into a locked room where liquor could be stored. The coal door was sealed and locked one night when shelving was being placed in the room. The staff members left and returned the next day to find that the formerly sealed door was now standing open. No one had been in the room since the night before and the restaurant had been empty the entire time. The coal door opened several more times on its own in the weeks that followed but then the phenomenon ceased.

But not everyone who worked here was convinced the place was haunted ---- at least not at first. The once skeptical Justin Harrison told me of the event that occurred which convinced him that there might be something to the reputed haunting in the house after all. He was working one day and had a roll of paper towel sitting nearby on a table. He left the room and came back in by way of a swinging door. As he did so, the paper towel roll suddenly spun around and began unraveling the towel from the roll, spinning off onto the floor. Justin was startled at first and then began to suspect that something other than a ghost was at work.

With this in mind, he rolled the towel back onto the roll and placed it on the table in the same spot where it had been. It was the air from the swinging door, he realized, that had caused the towel roll to spin. So, he took hold of the door and swung it open at the same speed that he had entered through it a few moments before --- and nothing happened! He began to swing the door back and forth, easy at first and then violently, trying as hard as he could to make the paper towel roll move. But nothing he did caused more than a flutter from the loose end of the roll. At that point, Justin explained to me later, he began to consider the idea that there was more to the house than first met the eye. He finally believed the McMackin House might actually be haunted.

Dinner, Spirits .... And Even Ghosts at the McMackin House

In the fall of 2002, I accepted an invitation from Hal Harrison to come and visit the McMackin House. I planned to come in November, after the busy time of tours, book signings and speaking engagements for October had come to an end. Investigations and visits like this were always fun to do once the hectic season was over and I certainly needed a break by then. Besides that, Hal had offered me a free dinner (and one for a guest as well) if I would come and see the house and hear about the hauntings. He was hoping to garner some publicity for the place through my website and books. I had warned him though that I wouldn't write about it unless I felt there was some compelling history that the place really was haunted. Hal agreed to this and said that he looked forward to my visit.

Once I had confirmed the visit, I called my friend Luke Naliborski and asked him if he wanted to come along with me to Salem. He quickly agreed and one thing you have to know about those of us who do the Alton Hauntings Tours --- there is not a one of us who will turn down a free meal!

It was a dark and stormy night..... No kidding. We drove about an hour through a torrential downpour get to Salem from Alton and we arrived, dripping wet, a few minutes before I told Hal we would be there. We hurried inside with our ghost hunting cases, packed full of equipment, cameras and tape recorders, and asked for Hal at the front desk. We were ushered into another room, where we assumed a table was waiting for us. We were right but it was not just one table --- it was a couple of dozen. All of them were jammed with people, looking expectantly towards the door and obviously waiting for our arrival. I had no idea what was going on.

Hal hurried over. I had met him once before but did not remember the rather sheepish grin that he had on his face. I asked him what was going on and he explained that he had invited a "few people" (about 55!) over for the investigation that we were doing and hoped that I didn't mind. Oh, and he almost forgot to mention ---- he also sort of told them that I would speak for a few minutes before dinner was served and tell them a little bit about ghosts.

I guess our meals weren't so "free" after all!

Good-naturedly, I agreed to go along with the new schedule for the evening. I was smiling on the outside but, inside, I was groaning in agony. After a month and a half of hosting tours, giving lectures and signing books, I was looking forward to a night of hunting ghosts. Oh well, I told myself, at least we'll get to do some ghost hunting after dinner. Little did we know that this was not going to go according to plan either.

After I spoke for a little while, dinner was served. Actually, dinner was served to everyone else when I started talking and I got to eat mine cold, although by the look on Luke's face, I wasn't missing much. And he was right. I can't say for sure why this business was ultimately unsuccessful but it's possible that the food may have had something to do with it.

Once dinner was over with, it looked like we were finally going to get a chance to investigate the place. The restaurant was largely empty and preparing to close soon, so we would have the whole place almost to ourselves. As Luke and I contemplated unloading our equipment, we waited anxiously for Hal to usher all of his guests out the door so that we could get started. We waited and waited, then waited some more. As time passed (and Luke checked his watch, having to get up early for work in the morning), the guests continued to stick around. With about 40 of them still hanging out, we were informed that they were waiting for us to start, hoping to see a real paranormal investigation in action. One problem was that we couldn't actually do an investigation with all of these people hanging around! A second problem was that we couldn't tell them that. It's tough to make people understand ---- when it's their house or their business --- how disruptive inviting over all of their friends and neighbors "to see the show" can be. Under better circumstances, we probably could have reasoned with them but I should likely mention that the longer we stayed there, the more everyone indulged on the other type of "spirits" the McMackin House offered.

This is a great place to mention two of our "biggest fans" that night. They were two ladies who were actually members of the McMackin family. Hal had invited them over for the evening and they met Luke and I with enthusiasm ---- a lot of enthusiasm. These two obviously wealthy and refined ladies of perhaps late middle-age (I'm being polite) were very interested in getting involved with the investigation. And the more cocktails that they consumed, the more interested they were! Let's just say that as the night progressed, Luke and I found it harder and harder to detach ourselves from them. Eventually, we started ducking out of sight every time that we saw them weaving around a corner. They were nice ladies, and probably a lot of fun under the right circumstances, but they wreaked havoc on our evening.

After a short discussion, Luke and I abandoned the idea that we were going to be able to do an actual investigation. This meant that most of our equipment ended up being packed back into the car. The last thing that we needed was for a couple of inebriated guests to be handling delicate equipment while we were out of the room. We finally decided that we would get the owner's to take us on a tour of the place and tell us about the weird happenings that had occurred. This was our best bet to get to see everything because we weren't able to stay as late as it would take for everyone to pass out and leave us in peace.

We started our tour, with about 30 people trailing behind (the rest had floated into the bar and had stayed there), and I have to admit that walking about the house was like taking a trip back into the past. There were a number of unusual and unique aspects to the house, some known and most unknown.

Perhaps the most eccentric of the strange additions to the house was the fence that was located in the back yard. If you walked around to the rear of the house, you would see a crumbling stone wall that crossed the yard and extended to the alley. The fence ran near to the original carriage house of the estate. Once surrounded by stables, it was used to house the hearses that were part of the funeral business and it was later converted to living quarters for the old groundskeeper who once tended the place. Even the most casual visitor would admit that the fence seemed odd, but if you looked closely and you would see that most of it was made up of old tombstones that had been cemented into place. This had to be one of the strangest fences in the state.

The tour of the interior of the house began inside of the front doors. Directly ahead of us, we could see the McMackin House lounge, which was once a garage during the days when this was a funeral home. Doors were once located at either end, since the hearse often had to be moved in a hurry. In the early days, it was also the town ambulance. It was in this room where we were able to ditch some of our most intoxicated "investigation assistants". Of course, the two ladies mentioned earlier refused to go away quietly. Luke and I found that it we stopped too suddenly, they were liable to trip over us.

In the main section of the house, we entered what was dubbed the "Adventurer's Room" because no one ever knew what would happen in there next. And this went for the ghosts, as well as for the changing displays and decorations that constantly surprised the patrons. Originally, this room had been two bedrooms in the house, one of which belonged to Flora Jane McMackin. Her daughter later told me that she once saw her mother reflected in a mirror in this room, long after her death.

Next door to this room was the Great Hall. This entryway from the front veranda still held the history and charm of the original home, opening up into another dining area. Glass cases that were located here once held political and military memorabilia collected by Charles McMackin. The Great Hall was also noted for its eerie ghost sightings, as well as for its history. It was here that restaurant staffers, customers and McMackin family members before them, often glimpsed the small figure of little Matthew McMackin, who died here from influenza in 1915. The small boy was seen walking and playing in this area and then he disappeared around the corner into the McMackin Room, which was the original parlor of the house.

It's around this corner where another ghostly sighting took place as well. On a number of occasions, staff members saw what appeared to be a glowing white light that skirted the edge of the corner and then disappeared into the parlor. Could this also have been Matthew's ghost? Perhaps it was but it still remained a mystery ---- and the only connection that our "investigation" that night had to the paranormal.

During the tour of the house, Luke was carrying his infrared video camera with him and he filmed a strange image around this area. Just as we rounded the corner and entered the parlor (following the same path as the light and the ghost of the boy), the video camera picked up the image of a white, shimmering light that was roughly the size of a human fist. It shot into the room at high speed, moving back and forth erratically, and it curved to the right, then to the left to circle the head of one of the McMackin relatives who accompanied us. It then shot upward to the right and vanished into the wall. Later analysis of the image showed no natural or artificial explanation for what this bizarre light could be.

Beyond the former bedrooms and the parlor, and facing the street, was the old veranda of the house. This area was once the perfect place for the family to sit and watch the world go by on busy Broadway Street. In the summer months, it was used as a place for

The old veranda of the house where the ghostly woman often appeared, looking for a table

entertaining and as a sleeping room for the children. In those days, before air conditioning, the sleeping porch would have offered a welcome respite during hot weather. It was in this area of the house, where the most famous ghost of the McMackin place appeared.

This phantom appeared to be an ordinary customer and she would come into the house and request a table for one from the hostess. She then would either stand near the door or seat herself on a bench that is next to the door. When the hostess returned, or even looked up from her seating chart, she would always find that the woman had vanished. Staff members here believed that this lovely young spirit may have been the ghost of Mary Belle Wells, the wife of Omar McMackin, who died after her hair caught fire in 1915.

At the time of our visit, the parlor had been turned into the formal dining room of the McMackin House and It had both history and hauntings of its own. It was in this room that the family and their often important guests would gather to discuss business and politics. A couch that was once located in this room is now on display at the Abraham Lincoln home in Springfield, Illinois. It was in this room where pictures flew from the walls and glass table tops shattered as a cry for attention for the portraits that were ignored for so long. But that's not the only mark the haunting left on it...

Cold, eerie chills often came over people who dined in this room and there was also another strange happening linked to the room's past. One corner of the room, near the front window, was once a favorite resting place for Uncle Merryfield McMackin. He liked to sit there and smoke his pipe, gazing out the window and taking part in discussions with others in the room. He liked the spot so much that some pondered the idea that he never left it! It was once common for visitors in this room to actually hear the sound of a man's deep laughter, followed by the fragrant wafting of pipe smoke through the room. There was no smoking allowed in this part of the building and yet the smell seemed to come from somewhere ---- perhaps from the other side?

Just beyond the old parlor was the Governor's Library. The room had been so-named due to the fact that every governor from the state of Illinois between 1905 and 1990 visited this house. He was always entertained in this room. It was originally a sitting room and offered access (now closed off behind a secret, turning bookcase) to the living quarters of Helen McMackin's dear friend, Beth Dunham. Like much of the rest of the house, memories of the past still haunted this room as well. It was here where visitors and guests reported mysterious cold chills that they were unable to explain. One guest described the cold air that washed over him as being like "air from a cave".

We found the McMackin House to be a place that was literally filled with the past, with both history and haunts. Unfortunately, this was our last chance to visit the place. I moved away from the area and soon received word that the restaurant had closed down. We certainly didn't meet any of the deceased McMackin's on the night we were there but we certainly learned a number of other lessons. It's interesting that an investigator often seems to learn more on the nights when things go wrong, as opposed to when they go right. I can say that this was definitely the case on that night ---- and on many others as well.

4. SOLITARY CONFINEMENT
A Haunted Night at the Eastern State Penitentiary
WITH TROY TAYLOR

As many readers know, I have always been fascinated by the history of crime in America, especially when it connects to ghosts and hauntings. I have found that when compiling a list of places where ghosts are most frequently found, prisons and jails come in high on the list. The amount of pain, trauma and terror experienced by the men who are incarcerated often leaves a lasting impression behind. The horrible events that occur in some of these places may also cause the spirits of the men who

lived and died here to linger behind as well. Jails and prisons can be terrifying places
---- for those in this world and the next.

America's Prisons

One of the first institutions brought to America by the early settlers was the jail, a place where lawbreakers could be held while they awaited trial and subsequent punishment. There were more than 150 offenses in those days for which the punishment was death and for the rest, there was whipping, branding, beatings or public humiliation. At that time, the jail was not a place where criminals were kept for punishment. In fact, the idea of a prison, or penitentiary, was a purely American institution that would have a profound effect on both this country and around the world.

The first state prison was the notorious Newgate, established in Connecticut in 1773. It was actually an abandoned copper mine where prisoners were chained together and forced into hard labor about 50 feet underground. Newgate became the first "hell hole" of American prisons, but it would not be the last. Almost immediately, social reformers appeared, but it has been questioned whether or not their efforts to achieve humane treatment helped or harmed the prisoners. The first reform was attempted in 1790 at Philadelphia's Walnut Street Jail. It was renovated by the Quakers for the jail was described as being a scene of "universal riot and debauchery.. with no separation of those accused but yet untried... from convicts sentenced for the foulest crimes."

The jail was remodeled in 1790 and for the first time, men and women were housed separately in large, clean rooms. Debtors were placed in another part of the jail from those being held for serious offenses and children were removed from the jail entirely. Hardened offenders were placed in solitary confinement in a "penitentiary house" and prisoners were given work and religious instruction. Within a short time though, the Walnut Street jail became overcrowded and a new institution had to be constructed.

Around this same time, two new prisons were built and would soon become models for the rest of the nation. Eastern Penitentiary was built in Philadelphia in 1829 to further the Quaker's idea of prisoner isolation as a form of punishment. Prisoners were confined in windowless rooms with running water and toilets. They would come into contact with no living persons, save for an occasional guard or a minister who would come to pray with them and offer spiritual advice. This extreme isolation caused many of the prisoners to go insane and it comes as no surprise that the prison is believed to be haunted today.

Also in 1829, a rival system, which gained wider acceptance, was started with the building of a prison in Auburn, New York. Here, the prisoners worked together all day at hard labor and then were isolated at night, as they were at the Eastern Penitentiary.

Even though they worked together, inmates were forbidden to talk to one another and were forced to march from place to place in the prison with their eyes always directed downward. The warden of the prison was Elam Lynds, who believed the purpose of the system was to break the spirit of the prisoners. He personally whipped the men and urged the guards to treat the prisoners with brutality and contempt. One standard punishment was the "water cure", which consisted of fastening a prisoner's neck with an iron yoke and then pouring an ice-cold stream of water onto his head. At other times, the man would be chained to a wall and then the water would be turned on him through a high-pressure hose. While the pain was unbearable, it left no marks.

The Auburn system began to be adopted throughout America because it was much cheaper to operate than the Pennsylvania system. The cells were much smaller and money was to be made from the inmate labor. And as the system spread, the treatment of the prisoner became even more imaginative. The striped uniform was first introduced at Sing Sing in New York and floggings, the sweatbox, the strait-jackets, the iron yoke, the thumb screws and the stretcher became widely used. The "stretcher" had a number of variations. A man might be handcuffed to the top of the bars of his cell so that his feet barely touched the floor, then left that way all day -- or his feet might be chained to the floor and his wrists tied to a pulley on the ceiling. When the rope was pulled, the prisoner was stretched taut.

"Sweatboxes" were metal chambers that were so small that the prisoner literally had to crawl inside. They might be left in such confinement all day and in some cases, the boxes were moved close to a furnace so that the heat inside of them would be intensified.

The Auburn system was based on cruelty and repression, with the idea that such treatment would reform prisoners and make them change their ways. Instead, it was a failure and led to riots, death and the closure of many of the institutions. Unfortunately, many of the practices have been adopted (in some degree) by modern prisons.

After the Civil War, new ideas began to be experimented with. In 1870, men like Enoch Cobbs Wines, and others who formed the American Prison Association, started the reformatory system. The Elmira Reformatory, the first of the new type, opened in New York in 1876. Although the reformatory plan was originally intended for all ages, prisoners at Elmira were limited to between the ages of 16 and 30. The principle of the plan was reformation, rather than punishment and was hailed as a great advance in humane treatment of prisoners.

By 1900, 11 states had adopted the reformatory system but by 1910, the plan was considered dead. Most guards and wardens were incapable of administering the grading program and fell back on favoritism rather than reformation. Because of this, many of the men who were paroled, and were allegedly "reformed", went right back out and committed new crimes. Today, many prisons are still called by the name of "reformatory" but are merely a part of the general prison system.

Despite some of the claims, there has been little advance in prisons since the introduction of the system in 1829, although thanks to reform wardens like Thomas Mott Osborne and Lewis E. Lawes, much of the outright cruelty and squalor of the earlier prisons has been considerably reduced.

Still, many of the extreme punitive concepts have persisted, as evidenced by the 1930's "super prison" of Alcatraz. This prison, called by some the "American Devil's Island", was the worst of the federal prisons and was said to be escape proof. According to some estimates, almost 60 percent of the inmates went stir crazy there. Alcatraz left an extreme mark on the prisoners and on the guards and staff members as well. It soon lost its original purpose of confinement for escape artists and troublemakers and became a place to put inmates who it was deemed deserved harsher treatment, like Al Capone. By 1963, Alcatraz was shut down, having proven to be a failure.

And some would consider the entire American prison system a failure as well. Many critics have charged that the prisons have failed to reform criminals or even to act as a deterrent to crime. Eventually, prisoners are simply released, mostly due to a lack of space, and they go right back out and commit new crimes. Many of the prisons themselves have returned to the status of "hell holes" as well. The brutal conditions often lead to permanent injury, insanity, trauma and death.

Is it any wonder that prisons and jails have become known as such haunted places?

Eastern State Penitentiary

After the changes at the Walnut Street Jail in 1790, the Quakers of Philadelphia began to search for a new method of incarceration for criminals in which "penitence" would become essential in the punishment of the lawbreaker. (Thus, we have the word "penitentiary"). The Quaker's concept of such incarceration would involve solitary confinement, a method already popular in Europe with members of monastic orders. It was believed that if monks could achieve peace through solitary confinement and silence, then criminals could eventually be reformed using the same methods.

After years of overcrowding at the Walnut Street jail, a new prison was proposed within the city limits of Philadelphia. Called Eastern State Penitentiary, it was designed to hold 250 prisoners in total solitary confinement and opened in 1829. An architect named John Haviland was hired and he set to work creating an institution in the popular "hub and spoke" design. It had been used in prisons throughout Europe and was highly effective, allowing for a constant surveillance of the prison from a central rotunda. The original design called for seven cell blocks to radiate outward from the center house and guard post.

Prisoners were confined in windowless rooms that were small, but were equipped with both running water and toilets. This was an amazing innovation for the time period as very few public or private buildings were equipped with indoor facilities. Of course, the reason for this was not for the comfort of the prisoner but to keep him out of contact with other people. The walls were thick and soundproof, so prisoners never saw one another. Each prisoner was also given his own exercise yard, surrounded by a brick wall, furthering the sense of extreme isolation. They would see no other inmate from the time they entered the prison until the time they were released.

Construction began on the prison in May 1822. The site selected for it was an elevated area that had once been a cherry orchard. Because of this, the prison later acquired the nickname of "Cherry Hill". As construction began, changes forced John Haviland to create new designs so that the prison could hold an additional 200 prisoners. At that time, the prison was the most expensive single structure ever built but Haviland's design would become so popular that it would be copied for nearly 300 institutions around the world.

Although the prison would not be completed until 1836, it began accepting prisoners in 1829. The first inmate was Charles Williams, who was sentenced to two years for burglary. Like all of the other prisoners who would be incarcerated here, Williams was stripped of his clothing, measured, weighed and given a physical examination. He was also given a number and was not referred to by his name until the day that he was released. A record was made of his height, weight, age, place of birth, age, complexion, color of hair and eyes, length of feet and if he was able to write, the prisoner placed his name on the record.

After the prisoner was examined, he was given a pair of wool trousers, a jacket with a number sewn on it, two handkerchiefs, two pairs of socks and a pair of

shoes. Then, a mask that resembled a burlap bag was placed over his head so that he would not be able to see the prison as he was taken to his cells. It was believed that if an inmate were unable to see which direction to go if he slipped out of his cell, it would be harder for him to escape. The masks were eventually discontinued in 1903.

After that, he was taken to his cell. As he entered it, he would be forced to stoop down (as a penitent would) because the doorways were shortened to remind the prisoners of humility. Above him would be the only lighting in the cell, a narrow window in the ceiling that was called the "Eye of God".

Silence had to be maintained at Eastern State at all times. The guards even wore socks over their shoes while they made their rounds. By doing this, they moved in secret around the prison and while the inmates could not hear them, the officers could hear any sounds coming from inside the cells. The prisoners were not allowed any sort of books or reading material and could not communicate with anyone in any way. If they were caught whistling, singing or talking (even to themselves), they were deprived of dinner or were taken to one of the punishment cells. Any prisoner who repeatedly broke the rules was taken to a punishment cell and was restricted to a half-ration of bread and water.

Even though communication was forbidden, most of the prisoners attempted it anyway. The easiest way to do this was to attach a note to a small rock and toss it over the wall into the next exercise yard. It was probably the quietest form of communication and the most popular. Other forms of contact ranged from coded tapping on the walls to whistling softly and even muffled speech. Since there were vents for heat in every cell, a limited amount of contact could be made through the ducts. They could also tap on the vents and be heard by several prisoners at once. However, if they were caught, they knew with certainty that they would be punished.

At first, punishment at Eastern State was mild compared to other institutions. Most prisons used the lash, a leather strap that was administered to the back, but officials at Eastern State believed that solitary confinement in the 8 x 12 stone cells was punishment enough. However, as the prisoners began to repeatedly break the rules, the punishments became more intense -- going far beyond the plans that had been conceived by the Quakers. The most common forms of punishment created by the prison staff became the Straitjacket, the Iron Gag, the Water Bath and the Mad Chair.

The straitjacket was commonly used by mental institutions to restrain crazed patients and to keep them from hurting themselves or others. At Eastern State, the jacket was used in a different way. Inmates would be bound into the jacket until their face, hands and neck became numb. Eventually, they would turn black from a lack of blood flow and the inmate would usually pass out. The use of the straitjacket was finally discontinued around 1850.

The Mad Chair was another form of punishment, or restraint, adapted from mental asylums. Here, the prisoner would be tied to the chair by chains and leather straps and held so firmly that he was unable to move at all. After long periods of time, his limbs would become very painful and swollen. The offending prisoners would often find themselves strapped into the chairs, unable to move a muscle, for periods of time befitting their punishments. These periods could last anywhere from a few hours to days. Prisoners who spent any length of time in the chair would find themselves unable to walk for hours (or even days) afterward. Their limbs were often a bluish-black color, caused by the lack of circulation, and it could take a week or more before they returned to their normal color.

The Water Bath was another punishment that was adapted from "treatments" at mental hospitals at the time. It involved either dunking, or drenching, a prisoner in ice cold water and then hoisting them up in chains to spend the night attached to the wall. This punishment was especially popular with the more brutal guards during the winter months, when the water would freeze onto the inmate's skin.

The Iron Gag was the most commonly used punishment ---- and the one most feared by the prisoners. It was a device that was placed over the inmate's tongue while his hands were crossed and tied behind his neck. His arms were then pulled taut and the hands secured just behind the man's neck. The gag was then attached to his tongue and his hands and locked into place. Any movement of the hands would tear at the gag and cause intense pain. The inmate would be bleeding and in agony by the time that he was released from his bonds.

These punishments and tortures had not been planned by the Quakers who devised the penitentiary system. They had been improvised by the guards at Eastern State, with full blessing from prison officials. It's no surprise that these officials were investigated for the first time concerning the inhumane treatment of prisoners in 1834, which was two years before the prison was officially opened. Investigations continued over the years and revealed chilling and horrific punishments that had not been conceived of by even the early guards. For example, Block 13, which was constructed in 1925, contained especially small cells that had no light and no ventilation. Prisoners who broke the rules were incarcerated in these cells but when they were discovered by inspectors years later, authorities were ordered to tear down the walls between them and make them larger chambers. Another dark discovery was made when inspectors uncovered "the Hole" under Block 14. It was a pit that had been dug under the cell block that was reserved for especially troublesome inmates. They were often kept for weeks in this black, rectangle of earth, chasing away rats and vermin and subsisting on only one cup of water and one slice of bread each day.

While punishments and seclusion were undoubtedly hard on the health of the prisoners, the diseases within the prison were even worse. During the first few years of the prison, poor planning caused the odor of human waste to constantly invade every part of the building. This was caused by the design of the vents and by the plumbing and heating methods that were used. Water was supplied to every cell for the toilets and for the running water. Since the prisoners were only permitted to bathe every three weeks, they were forced to wash themselves in the basins inside of their cells. To heat the water and the rest of the prison, coal stoves were placed in tunnels underneath the floors. Since the sewer pipes from the toilets ran alongside the pipes for the fresh water, the coal stoves also heated the waste pipes. Because of this, the prison always smelled like human waste. The problem was finally corrected in later years because of the frequency of illnesses among the prisoners and the guards.

But most damaged of all was the mental health of the inmates. The inmates at Eastern State often went insane because of the isolated conditions and so many cases were reported that eventually the prison doctors began to invent other reasons for the outbreaks of mental illness. It was believed at that time that excessive masturbation could cause insanity. Because of this, the doctor's log book of the period listed many cases of insanity, always with masturbation as the cause. It was never documented that the total isolation caused any of the men's breakdowns.

Without question, being imprisoned at Eastern was mind-numbing at best. The prisoner was required to remain in his cell all day and all night in solitary confinement, thinking of nothing but their crimes. The system was brutal on the inmates but hard for the warden and guards as well. The first warden at Eastern was Samuel Wood and it was up to him to insure that the punishment of total solitary confinement was carried out. He and his family were required to reside on the premises of the prison and were not allowed to leave for periods of more than 18 hours without permission from the prison commission.

One of the biggest problems in the early days at Eastern was keeping the guards sober. It was so boring making the rounds and maintaining total silence that the guards often drank to combat the monotony. At one point, the guards were even given a ration of alcohol during the workday so that they would not drink too much. Not surprisingly, they found ways around this and guards were often found asleep at their posts, passed out from too much liquor. Eventually, a rule was passed that promised immediate termination for anyone found intoxicated while on duty.

In time, Eastern State Penitentiary became the most famous prison in America and tourists came from all over the country to see it. Some sightseers traveled from even further abroad. Perhaps the most famous penitentiary tourist was the author Charles Dickens. He came to the prison during his five-month tour of America in 1842 and named it as one of his essential destinations, right after Niagara Falls. Although he came to the prison with the best of intentions, he really did not believe the officials knew what damage the isolation was doing to the minds of the prisoners. He later wrote about his trip to the prison in 1845 and stated that "the system here is rigid, strict, and hopeless solitary confinement... I believe it, in its effects, to be cruel and wrong." He went on to write about the inhumane treatment of the inmates and after speaking to many of them, came to believe that the solitary conditions were a "torturing of the mind that is much worse that any physical punishment that can be administered."

Dickens wrote about a number of the prisoners that he encountered during his visit, including a man who had turned every inch of the interior of his cell into a breathtaking mural. Dickens was stunned when he saw it and exclaimed that it was one of the most amazing works of art that he had ever seen. He tried to speak to the man who had created it but was shocked when he realized that the prisoner's eyes and expression were totally blank. Although he did not rant, rave or weep hysterically, Dickens knew that the man had gone totally insane.

And this man was just one of the thousands who were incarcerated at the prison during its years of silence. The loneliness, misery and solitude drove many of them to madness. The conditions of the place drove many of the inmates over the brink, leaving little doubt as to why insanity and escape attempts were a major problem at Eastern State Penitentiary throughout the 1800's and beyond.

Although it wasn't easy for a prisoner to escape, there were many that tried. The only way to get out was to scale the wall of the exercise yard and then make to the high wall or the front gate. This had to be done without attracting the attention of the guards and with the added disadvantage of not knowing the prison layout. Each of the inmates had been brought into the prison and marched to their cells with hoods over their heads. This way they could not see their surroundings.

In spite of this, the first escape came in 1832. Prisoner number 94, a prison baker named William Hamilton, was serving dinner in the warden's apartment. The warden stepped out of the room and Hamilton managed to tie several sheets together and lower himself out the window. He was not caught until 1837 and when he was, he was returned to his old cell.

There were other escapes as well, but the most memorable came in 1926. Eight prisoners took turns tunneling under cells 24 and 25. They went down about eight feet and then started digging toward the outer wall. The tunnel had been extended nearly 35 feet before they were caught. A similar tunnel actually succeeded in making it out of the prison in April 1945. A group of prisoners, using wood from the prison shop for reinforcement, managed to dig a shaft under the prison and beyond the wall. After it was completed, the men went out at slightly different times to avoid being noticed. By the time they all reached the tunnel's exit, the guards had realized that they were missing and the last two were caught climbing out of the tunnel. The others were apprehended a few blocks away.

The method of total solitary confinement was finally abandoned in the 1870's. It was largely considered a failure in that it was too expensive to manage and had shown little in the way of results. It was decided that Eastern State would become a regular prison. From this point on, being sent to solitary confinement was a punishment and no longer the accepted norm at the prison.

The prisoners were no longer confined to their cells only and a dining hall and athletic field were built. Since the prisoners no longer needed the individual exercise yards, the areas were converted into cells to help with the overcrowding that was starting to affect the prison. Between 1900 and 1908, many of the original cells were also renovated and what had once been a small chamber for one man, became close quarters for as many as five. Along with these changes came new cell blocks, a wood shop, a new boiler room and other buildings where the prisoners could labor. There were also art and educational programs added as the prison system began to try and rehabilitate the inmates rather than merely punish them. The work done by the inmates also helped both the prisoners and the prison itself. No work was contracted out and the goods that were made in the shops were sold and the proceeds helped to pay for the prison's expenses for many years.

Eastern State underwent sweeping reforms in 1913 after the structure overflowed with a population of 1,700. But despite the renovations that followed, talk began to circulate in the 1960's about closing the place down. By this time, it was in terrible shape and the only way to keep it in operation was to renovate it again. The buildings were still overcrowded, walls had crumbled in some locations and in others, ceilings were starting to collapse. The cost of repairing the prison was nearly as high as building a new one.

By 1970, Pennsylvania Governor Shafer announced that four new prisons would be built to replace Eastern State. Most of the men from Eastern State would be transferred to Graterford Prison, which would be located about 25 miles from Philadelphia. Construction began immediately on this institution to help relieve the overcrowding and the concern about the conditions at the old prison. As Graterford was completed in 1971, prisoners began to be sent there.

On April 14, 1971, Eastern State was completely empty. The last of the men were transferred out and the prison was shut down until a short time later, when it became the Center City Detention Center.

Prison riots at the New Jersey State Prison at Trenton later that year forced Eastern State to open its doors once again. Because of the overcrowding and the riots at the New Jersey prison, a number of the inmates had to be relocated. Eastern State was the closest available facility and they were temporarily moved here. The place operated with a skeleton crew for eight months and then was shut down again.

Once more, the prison stood empty and silent.

The Haunting of Eastern State Penitentiary

During the early years of the Twentieth Century, when the penitentiary was still in operation, the first rumors of ghosts began to circulate at the prison. The walls of the place had an almost tangible oppressiveness about them and it was not hard to believe that the generations of prisoners who had lived, died and lost their sanity within the penitentiary could still be lingering behind. However, the first real ghost story of Eastern State surrounded not the prison itself but perhaps the most famous (or infamous) prisoner to ever be incarcerated here -- Al Capone.

Following the bloody events of the St. Valentine's Day Massacre in Chicago, Capone slipped out of town in May 1929 to avoid the heat that was still coming down from the massacre and to avoid being suspected in the deaths of several of the men believed responsible for the killing of the Moran gang. While in Philadelphia, Capone, along with his trusted bodyguard Frankie Rio, was picked up on charges of carrying a concealed weapon and was sentenced to a year in prison. The men eventually ended up in the Eastern State Penitentiary.

Capone continued to conduct business from prison. He was given a private cell and allowed to make long-distance telephone calls from the warden's office and to meet with his lawyers and with Frank Nitti, Jack Guzik and his brother, Ralph, all of whom made frequent trips to Philadelphia. An article in the *Philadelphia Public Ledger* for August 20, 1929, described Capone's cell: "The whole room was suffused in the glow of a desk lamp which stood on a polished desk.... On the once-grim walls of the penal chamber hung tasteful paintings, and the strains of a waltz were being emitted by a powerful cabinet radio receiver of handsome design and fine finish..." The place was obviously unlike the cells that were being used by other prisoners of the time! He was released two months early on good behavior and when he returned to Chicago, he found himself branded "Public Enemy Number One".

It was while he was incarcerated in Pennsylvania that Capone first began to be haunted by the ghost of James Clark, one of the St. Valentine's Day Massacre victims and the brother-in-law of his rival, George Moran. While in prison, other inmates reported that they could hear Capone screaming in his cell, begging "Jimmy" to go away and leave him alone. After his release, while living back in Chicago at the Lexington Hotel, there were many times when his men would hear him begging for the ghost to leave him in peace. On several occasions, bodyguards broke into his rooms, fearing that someone had gotten to their boss. Capone would then tell them of Clark's ghost. Did Capone imagine the whole thing, or was he already showing signs of the psychosis that would haunt him after his release from Alcatraz prison?

Whether the ghost was real or not, Capone certainly believed that he was. The crime boss even went so far as to contact a psychic named Alice Britt to get rid of Clark's angry spirit. Not long after a séance was conducted to try and rid Capone of the vengeful spirit, Hymie Cornish, Capone's personal valet also believed that he saw the ghost. He entered the lounge of Capone's apartment and spotted a tall man standing near the window. Whoever the man was, he simply vanished. Years later, Capone would state that Clark's vengeful specter followed him from the Eastern State Penitentiary -- to the grave.

Whispers and rumors of ghosts had echoed from the prison walls for many years before the penitentiary was actually closed down. By the time the building's last living prisoners were removed though, anyone who had spent any time in the place were certain that something supernatural was taking place at Eastern State. It has been said that when the last guards made their rounds through the prison, this last foray into the darkness caused them to utter chilling stories to one another -- and to anyone else who would listen and not think them insane. They spoke of the sounds of footsteps in the corridors, pacing feet in the cells, eerie wails that drifted from the darkest corners of the complex and dark shadows that resembled people flitting past now darkened doorways and past windows and cells. It seemed that the abandoned halls, corridors and chambers were not so empty after all! Those who left the penitentiary on that final day had become convinced that a strange presence had taken over the building and most breathed a sigh of relief to be gone.

But if ghosts lingered in the building, they would soon be sharing the place with a handful of those from among the living. In the middle 1970's, the empty prison was designated as a National Historic Landmark and was eventually purchased by the city of Philadelphia to be used as a tourist attraction. The Pennsylvania Prison Society of Philadelphia was placed in charge of operating and promoting it as a historic site and they continue to conduct tours of the penitentiary today.

And from these tours and forays into the prison, came more the tales of ghosts and hauntings. Without question, the prison was designed to be a frightening place and in recent times, it has become even more so. The prison still stands as a ruin of crumbling cellblocks, empty guard towers, rusting doors and vaulted, water-stained ceilings. It is a veritable fortress and an intimidating place for even the most hardened visitors. But does the spooky atmosphere of the place explain the ghostly tales as merely tricks of the imagination? Those who have experienced the spirits of Eastern State say that it does not.

"The idea of staying in this penitentiary alone is just overwhelming... I would not stay here overnight," stated Greta Galuszka, a program coordinator for the prison.

Over the years, volunteers and visitors alike have had some pretty strange experiences in the prison. In Cell Block 12, several independent witnesses have reported the hollow and distant sound of laughter echoing in certain cells. No source can ever be discovered for the noises. Others have reported the presence of shadowy apparitions in the cells and the hallways, as though prisoners from the past can find no escape from this inhuman place. Several volunteers believe that they have seen these ghostly figures in the "six block", while others have seen them darting across corridors and vanishing into rooms. Eastern State's Death Row has also been the scene of strange encounters and chilling visitations by the same shadowy figures encountered by others.

A locksmith named Gary Johnson was performing some routine restoration work one day when he had his own odd encounter. "I had this feeling that I was being watched," he recalled, "but I turned and I'm looking down the block and there's nobody there. A couple of seconds later and I get the same feeling... I'm really being watched! I turn around and I look down the block and shoooom.... this black shadow just leaped across the block!" Johnson still refers to the prison as a "giant haunted house."

Angel Riugra, who has also worked in the prison, agrees. "You feel kinda jittery walking around because you feel something there, but when you turn around, you don't see anything," he said. "It's kinda weird, it's spooky!"

One of the most commonly reported specters in the prison is encountered by staff members and visitors alike among the older cellblocks. The phantom is always described as being a dark, human-like figure who stands very still and quiet. The figure usually goes unnoticed until the visitor gets too close to him and he darts away. The sightings never last for long but each person who has encountered the apparition state that it gives off a feeling of anger and malevolence. Could this be a prisoner who has remained behind in protest of the inhumane treatment that he and so many others received in this cruel and brutal place? Perhaps -- and it's likely that this single spirit does not walk here alone.

Another of the penitentiary's most frequently seen phantoms is a ghost that stands high above the prison walls in a guard tower. It has been assumed for many years that this is the spirit of a former guard who is still standing his post after all of these years. One has to wonder why a guard, who was free to leave this place at the end of the day, would choose to remain behind at the prison. But perhaps he has no choice -- we can only speculate as to what dark deeds this lonesome man may have been witness to, or perhaps had taken part in, during his years at the prison. Maybe he is now compelled to spend eternity watching over the walls that held so many prisoners in days gone by.

As intimidating as all of this sounds though, it is the history and the hauntings of the prison that continue to bring people back. Many of the staff members, while unsettled by the strange events that sometimes occur, are nevertheless fiercely protective of the place and are determined to see that it is around for many years to come. Even so, they can't help but feel that forces are at work inside of the prison.

"So much did happen here," Greta Galuszka added, "that there's the potential for a lot of unfinished business to be hanging around. And I think that's my fear --- to stumble upon some of that unfinished business."

Spending the Night at Eastern State with The Learning Channel

In June 2003, I had the opportunity to spend the night at Eastern State Penitentiary with a crew from Digital Reality Television, who was producing a series for The Learning Channel called *Mysterious Worlds*. The episode that I was involved with dealt with ghosts and hauntings and aired in October of that same year. The show was called "*America's Ghost Hunters*" and it became one of my favorite television shows to be a part of. I have worked with a variety of different shows over the years and many of them have been less than satisfying experiences. "*America's Ghost Hunters*" however was an exception.

I was first contacted about the show by producer Michael Brockhoff. He explained that the premise of the episode was to bring together researchers and groups who specialized in various aspects of paranormal investigation. Each of them would be filmed separately and then we would be brought together for the final segment of the show in one haunted location. After much discussion, I mentioned Eastern State Penitentiary to him as a possible site for the last segment. The prison had a history of hauntings and the officials there would be open to the idea of us not only spending an entire night there but would also be comfortable with us talking about the possibility of ghosts in the building. I would later find out that even their own public tours make mention of the possibility of spectral prisoners still lingering behind.

I met with Michael Brockhoff, and producer Steve Rice, when they came to Alton, Illinois to film the first segment that I did for the show. My "specialty" for the program was "historical research", meaning that I looked for independent sightings or encounters with spirits from a single location. I had already documented such activity in Alton at the First Unitarian Church and had a number of witnesses who had reported a haunting without realizing that others were experiencing the same thing. I called my friend Luke Naliborski to help with a television version of an "investigation" of the church and we spent most of the day filming. After that, Michael, Steve and I started making plans for our upcoming trip to Philadelphia. (See Luke's story about filming at the church elsewhere in the book)

Meanwhile, other members of what would be the final team were also filming segments in various parts of the country. Each of them would film an investigation using their "specialty" for a separate segment and then each would be put to use at Eastern State. The teams included Tonya Hacker and Tammy Wilson from Oklahoma, who were working with EVP; a group called Seven Paranormal Research from North Carolina, who had trained a dog to be able to pick up anomalous energy fields in a haunting; and investigators from the AGHOST group in Seattle, who had put together a computer system with a multi-sensor array to measure several energy fields at once. Although I had corresponded with several of these investigators in the past, I would be meeting them for the first time in Philadelphia.

On June 6, 2003, I flew into Philadelphia and met with Michael and Steve at the hotel. I spent that first evening seeing a little of the city and tracking down the best Philly cheesesteaks in town (Pats!). The following morning, I spent several hours working on sit-down interviews with the cast and crew and then went to the prison to check out the layout of the place during the daylight hours. After walking around for a couple of hours, I met with some of the staff members and one of them was kind enough to take me on a tour of areas of the prison that are not open to the public. I would later have access to these same spots during our shoot but would find that they looked totally different after darkness had fallen. It was a very wet and gloomy weekend in the city and the prison seemed especially eerie with an overcast sky and the constant dripping of water in places where the buildings had fallen into ruin. I photographed a good portion of the place before leaving for the afternoon. The rest of the day was spent checking out local bookstores and historic sites and then after dinner, I returned to my hotel for some rest. I had a long night ahead of me and this would be my last chance to sleep for about 36 hours.

Later that night, the entire group of investigators returned to the prison or, in some cases, came there for the first time. We spent the next hour to so getting set up for the night ahead. Members of the crew had already arrived and had set up a "safe area" for equipment storage, food and coffee, just off the rotunda at the center of the prison. Here, we became acclimated with maps of the prison and instructions on what we would be doing for the night ahead. Michael Brockhoff had asked me to coordinate everyone as much as possible and had assigned me a couple of tasks for the night. In addition to photographing the prison as thoroughly as possible, he also wanted me to supervise the investigations and to rotate among the different groups as much as I could. This would give me the opportunity to explore the prison and also to see what sort of activity the various groups and individuals might be picking up.

To start with though, I was supposed to take everyone on a historical tour through the prison and to explain what was located where and when it was all used. I had pretty thoroughly researched the site and had been filling in my information after I had arrived so, accompanied by the researchers and a camera and sound crew, we covered a large portion of the penitentiary. After that, we were ready to begin our investigations.

Split up into different groups, everyone went their separate directions and started setting up for the night. My job was to "float" between them as much as possible but this was not easy to do since in the majority of cases, the various experiments that were being conducted had to be run without any interference. This was notably the case with the EVP recordings that were being done by Tonya Hacker and Tammy Wilson. I went to speak with them as they were setting up and we discussed their methods for finding legitimate recordings. Both of them were using external microphones that night (so as to avoid sounds from the recorder itself) and were willing to admit that it was going to be tough to try and set up units to record without them being monitored at all times. Between the researchers and the crew, there were quite a few people moving around inside of the buildings and so voices on the tapes might not necessarily be ghostly, they realized. They finally decided to try "interactive recording", meaning that they would ask questions on tape and then pause for replies, hoping that they might get more answers that way than with simply leaving the recorders set up in different parts of the prison. The evening would prove to be interesting for them and while both told me the following morning that the results of their recordings were "inconclusive" without further study, they did feel that they had captured some fairly mysterious sounds on tape, including voices that came from otherwise empty parts of the building.

A couple of sections of the prison seemed to be more active than others that night and one of them was the central guard tower, which, according to the building's tradition, had long been haunted by a spectral guard from when the prison was still in operation. I returned to the guard tower several times throughout the evening and at one point, stayed there for almost as hour. I did not experience anything unusual but members of the Seven Paranormal Research team, including Jim Hall, certainly did. While exploring the area, their trained dog detected a very strong presence -- one that was verified by more than one electromagnetic field meter. I can vouch for the fact that there were no artificial fields in the tower that night, so what the dog may have been sensing is unknown. I asked Jim and Kady Harrington how exactly the dog was able to assist them with their investigations and they explained what turned out to be a fairly simple method to me. They began bringing him to their investigations and he began to react in an erratic manner while in the presence of electromagnetic fields that could be verified with equipment. Eventually, he began to lead the investigators to these fields and had been doing so ever since. I asked them if the dog could simply be behaving in a way that would earn him a reward and they told me that they had considered this and so they never rewarded him for his work. In that way, they did not get any false reactions from him. He certainly seemed to know what he was doing that night. I had the chance to observe him a couple of times and despite a number of things that might have set off a less-focused animal, the only time that he ever reacted in the way that he did in investigation situations was in the guard tower. Interestingly, the equipment also picked up readings here and one of their team members reported the uncomfortable presence of a man on the stairs.

Aside from the guard tower, the most active location that we experienced and investigated that night was in the former "Death Row" section of the prison. To be honest, this section was only somewhat accurately named. It was used as an incarceration unit for Pennsylvania prisoners who had been sentenced to death but no executions were actually carried out here. This cell block was the last addition made to the prison and it was completed in 1959 and became the only block in the prison with electronic doors. The lower level was used to house dangerous prisoners, who were placed here as punishment, and the upstairs held those sentenced to death. When their execution dates came about, the prisoners were then transferred to the State Correctional Institution at Rockville for their date with "Old Sparky". Because the prisoners in the lower level of the block were so

The prison's death row has long been the site of paranormal reports and it would remain active during our overnight stay in the penitentiary.

dangerous, a separate row of bars was installed down the center of the corridor. The guards were supposed to walk behind the second section so that they would be out of reach of the inmates, but one of the staff members here told me that they rarely did this because it showed weakness to the prisoners. This was the section of the prison that held the worst of the worst ---- and so it was no surprise to me to learn that there had been a number of paranormal happenings reported here over the years.

Because most of this building is not open to the general public, most of the reports of unidentified sounds, cold chills and voices have been reported by staff members and paranormal investigators. According to a friend who was a consultant for another television show, a producer on that show claimed to be pushed down the stairs that go from the first level to the upper one. It was in the upper cell block that Ross Allison and Dutch Jackson, from the AGHOST group in Seattle, decided to place their electronic testing equipment at the beginning of the night. The equipment used a laptop computer to measure any fluctuations that might take place in the energy field of the building. Over a two hour period, they picked up not only changes in the electromagnetic field but also nearly constant movements that were picked up by the motion detectors. At the time, the entire block was sealed off and no one was inside. Even before they had set up, tests of the equipment picked up moving and changing magnetic fields --- where there was no electricity --- inside of several cells.

And, as it turned out, the only paranormal encounter that I experienced for myself also occurred that night in the Death Row cell block. I had no idea at the time that anything out of the ordinary was occurring however. I would not discover this until after I returned home and had the film in my cameras developed. Of all of the eerie photos taken that night, only one of them remains unexplained. It was number 12 on the roll and was taken merely as a documentation of the location, using Kodak 800 ASA color film. There was no strap on the camera and nothing in front of me

The unexplained photo taken by Troy Taylor in the Death Row Block at Eastern State. There was nothing in front of the camera at the time it was taken.

that would have caused the anomaly to appear. After the photo was developed, the negative and the print were studied by technicians at Kodak, as well as by two independent photographers with no connection to the paranormal field. No one could provide any explanation as to what the image in the photo might be.

So, is the Eastern State Penitentiary haunted? In the end, that must be up to the reader to decide but I have always been of the opinion that In locations where violent and traumatic events take place, those events often leave an impression behind. In no place, would this be more true than at Eastern State, a place with a long, rich history of violence, bloodshed and terror. If the events of the past really do create the hauntings of today ---- then Eastern State Penitentiary is a very haunted place indeed.

5. SUICIDE & SPIRITS

The Haunting of the Lemp Mansion
WITH TROY TAYLOR

One of the first locations that we began visiting with the American Hauntings Tours was the infamous Lemp Mansion in St. Louis, Missouri. Long regarded as one of the most haunted houses in America, the historic mansion was once home to the Lemp family, creators of an American beer empire that was unlike any other for many years. Not long after visiting the old house for the first time, I began to realize that the reputation that it had gained was well-deserved.

The Lemp family came to prominence in the middle 1800's as one of the premier brewing families of St. Louis. For years, they were seen as the fiercest rival of Anheuser-Busch and the first makers of lager beer in America but today, they are largely forgotten and remembered more for the house they once built than for the beer they once brewed. That house stands now as a fitting memorial to decadence, wealth, tragedy and suicide. Perhaps for this reason, there is a sadness that hangs over the place and an eerie feeling that has remained from its days of disrepair and abandonment. It has since been restored into a restaurant and inn, but yet the sorrow seems to remain. By day, the mansion is a bustling restaurant, filled with people and activity, but at night, after everyone is gone and the doors have been locked tight ----- something still walks the halls of the Lemp Mansion.

Are the ghosts here the restless spirits of the Lemp family, still unable to find rest? Quite possibly, for this unusual family was as haunted as their house is purported to be today. They were once one of the leading families in St. Louis but all that would change and the eccentricities of the family would eventually be their ruin.

The story of the Lemp brewing empire began in 1836, when Johann Adam Lemp came to America from Germany. He had learned the brewer's trade as a young man and when he came to St. Louis, after spending two years in Cincinnati, he opened a small mercantile store and began selling dry goods, vinegar and his own brand of beer. He soon closed the store and turned his attentions to a small factory that made strictly vinegar and beer. It is believed that during this period, Lemp introduced St. Louis to the first lager beer, which was a crisp, clean beer that required a few months of storage in a cool dark place to obtain its unique flavor. This new beer was a great change from the English-type ales that had previously been popular and the lighter beer soon became a regional favorite. Business prospered and by 1845, the popularity of the beer was enough to allow him to discontinue vinegar production and concentrate on beer alone.

His company expanded rapidly, thanks to the demand for the beer, and Lemp soon found that his factory was too small to handle both the production of the beer and the storage needed for the lagering process. He found a solution in a limestone cave that was just south of the city limits at the time. The cave had been recently discovered and its proximity to the Mississippi River would make it possible to cut ice during the winter and keep the cave cold all year around.

Lemp purchased a lot over the entrance to the cave and then began excavating and enlarging it to make room for the wooden casks needed to store the beer. The remodeling was completed in 1845 and caused a stir in the city. Other brewers were looking for ways to model their brews after the Lemp lager beer and soon these companies also began using the natural caves under the city to store beer and to open drinking establishments. The Lemp's own saloon added greatly to the early growth of the company. It was one of the largest around and served only Lemp beer and no hard liquor. This policy served two purposes in that it added to beer sales and also created a wholesome atmosphere for families as beer was considered a very healthy drink, especially to the growing numbers of German immigrants in the city.

The Lemp's Western Brewing Co. continued to grow during the 1840's and by the 1850's was one of the largest in the city. Adam Lemp died on August 25, 1862, a very wealthy and distinguished man. The Western Brewery then came under the leadership of William Lemp, Adam's son, and it then entered its period of greatest prominence.

William Lemp had been born in Germany in 1836, just before his parents came to America. He spent his childhood there and was brought to St. Louis by his father at age 12. He was educated at St. Louis University and after graduation, he joined his father at Western Brewery. At the outbreak of the Civil War, he enlisted in the Union Army and soon after leaving the military, he married Julia Feickert and the couple would have nine children together.

After the death of Adam Lemp, William began a major expansion of the Western Brewery. He purchased a five-block area around the storage house on Cherokee, which was located above the lagering caves. Here, he began the construction of a new brewery and by the 1870's, the Lemp factory was regarded as the largest in the entire city. By1876, it was producing 61,000 barrels of beer each year. A bottling plant was added the following year and artificial refrigeration was added to the plant in 1878. This would be the first year that the brewery's production would reach over 100,000 barrels.

By the middle 1890's, the Lemp brewery was known all over America. They had earlier introduced the popular "Falstaff" beer, which is still brewed by another company today although the familiar logo once had the name "Lemp" emblazoned across it. This beer became a favorite across the country and Lemp was the first brewery to establish coast-to-coast and then international, distribution of its beer. The brewery had grown to the point that it employed over 700 men and as many as 100 horses were needed to pull the delivery wagons in St. Louis alone. It was ranked as the eighth largest in the country and construction and renovation continued on a daily basis. The entire complex was designed in an Italian Renaissance style with arched windows, brick cornices and eventually grew to cover a five city blocks.

William Lemp Sr.

In addition to William Lemp's financial success, he was also well-liked and popular among the citizens of St. Louis. He was on the board of several organizations, including a planning committee for the 1904 World's Fair and many others. His family life was happy and his children were either involved in the business or successful in their own right.

During the time of the Lemp Brewery's greatest success, William Lemp also purchased a home for his family a short distance away from the brewery complex. The house was built by Jacob Feickert, Julia Lemp's father, in 1868. In 1876, Lemp purchased it for use as a residence and as an auxiliary brewery office. Although already an impressive house, Lemp immediately began renovating and expanding it and turning it into a showplace of the period. The mansion boasted 33 rooms, elegant artwork, handcrafted wood decor, ornately painted ceilings, large beautiful bathrooms and even an elevator that replaced the main staircase in 1904. The house was also installed with three room-sized, walk-in vaults where paintings, jewelry and other valuables were stored. It was a unique and wondrous place and one fitting of the first family of St. Louis brewing.

And the mansion was as impressive underground as it was above. A tunnel exited the basement of the house and entered into a portion of the cave that Adam Lemp had discovered for his beer lagering years before. Traveling along a quarried shaft, the Lemp's could journey beneath the street, all the way to the brewery. The advent of mechanical refrigeration also made it possible to use parts of the cave for things other than business, as will be evident later in this account.

Ironically, in the midst of all of this happiness and success, the Lemp family's troubles truly began.

The first death in the family was that of Frederick Lemp, William Sr.'s favorite son and the heir apparent to the Lemp empire. He had been groomed for years to take over the family business and was known as the most ambitious and hard working of the Lemp children. In 1898, Frederick married Irene Verdin and the couple was reportedly very happy. Frederick was well-known in social circles and was regarded as a friendly and popular fellow. In spite of this, he also spent countless hours at the brewery, working hard to improve the company's future. It's possible that he may have literally worked himself to death.

In 1901, Frederick's health began to fail. He decided to take some time off in October of that year and temporarily moved to Pasadena, California. He hoped that a change of climate might be beneficial to him. By December, he was greatly improved and after his parents visited with him after Thanksgiving, William returned to St. Louis with hopes that his son would be returned to him soon. Unfortunately, that never happened. On December 12, Frederick suffered a sudden relapse and he died at the age of only 28. His death was brought about by heart failure, due to a complication of other diseases.

Frederick's death was devastating to his parents, especially to his father. Brewery secretary Henry Vahlkamp later wrote that when news came of the young man's death, William Lemp "broke down utterly and cried like a child... He took it so seriously that we feared it would completely shatter his health and looked for the worst to happen."

Lemp's friends and co-workers said that he was never the same again after Frederick's death. It was obvious to all of them that he was not coping well and he began to slowly withdraw from the world. He was rarely seen in public and chose to walk to the brewery each day by using the cave system beneath the house. Before his son's death, Lemp had taken pleasure in paying the men each week. He also would join the workers in any department and work alongside them in their daily activities or go personally among them and discuss any problems or any questions they had. After Frederick died though, these practices ceased almost completely.

On January 1, 1904, William Lemp suffered another crushing blow with the death of his closest friend, Frederick Pabst. This tragedy changed Lemp even more and soon he became indifferent to the details of running the brewery. Although he still came to the office each day, he paid little attention to the work and those who knew him said that he now seemed nervous and unsettled and his physical and mental health were both beginning to decline. On February 13, 1904, his suffering became unbearable.

When Lemp awoke that morning, he ate breakfast and mentioned to one of the servants that he was not feeling well. He finished eating, excused himself and went back upstairs to his bedroom. Around 9:30, he took a .38 caliber Smith & Wesson revolver and shot himself in the head with it. There was no one else in the house at the time of the shooting except for the servants. A servant girl, upon hearing the sound of the gunshot, ran to the door but she found it locked. She immediately ran to the brewery office, about a half block away, and summoned William Jr. and Edwin. They hurried back to the house and broke down the bedroom door. Inside, they found their father lying on the bed in a pool of blood. The revolver was still gripped in his right hand and there was a gaping and bloody wound at his right temple. At that point, Lemp was still breathing but unconscious.

One of the boys called the family physician, Dr. Henry J. Harnisch, by telephone and he came at once. He and three other doctors examined William but there was nothing they could do. William died just as his wife returned home from a shopping trip downtown. No suicide note was ever found.

Immediately after the shooting, the house was closed to everyone but relatives and brewery employees were posted to intercept callers and newspapermen at the front gate. Funeral arrangements were immediately made and services took place the next day in the mansion's south parlor. The brewery was closed for the day and employees came to pay their respects before the private service was held.

After the service, a cortege of 40 carriages traveled to Bellefontaine Cemetery, although Julia, Elsa and Hilda were too grief-stricken to go to the burial ground. Eight men who had worked for Lemp for more than 30 years served as pallbearers and honorary pallbearers included many notable St. Louis residents, including Adolphus

Busch, the owner of the Anheuser-Busch brewery, who had liked and respected his principal competitor. William was placed inside the family mausoleum next to his beloved son, Frederick.

Lemp's terrible and tragic death came at a horrible time as far as the company was concerned. In the wake of his burial, all of St. Louis was preparing for the opening of the Louisiana Purchase Exposition, perhaps the greatest event to ever come to St. Louis. Not only had William been elected to the fair's Board of Directors, but the brewery was also involved in beer sales and displays for the event. William Jr. took his father's place and became active with the Agriculture Committee and with supervising the William J. Lemp Brewing Company's display in Agriculture Hall, where brewers and distillers from around the world assembled to show off their products.

William Lemp Jr.

In November 1904, William Lemp Jr. took over as the new president of the William J. Lemp Brewing Company. He inherited the family business and with it, a great fortune. He filled the house with servants, built country houses and spent huge sums on carriages, clothing and art.

In 1899, Will had married Lillian Handlan, the daughter of a wealthy manufacturer. Lillian was nicknamed the "Lavender Lady" because of her fondness for dressing in that color. She was soon spending the Lemp fortune as quickly as her husband was. While Will enjoyed showing off his trophy wife, he eventually grew tired of her and decided to divorce her in 1906. Their divorce, and the court proceedings around it, created a scandal that all of St. Louis talked about. When it was all over, the "Lavender Lady" went into seclusion and retired from the public eye.

But Will's troubles were just beginning that year. The Lemp brewery was also facing a much-altered St. Louis beer market in 1906 when nine of the large area breweries combined to form the Independent Breweries Company. The formation of this company left only Lemp, Anheuser-Busch, the Louis Obert Brewing Co. and a handful of small neighborhood breweries as the only independent beer makers in St. Louis. Of even more concern was the expanding temperance movement in America. The growing clamor of those speaking out against alcohol was beginning to be heard in all corners of the country. It looked as though the heyday of brewing was coming to an end.

The year 1906 also marked the death of Will's mother. It was discovered that she had cancer in 1905 and by March 1906, her condition had deteriorated to the point that she was in constant pain and suffering. She died in her home a short time later. Her funeral was held in the mansion and she was laid to rest in the mausoleum at Bellefontaine Cemetery.

In 1911, the last major improvements were made to the Lemp brewery when giant grain elevators were erected on the south side of the complex. That same year, the Lemp mansion ceased being a private residence and it was converted and remodeled into the new offices of the brewing company. Like most of its competitors, the

Lemp brewery limped along through the next few years and through World War I. According to numerous accounts though, Lemp was in far worse shape than many of the other companies. Will had allowed the company's equipment to deteriorate and by not keeping abreast of industry innovations, much of the brewing facilities had become outmoded. And to make matters worse, Prohibition was coming.

Brewers were stunned a short time later by the passing of an amendment that made the production, sale and consumption of alcohol illegal in America and by the Volstead Act, which made prohibition enforceable by law. This seemed to signal the real death of the Lemp brewery. As the individual family members were quite wealthy aside from the profits from the company, there was little incentive to keep it afloat. Will gave up on the idea that Congress would suddenly repeal Prohibition and he closed the Lemp plant down without notice. The workers learned of the closing when they came to work one day and found the doors shut and the gates locked.

Will decided to simply liquidate the assets of the plant and auction off the buildings. He sold the famous Lemp "Falstaff" logo to brewer Joseph Griesedieck for the sum of $25,000. Griesedieck purchased the recognizable Falstaff name and shield with the idea that eventually the government would see Prohibition for the folly that it was and that beer would be back. Lemp no longer shared the other man's enthusiasm though and in 1922, he saw the brewery sold off to the International Shoe Co. for just $588,000, a small fraction of its estimated worth of $7 million in the years before Prohibition. Sadly, virtually all of the Lemp company records were pitched when the shoe company moved into the complex.

With Prohibition finally destroying the brewery, the 1920's looked to be a dismal decade for the Lemp family. As bad as it first seemed though, things almost immediately became worse with the suicide of Elsa Lemp Wright in 1920. She became the second member of the family to take her own life.

Elsa was born in 1883 and was the youngest child in the Lemp family. With the death of her mother in 1906, she became the wealthiest unmarried woman in the city after inheriting her portion of her father's estate. In 1910, she became even richer when she married Thomas Wright, the president of the More-Jones Brass and Metal Co. They moved into a home in Hortense Place in St. Louis' Central West End. During the years between 1910 and 1918, their marriage was reportedly an unhappy and stormy one. They separated in December 1918 and in February 1919, Elsa filed for divorce. Unlike the sensational divorce of her brother, Elsa's legal battle was kept quiet and the details were not revealed. It was granted however in less than an hour and the reasons were cited as "general indignities".

However, by March 8, 1920, Elsa and Thomas had reconciled and the two were remarried in New York City. They returned home to St. Louis and found their house filled with flowers and cards from friends and well-wishers.

The night of March 19 was a restless one for Elsa. She suffered from frequent bouts of indigestion and nausea and her ailments caused periods of severe depression. She was awake for most of this night and slept very little. When her husband awoke the next morning, Elsa told him that she was feeling better but wanted to remain in bed. Wright agreed that this was the best thing for her and he went into the bathroom and turned on the water in the tub. He then returned to the bedroom for a change of underwear, retrieved them from the closet and went back into the bathroom. Moments after he closed the door, he heard a sharp cracking sound over the noise of the running water.

Thinking that it was Elsa trying to get his attention, Wright opened the door and called to his wife. When she didn't answer, he walked into the bedroom and found her on the bed. Her eyes were open and she seemed to be looking at him. When Wright got closer, he saw a revolver on the bed next to her. Elsa tried to speak but couldn't and a few moments later, she was dead. No note or letter was ever found and Wright could give no reason as to why she would have killed herself. He was not even aware that she owned a gun.

The only other persons present that morning were members of the household staff. None of them heard the shot and none of them saw any sign that Elsa intended to end her life. They quickly summoned Dr. M.B. Clopton and Samuel Fordyce, a family friend. Strangely, the police were not notified of Elsa's death for more than two hours and even then, the news came indirectly through Samuel Fordyce. Wright became "highly agitated" under the scrutiny of the police investigation that followed and his only excuse for not contacting the authorities was that he was bewildered and did not know what to do.

And while the mysterious circumstances around Elsa's death have had some suggesting that there was more to the story than was told, her brothers seemed to find little out of the ordinary about her demise. Will and Edwin rushed to the house as soon as they heard about the shooting. When Will arrived and was told what had happened, he only had one comment to make.

"That's the Lemp family for you", he said.

Will was soon to face depression and death himself. He had already slipped into a dark state of mind following the end of the Lemp's brewing dynasty, but he took an even sharper turn for the worse after the sale of the plant to the International Shoe Co. Will soon began to follow in the footsteps of his father and he became increasingly nervous and erratic. He shunned public life and kept to himself, complaining often of ill health and headaches.

By December 29, 1922, he had reached the limit of his madness.

On that morning, Lemp secretary Henry Vahlkamp arrived at the Lemp brewery offices around 9:00. When he came in the front door, he found Will already in his office. The two of them were joined shortly after by Olivia Bercheck, a stenographer for the brewery and Lemp's personal secretary.

Vahlkamp later recalled that Lemp's face was flushed that morning and that when he entered his employer's office, he had an elbow on the desk and he was resting his forehead on his hand. He asked Lemp how he was feeling and Will replied that he felt quite bad.

"I think you are looking better today than you did yesterday," Vahlkamp noted in an effort to cheer up the other man.

"You may think so," Will replied, "but I am feeling worse."

Vahlkamp then left and went to his own office on the second floor of the converted mansion.

Moments after this exchange, Miss Bercheck telephoned Will's second wife, Ellie, about instructions for the day's mail and as she was speaking to her, Lemp picked up the other line and spoke to his wife himself. The secretary recalled that he spoke very quietly and she did not hear what turned out to be his last words to his wife. After Lemp finished the conversation, Bercheck asked him a question about some copying that she was doing from a blueprint. He first told her that what she had was fine and then he changed his mind and suggested that she go down to the basement and speak to the brewery's architect, Mr. Norton.

While she was on her way downstairs, she heard a loud noise. Because there were men working in the basement, she thought nothing of it, assuming that someone had dropped something. When she came back upstairs though, she found Will lying on the floor in a pool of blood. Another employee had also been working upstairs but when he heard the same loud noises that Miss Bercheck later reported, he recognized it as a gunshot. He ran upstairs to find Will lying on the floor with his with his feet under the desk. He called for help and men from the office across the hall came over and put a pillow under Will's head.

Apparently, just after speaking to Miss Bercheck, Lemp had shot himself in the heart with a .38 caliber revolver. He had unbuttoned his vest and then fired the gun through his shirt. When discovered, Lemp was still breathing, but he had expired by the time a doctor could arrive.

Captain William Doyle, the lead police investigator on the scene, searched Lemp's pockets and desk for a suicide note, but as with his father and his sister before him, Will left no indication as to why he had committed suicide.

Oddly, Lemp seemed to have no intention of killing himself, despite being depressed. After the sale of the brewery, he had discussed selling off the rest of the assets, like land parcels and saloon locations, and planned to then just "take it easy". Not long after that announcement, he had even put his estate in Webster Groves up for sale, stating that he planned to travel to Europe for awhile. Even a week before his death, he had dined with his friend August A. Busch, who said that Lemp seemed "cheerful" at the time and that he gave no indication that he was worrying about business or anything else. "He was a fine fellow," Busch added, "and it is hard to believe that he has taken his own life."

The funeral of William Lemp Jr. was held on December 31 at the Lemp mansion. The offices were used as the setting for the services for sentimental reasons, staff members said. He was interred in the family mausoleum at Bellefontaine Cemetery, in the crypt just above his sister Elsa.

With William Jr. gone and his brothers involved with their own endeavors, it seemed that the days of the Lemp empire had come to an end at last. The two brothers still in St. Louis had left the family enterprise long before it had closed down. Charles worked in banking and finance and Edwin had entered a life in seclusion at his estate in Kirkwood in 1911. The great fortune they had amassed was more than enough to keep the surviving members of the family comfortable through the Great Depression and beyond.

But the days of Lemp tragedy were not yet over.

In 1933, Prohibition was officially repealed and almost immediately, beer was once again being brewed in St. Louis. The future was bright once more for many of the local companies but dark days were still ahead for the remaining members of the Lemp family.

By the late 1920's, only Charles and Edwin were left in the immediate family. Throughout his life, Charles was never much involved with the Lemp Brewery. His interests had been elsewhere and when the family home was renovated into offices, he made his residence at the Racquet Club in St. Louis. His work had mostly been in the banking and financial industries and he sometimes dabbled in politics as well. In 1929, Charles moved back to the Lemp mansion and the house became a private residence once more.

Despite his very visible business and political life though, Charles remained a mysterious figure who became even odder and more reclusive with age. He remained a bachelor his entire life and lived alone in his old rambling house with only his two servants, Albert and Lena Bittner for company. By the age of 77, he was arthritic and quite ill. Legend has it that he was deathly afraid of germs and wore gloves to avoid any contact with bacteria. He had grown quite bitter and eccentric and had developed a morbid attachment to the Lemp family home. Thanks to the history of the place, his brother Edwin often encouraged him to move out, but Charles refused. Finally, when he could stand no more of life, he became the fourth member of the Lemp family to commit suicide.

On May 10, 1949, Alfred Bittner, one of Charles' staff, went to the kitchen and prepared breakfast for Lemp as he normally did. He then placed the breakfast tray on the desk in the office next to Lemp's bedroom, as he had been doing for years. Bittner later recalled that the door to the bedroom was closed and he did not look inside. At about 8:00, Bittner returned to the office to remove the tray and found it to be untouched. Concerned, he opened the bedroom door to see if Charles was awake and discovered that he was dead from a bullet wound to the head. When the police arrived, they found Lemp still in bed and lightly holding a .38 caliber Army Colt revolver in his right hand. He was the only one of the family who had left a suicide note behind. He had dated the letter May 9 and had written "In case I am found dead blame it on no one but me" and had signed it at the bottom.

Oddly, Charles had made detailed funeral arrangements for himself long before his death. He would be the only member of the family not interred at the mausoleum at Bellefontaine Cemetery and while this might be unusual, it wasn't nearly as strange as the rest of the instructions that he left behind. In a letter that was received at a south St. Louis funeral home in 1941, Lemp ordered that, upon his death, his body should be immediately taken to the Missouri Crematory. His ashes were then to be placed in a wicker box and buried on his farm. He also ordered that his body not be bathed, changed or clothed and that no services were to be held for him and no death notice published, no matter what any surviving members of his family might want.

On May 11, 1949, Edwin Lemp picked up his brother's remains at the funeral home and took them to the farm to be buried. And while these instructions were certainly odd, they were not the most enduring mystery to the situation. You see, even after all of these years, there is no indication as to where Charles Lemp's farm was located....

The Lemp family, which had once been so large and prosperous, had now been almost utterly destroyed in a span of less than a century. Only Edwin Lemp remained and he had long avoided the life that had turned so tragic for the rest of his family. He was known as a quiet, reclusive man who had walked away from the Lemp Brewery in 1913 to live a peaceful life on his secluded estate in Kirkwood. Here, he communed with nature and became an excellent cook, gourmet and animal lover. He collected fine art and entertained his intimate friends.

Edwin managed to escape from the family "curse" but as he grew older, he did become more eccentric and developed a terrible fear of being alone. He never spoke about his family or their tragic lives, but it must have preyed on him all the same. His fears caused him to simply entertain more and to keep a companion with him at his estate almost all the time.

His most loyal friend and companion was John Bopp, the caretaker of the estate for the last 30 years of Edwin's life. His loyalty to his employer was absolute and it is believed that Bopp was never away from the estate for more than a few days at a time. He never discussed any of Lemp's personal thoughts or habits and remained faithful to Edwin, even after his friend's death.

Edwin passed away quietly of natural causes at age 90 in 1970. The last order that John Bopp carried out for him must have been the worst. According to Edwin's wishes, he burned all of the paintings that Lemp had collected throughout his life, as well as priceless Lemp family papers and artifacts. These irreplaceable pieces of history vanished in the smoke of a blazing bonfire and like the Lemp empire ---- were lost forever.

The Lemp family line died out with Edwin and while none of them remain today, it's almost certain that some of them are still around.

The Haunting of the Lemp Mansion

After the death of Charles Lemp, the grand family mansion was sold and turned into a boarding house. Shortly after that, it fell on hard times and began to deteriorate, along with the nearby neighborhood. In later years, stories began to emerge that residents of the boarding house often complained of ghostly knocks and phantom footsteps in the house. As these tales spread, it became increasingly hard to find tenants to occupy the rooms and because of this, the old Lemp Mansion was rarely filled.

One strange account from the days following Charles' death was told by a young woman who decided to sneak into the house with some friends one day in 1949. The house was still vacant at the time but the group managed to get into the front door and they started up the main staircase to the second floor. They climbed the steps to the first landing and then prepared to go up the last set of stairs to the upper level. Just as they reached the landing, they looked up and saw a filmy apparition coming down the steps toward them! The young girl much later described it as an almost human-shaped puff of smoke. The group took one look at it and ran! When she told this story for the first time in the late 1990's, the woman, who was quite elderly by this time, stated that she had never been back in the mansion again.

The decline of the house continued until 1975, when Dick Pointer and his family purchased it. The Pointer's began remodeling and renovating the place, working for many years to turn it into a restaurant and an inn. But the Pointer's were soon to find out that they were not alone in the house. The bulk of the remodeling was done in the 1970's and during this time, workers reported that ghostly events were occurring in the house. Almost all of the workers confessed that they believed the place was haunted and told of feeling as though they were being watched, spoke of strange sounds and complained of tools that vanished and then returned in different places from where they had been left.

At one point in the renovations, a painter was brought in to work on the ceilings and he stayed overnight in the house while he completed the job. One day, he was in his room and ran downstairs to tell one of the Pointer's that he had heard the sound of horse's hooves on the cobblestones outside of his window. Pointer convinced the painter that he was mistaken. There were no horses and no cobblestones outside of the house. In time, the man finished the ceilings and left, but the story stayed on Pointer's mind. Later that year, he noticed that some of the grass in the yard had turned brown. He dug underneath it and found that beneath the top level of the soil was a layer of cobblestones! During the Lemp's residency in the house, that portion of the yard had been a drive to the carriage house! Pointer had the cobblestones removed and then used them as floor stones in one area of the mansion's basement.

Later in the restoration, another artist was brought in to restore the painted ceiling in one of the front dining rooms. It had been covered over with paper years before. While he was lying on his back on the scaffolding, he felt a sensation of what he believed was a "spirit moving past him". It frightened him so badly that he left the house without his brushes and tools and refused to return and get them. Some time after this event, an elderly man came into the restaurant and told one of the staff members that he had once been a driver for the Lemp family. He explained that the ceiling in the dining room had been papered over because William Lemp hated the design that had been printed on it. The staff members, upon hearing this story, noted that the artist had gotten the distinct impression that the "spirit" he encountered had been angry. Perhaps because he was restoring the unwanted ceiling?

During the restorations, Mr. Pointer's son, Richard "Dick" Pointer, lived alone in the house and became quite an expert on the ghostly manifestations. One night, he was lying in bed reading and he heard a door slam loudly in another part of the house. No one else was supposed to be there and he was sure that he had locked all of the doors. Fearing that someone might have broken in, he and his dog, a large Doberman named Shadow, decided to take a look around. The dog was spooked by this time, having also heard the sound, and she had her ears turned up, listening for anything else. They searched the entire house and found no one there. Every door had been locked, just as Pointer had left them. He reported that the same thing happened again about a month later, but again, nothing was found.

After the restaurant opened, staff members began to report their own odd experiences. Glasses were seen to lift off the bar and fly through the air, sounds were often heard that had no explanation and some even glimpsed actual apparitions who appeared and vanished at will. In addition, many customers and visitors to the house reported some pretty weird incidents. It was said that doors locked and unlocked on their own, the piano in the bar played by itself, voices and sounds came from nowhere and even the spirit of the "Lavender Lady", Lillian Handlan, was spotted on occasion.

Late one evening, Dick was bartending after most of the customers had departed and the water in a pitcher began swirling around of its own volition. Pointer was sure that he was just seeing things but all of the customers who remained that night swore they all saw the same thing. Then one night in August 1981, Dick and an employee were startled to hear the piano start playing a few notes by itself. There was no one around it at the time and in fact, there was no one else in the entire building. The piano has continued to be the source of eerie occurrences as the years have passed. No matter where it has been located in the house, whether in the main hallway upstairs or in one of the guest rooms, the piano keys have reportedly tinkled without the touch of human hands.

And while the ghostly atmosphere of the place has admittedly attracted a number of patrons, it has also caused the owners to lose a number of valuable employees of the house. One of them was a former waitress named Bonnie Strayhorn, who encountered an unusual customer while working one day. The restaurant had not yet opened for business but she saw a dark-haired man seated at one of the tables in the rear dining room. She was surprised that someone had come so early, but she went over to ask if he would like a cup of coffee. He simply sat there are did not answer. Bonnie frowned and looked away for a moment. When she looked back, just moments later, the man was gone! She has continued to maintain that the man could not have left the room in the brief seconds when she was not looking at him. After that incident, she left the Lemp Mansion and went to work in a non-haunted location.

In addition to customers, the house has also attracted ghost hunters from around the country. Many of them have come due to the publicity that has been achieved by the house as a haunted location. The mansion has appeared in scores of magazines, newspaper articles, books and television shows over the years but it first gained notoriety back in the 1970's when it was investigated by the "Haunt Hunters". These two St. Louis men, Phil Goodwilling and Gordon Hoener, actively researched ghost stories and sightings in the area and during that period, even conducted a class on ghosts for St. Louis University. They promised their students that they would take them to a real haunted place and decided that the Lemp Mansion fit the bill. In October 1979, they brought the class to the house and brought along a local television crew to film the event.

Goodwilling and Hoener divided the students up into small groups and gave them all writing "planchettes" to try and contact the spirits. The devices, like Ouija boards, were used to spell out messages from the ghosts. Each of the groups of students was divided into groups of four.

One of the groups asked: "Is there an unseen presence that wishes to communicate?"

"Yes", came the answer. It scrawled out on a large piece of paper as the planchette, with its pencil tip, moved across the surface.

The students asked another question: "Will you identify yourself?"

The planchette scratched out a reply: "Charles Lemp."

Goodwilling later noted that the students who received this message were the most skeptical in the class. He also noted that no one in the room that night, with the exception of Dick Pointer, had any idea that Charles had committed suicide. At that time, the history of the house had not been widely publicized.

After the name was revealed, the spirit added that he had taken his own life. When asked why he did this, the spirit replied in three words: "Help, death, rest."

It might also be added that by the time this séance was over, the four students were no longer the most skeptical in the class.

In November, the Haunt Hunters returned to the house and this time brought along a camera crew from the popular show of the era, *Real People*. Goodwilling and Hoener participated in a séance with two other participants, neither of which had any idea about the past history of the mansion. They once again made contact with a spirit who identified himself as "Charles Lemp" and he was asked again why he had committed suicide. The spirit reportedly used a derogatory term and then added "... damn Roosevelt." Apparently, the Lemp's had not been fond of the politics practiced by Franklin D. Roosevelt during their time.

But the séance continued with the next question from the group: "Is there a message for someone in this house?"

The answer came: "Yes, yes, Edwin, money"

The group then asked if there was anything they could do to free the spirit from being trapped in the house? "Yes, yes," the ghost replied. Unfortunately though, they were unsuccessful in finding out what they could do to help.

Goodwilling felt that if the spirit was actually Charles Lemp, then he might have stayed behind in the house because of his suicide. He might have had a message for his brother, Edwin Lemp, who he tried to contact during the séance. He may have believed that Edwin was still alive and based on the conversation, was trying to pass along a message about money. Could this be what caused Charles Lemp's ghost to remain behind?

Most importantly perhaps to the reader is the question of whether the Lemp Mansion still remains haunted today. Most can tell you that it does and the current owners of the house accept this as just part of the house's unusual ambience. One of the owners, Paul Pointer, helps to maintain the place as a wonderful eating and lodging establishment. He takes the ghosts as just another part of the strange mansion. "People come here expecting to experience weird things," he said, " and fortunately for us, they are rarely disappointed."

Nights at the Lemp Mansion

I first heard about the Lemp Mansion and its hauntings back in the early 1990's, when the first (wildly skewed) stories about the ghosts began to appear in what few ghost books were available in those days. At the first opportunity that I had, I traveled to St. Louis to see the house and a couple of years later, spent the night here for the first time. Even then, it was an amazing house, although the "bed and breakfast" service was definitely in its early stages. I stayed there on a scorching June night with a few friends and aside from a couple of struggling window units, there was no cooling system in the place. The house was stifling until about 2:00 a.m., when it finally started to cool down. I remember that we were given some fruit and muffins to keep until breakfast in the morning, along with a large bucket of ice. It was so hot though that the ice was melted within about 20 minutes.

On the bright side though, we had the entire house to ourselves and Paul Pointer told us that we could roam anywhere we wanted to in the place. We took him up on it and scoured the mansion from top to bottom in search of not only ghosts but an entrance to the legendary caverns that were supposed to exist under the house. The book that I had read, which featured the Lemp Mansion, had been badly out of date and stated that the caves were accessible from the mansion. Later, when I started researching the house for my own writings on the Lemp's, I would find out that the cave entrance had been closed for many years. I wouldn't give up on the idea of getting into the cave though, as you'll see later in this chapter.

My first stay in the Lemp Mansion was largely uneventful, although there was one incident that occurred that I have never been able to explain. At some point, around 3:00 a.m., we heard someone on the main staircase that leads from the front foyer to the second floor. We were sitting in the hallway at the top of the stairs, talking quietly, when we heard what sounded like heavy footsteps. One of my friends got up and walked over to see if someone, perhaps one of the staff members, had returned to the mansion. She called the rest of us over when she noticed that, although we could all still hear someone walking, there was no one on the staircase! All of us witnessed this eerie phenomenon, which continued for several minutes and went up and down the stairs several times.

While it was occurring, I went down the stairs to see if I could sense anyone going past me, a temperature change or some sort of movement. I never felt a thing but there was no denying that we could hear someone walking. Strangely though, and I am hardly a lightweight, my own shoes made no sound on the wooden steps.

The footsteps continued on for a few minutes and then stopped. We looked under the steps, up and down them and even tried measuring and jumping up and down on them. We could never duplicate the sounds that we heard. They sounded exactly like someone with heavy boots walking back and forth and if they were anything else ---- I can't begin to imagine what it was.

I visited the mansion a number of other times as the years went by but it wouldn't be until 2003 when I would spend another night there. This time, I did not spend the night inside the house but under it ---- in the famous caverns that had originally been used by the Lemp's to lager their beer!

A reporter for the *Missouri Republican* newspaper once wrote that Lemp's cave had three separate chambers and that each one of them contained large casks that were capable of holding 20-30 barrels of beer. The lagering cellars were opened for use in 1845, but Lemp soon expanded them to store more than 3,000 barrels of beer at a time. The beer cellars had been created by simply clearing out the natural underground river channels that had been carved from the limestone. They were divided off by the construction of masonry and brick walls into artificial rooms. During the early period of the brewery's history, Lemp was still brewing the beer near the downtown riverfront and taking it by wagon to the cave for the lagering period. After the death of Adam Lemp, his son, William, would construct a new brewery above the cave.

Around 1850, and around the time that the Lemp Brewery was just beginning to grow, fur trader Henri Chatillon built a home on a piece of property that adjoined Lemp's property at the crest of Arsenal Hill on Thirteenth Street. In 1856, Dr. Nicholas DeMenil purchased the house and land and he began enlarging and expanding the farm house a few years later. He added several rooms to the house and a magnificent portico that faced eastward and looked out over his large garden and the Mississippi River. The Greek Revival mansion became a favorite landmark for river pilots rounding a landmark known as Chatillon's Bend.

In 1865, DeMenil leased the southwest corner of the property to the Minnehaha Brewery and they built a small, two-story frame brewery on the site. For several years, DeMenil had been using a cave that was located beneath his house as a place to store perishable goods and he also leased a portion of this cave to Charles Fritschle and Louis Zepp, the owners of the brewery. Like Adam Lemp, they planned to use the caverns as a place to lager beer and over the course of the next year, they made a number of improvements to the cave. Unfortunately, the brewery went out of business in 1867 and DeMenil acquired the buildings.

During the years of both operations, the Lemp's and the Minnehaha Brewery were using different parts of the same cave. A wall had been constructed between the two businesses but the Lemp's had little to fear from this short-lived competition. It is also believed that they must have been on good terms with Dr. DeMenil. When the Lemp family renovated their home just down the street from the DeMenil mansion, an arrangement was made to run three pipelines through DeMenil's cave, furnishing the Lemp mansion with hot water, cold water and beer from the brewery complex down the street.

The Lemp's continued to use the cave until the time when artificial refrigeration was installed at the factory. After that, the cave no longer played a role in beer production, so it was turned into a private playground for the Lemp family. A tunnel exited the basement of the house and entered into a portion of the cave that Adam Lemp had discovered for his beer lagering years before. Traveling along a quarried shaft, the Lemp's could journey beneath the street, all the way to the brewery. One large chamber was converted into a natural auditorium and a theater with constructed scenery of plaster and wire. Crude floodlights were used to illuminate the scene and the Lemp's were believed to have hired actors on the theater and vaudeville circuits of the day to come into the cave for private performances. This section of the cave was accessible by way of a spiral staircase that once ascended to Cherokee Street. This entrance is sealed today and the spiral stairs were cut away to prevent anyone from entering the cave.

East of the theater was another innovation of the Lemp family. Just below the intersection of Cherokee and DeMenil Streets was a large, concrete-lined pool that had been a reservoir back in the days of underground lagering. In the years that followed, the Lemp's converted it into a wading pool by using hot water that was piped in from the brewery's boiler house, which was located only a short distance away.

After Prohibition, the caves were abandoned and the entrances sealed shut. However, this was not the end for the Minnehaha portion of the cave. In November 1946, a pharmaceutical manufacturer named Lee Hess bought not only the Minnehaha portion of the cave but the old DeMenil Mansion and grounds as well. He set to work developing the cave as a tourist attraction. He erected a museum building and parking lot to serve what he dubbed "Cherokee Cave". The cave became a popular tourist attraction but some still tell stories about Hess and his strange obsession with the cavern. He nearly lost his entire fortune trying to develop it and only two rooms of the sprawling DeMenil house were used during his time there. He and his wife shared one room and Albert Hoffman, who managed the cave for Hess, lived in the other.

In April 1950, Cherokee Cave was opened to the public and it was a popular attraction for more than 10 years. Visitors to the cave were able to stroll along on a tour that took them to Cherokee Lake and the Petrified Falls and of course to the famed Spaghetti Room, where slender cave formations hung down from the ceiling like strands of pasta.

The cave remained open until 1960 and in 1961, it was purchased by the Missouri Highway department to clear the way for Interstate 55. Hess battled to the end of his life to keep the state from destroying the DeMenil Mansion and he eventually succeeded, although the cave museum and entrance could not be saved. The building and the entrance that Hess had created were demolished in 1964. Today, the only reminder of this unique place is a short street near Broadway and Cherokee in St. Louis called "Cave Street". The DeMenil Mansion became a historic site and museum.

For years after the Interstate tore though this historic portion of the city, it was believed that Cherokee Cave had been filled in and completely destroyed. It was later discovered that this was wrong and that portions of the cave still exist today. While not accessible to the public, the mystery of the place still remains alive.

Cave researchers and spelunkers have toured these passages in recent years but the last real documented visits took place in the middle 1960's. During the visit, accounts told of the labyrinth of rooms that were constructed by the Lemp's and revealed the remains of broken and rotted wooden casks where beer was once aged in the cellars. Visitors also passed through oversized doorways and into rooms lined with brick and stone. The wading pool remained as well, now filthy and covered with mud. The theater still existed, although it was hard to imagine audiences who might have assembled here to watch a performance. When the theater was built, the Lemp's tore out the natural formations of the cave and replaced with them with formations made from plaster and wood. Tinted in odd colors, this formed the backdrop for the stage.

And while many can attest to the haunting that occurs in the Lemp Mansion, once accessible from the cave, there are others who insist that the cave is haunted too. Stories have been told about strange sounds and shapes that have been seen and heard down here and cannot be explained away as the weird, but natural, happenings of a cave. In recent times, the brewery above the cave has occasionally been the site of a "haunted house" attraction that has been put on by the current owners of the Lemp Mansion Restaurant. While a standard attraction of that type, in some cases, the customers sometimes got a little more than they bargained for. On at least one occasion, the attraction was reportedly closed down after a staff member spotted someone in an off-limits area that led down to the cave entrances. The customers were stopped at the door while employees tracked down this wandering visitor and escorted them out. However, after a thorough search, there was no one found. The trespasser had completely vanished!

On other occasions, apparitions had been seen and one staff member, who entered the cave itself, claimed to hear the sound of someone with hard-soled shoes walking behind him in some of the abandoned passageways. Unnerved, he began walking faster, only to have the mysterious footsteps keep pace with him. Suddenly, perhaps thinking that it was only his imagination or an echo of the cave playing tricks on him, he stopped abruptly, fully expecting the tapping of the shoes to stop as well ----- but they continued on for several more steps before stopping too. Now, feeling quite frightened, he turned and illuminated the passage behind him with his flashlight but there was no one there! Needless to say, he immediately left the cave.

And the stories have continued to be told over the past few years. Forays into the caves for research purposes have added to the haunted lore of the place but unfortunately, it was unlikely, I thought, that I would ever get to experience this for myself. After discovering that the cave was no longer accessible from the house, I gave up on the idea of ever seeing it. The Lemp Caverns, and legendary Cherokee Cave, were now closed and forgotten, perhaps for all time. I had finally resigned myself to the fact that it was a place that I would never get to see.

Or that's what I thought at the time.

In March 2003, I received an invitation from some acquaintances, as well as my friend Luke Naliborski and Lemp Mansion owner Paul Pointer, to come along on an excursion into the one place in St. Louis that I never imagined that I would get to see ---- the Lemp Caverns and Cherokee Cave. Paul had offered a private tour of the caverns and I immediately said that I would come.

On a chilly night in early March, we assembled at the nearby Lemp Mansion and then followed Paul as he took us to one of the rear entrances to the brewery buildings, now the only access into the caves. We entered one of the buildings with the gigantic grain silos and first had the rare treat of touring the brewery building itself, even riding one of the original elevators to the top floor and going out on the roof for an incredible view of south St. Louis. The warehouse buildings of the brewery are utterly massive with huge open floors that once held the workings and storage casks

One of the vaulted chambers once used for storing beer in the lower levels of the abandoned Lemp Brewery.

for the beer. In later times, after artificial refrigeration, the beer had been stored in various locations in the building. As we would descend to the lower areas of the brewery though, we would literally go back in time to the earliest days of the company, when beer had to be stored in low, cool areas to lager.

Staircases and elevators began to take us lower into the brewery until we finally entered areas that were underground. Here, we found more of the massive rooms with curved archways, detailed stone and brick work and unique ceilings that had been built with individual, arched sections to add extra support for the gigantic stone buildings overhead. When the brewery had been opened, the foundations would have had to support incredible weight in machinery, men and the huge casks of beer.

In each section that we explored, as we went deeper underground, we found that remnants of the brewery, and the heyday of the Lemp empire, remained. In the upper sections, we found only occasional, worn away emblems in the shape of the famous Lemp shield (which later became the Falstaff logo), original light fixtures, hidden designs in doors and glass fixtures but little else. As we descended deeper underground however, the remains of the brewery became more noticeable and some locations appeared almost untouched, as though the last people to walk there before we did had been men who received a paycheck from the Lemp brewery each week.

Leaving the gigantic, arched rooms behind, we descended once again, this time through a smaller doorway, traveled along more passages and then went down a long, curved staircase to what would be considered the sub-basement of the brewery. This was at the same level as the first portion of the cave. It was through this level that the Lemp's would ascend to the brewery as they walked to work on many mornings, using the cave to travel from the mansion to their offices. It was here that William Lemp had walked as he began his descent into the depression and madness that would later claim his life. He became so withdrawn that he refused to appear in public and chose these subterranean passages to travel to the brewery each day.

Our flashlights illuminated this area of the complex, which seemed well on its way to being reclaimed by the cave that it had been carved out of. The floors were covered with mud, moss and algae in some places and water dripped constantly from the walls and the ceilings. The brick was slowly crumbling beneath the decades of dampness and moisture. It was this area of the brewery, the actual cave, where Adam Lemp had stored the first lager beer in St. Louis. There are several chambers that had been created here with high, curved ceilings and it was inside of these chambers where the original casks were placed. Ice was cut from the river during the winter months

The entrance to the Lemp Caverns from the Brewery. During the last days of his life, William Lemp often walked through this passageway as he traveled back and forth to the Brewery.

and then placed in the chambers to keep the beer cool. As it melted, the water would drain off into the sides of the chambers and into the water that flowed through the cave itself. On the sides of these long rooms, the cave water was visible and while extremely clear, left behind mineral deposits on the stone floor, making it plain that it was not fit to drink.

We then left the finished areas of the cave, with its stone floor and brick-lined walls, and entered a passageway that would take us into the wild areas of the cave that remained. To reach this section, we passed through a long, rugged corridor that was so damp and filled with moisture that many of the photographs that we took that night were so fogged that it was impossible to make out details. Several of my own photographs were lost but by continuing to clean my lens throughout the evening, I was able to take some of the first photos of the caverns that had been captured in years.

This long passageway, which led deeper into the cave, was littered with fallen stone, mud and refuse from the old days of the brewery. Above our heads were metal brackets and chains that had once been part of a conveyor belt system for transporting ice into the lager vaults. A motor from the conveyor belt is still resting on the side of the path through the passage. At the end of it, a metal ladder dangled from the ceiling and led upwards into a narrow, shadowy hole. During the early days of the brewery, this had been a shaft that was used to dump ice down into the cave. It was loaded onto cars on the conveyor belt and then mechanically moved to the lagering areas. This hole was sealed off many years ago and the metal ladder has fallen into disrepair.

Our first area of exploration took us to the left of the passage and we traveled down a wide tunnel toward what was once the Lemp's theater. In a number of areas, cave formations, mostly stalactites, were visible. Unfortunately though (as we would see in other parts of the cave), many of the formations had been broken off and damaged. This was presumably done in less enlightened times, when people didn't realize that such formations not only take hundreds of years to be created but are very harmful to the life of the cave. There are formations in the caverns that still exist but they are now somewhat rare.

The old Lemp theater is literally in ruins today. An archway at the back, which led to another chamber, was really one of the only remaining architectural pieces, as the false scenery that had been created for the theater now lay in heaping piles on the floor. It has long since been destroyed but some of the garish colors that had been painted on the plaster and stone can still be seen. Overhead, an old electric light bar that once illuminated the small stage does still remain. Its bulbs have long since been darkened and have been shattered though. I couldn't help but wonder as I stood here, looking around a room that was shrouded in a heavy mist, just how much privacy the Lemp's must have craved? I couldn't imagine huddling down here, far underground in this damp and dark chamber, just so I could attend private performances of popular programs. And how much did the Lemp's offer to be able to get the actors to put on these command performances? The theater remains an eerie and downright spooky place. I would not be surprised to learn that the ghosts of these actors still linger here ---- still walking a stage that vanished long ago.

The theater marks the end of this passage and so we turned back in the direction we had come from and once more ended up beneath the ice chute to the surface. Just beyond this is the famed "swimming pool" of the Lemp family. The pool was actually just a wading pool and it was only used for this purpose after electric refrigeration was installed in the brewery. Before this, it was a reservoir for run-off from the melting ice. To visit the site today, you can still see the smooth walls of the reservoir but over the years, it has been heavily clogged with falls of rock from the cave's ceiling and by copious amounts of mud and clay. It bears little resemblance to any sort of wading pool now and was certainly not inviting enough for me to want to consider rolling up my pant legs and walking in. The pool is still filled with water though, which is approximately two feet deep or

A staircase leading down into what had once been the passages of Cherokee Cave

so, and is a habitat for the blind, white fish that dwell in caves. The animals are fairly rare but they can be found in the old Lemp Caverns.

Once we traveled past the reservoir, we entered what I considered to be the actual passages of Cherokee Cave. Here, the natural contours of the cave had been opened up and the floor had been artificially smoothed and fitted with curbs on each side of the path to keep the majority of the water away. These improvements, along with the remains of electrical wiring and light boxes, had been left behind when Lee Hess had been forced to abandon the cave back in 1961. They were just a few of the signs of the commercial cave that we would find in the passages ahead.

As the trip progressed, the commercial aspects of the cave became more and more obvious. At one point, we reached a ravine that cut across the path and had to use a metal ladder to climb down and cross to stone steps on the other side. An alternate route opened to the right and we descended another flight of steps, which were nestled between metal hand rails had been installed nearly 50 years ago. Here, we discovered more signs of the commercial Cherokee Cave in stripped out electrical lines and carefully constructed walkways. It was this passage that had originally connected the cave and brewery to the Lemp Mansion. The entrance from the house has long since been sealed off and is no longer accessible but I looked forward to seeing it anyway. However, as we began to get nearer to the house, the water that now covered the floor grew deeper and deeper. To make matters worse, Paul began to get very concerned about the quality of air in this passageway. This has been a problem with some of the cave exploration that has been done in recent years. On one occasion, one member of a group of spelunkers had to be bodily carried out of the cave after passing out. We tried checking the air with a flame from a lighter and we watched as the flame grew weaker and weaker as we progressed along the passage. Eventually, it flickered and went out and we had to turn back. I was the last to return, feeling a great sense of loss for the now forgotten cave. I wondered if the others had the same sense of the history that we were privileged enough to be experiencing, walking where very few had walked in nearly half a century. This was, I realized, a haunted place ---- whether by ghosts or by time though, I was unable to say.

One final passage awaited us and led us deeper into the cave or, if we had visited Cherokee Cave when it was in business, would have led us out of the cave. This was the original shaft that had been opened by Lee Hess and would have ended at the cave's visitor center and parking lot if they had not been demolished in the early 1960's.

The passage made a sharp right turn, although ahead of us was a man-made basin that had been built to catch run-off from a small spring that flowed from the cave wall. A trickle of water was still running into the basin even now. We turned into this last passageway but only traveled for a short distance before coming to what had been dubbed "Cherokee Lake" by Lee Hess. A stone bridge had been built across the lake decades ago but the path on the opposite side of it ended abruptly at a stone wall. This wall had been placed here by the Missouri Department of Transportation during the construction of Interstate 55. When they had razed the visitor's center, to replace it with the highway, the cave had also been sealed off, bringing to an end an element of St. Louis' most mysterious and colorful history.

Our return journey back through the labyrinth of cave passages, doorways, staircases, lagering chambers and brewery corridors took us much less time to complete than it had when we were descending. I was surprised to discover that we had actually been underground for several hours.

I remember walking back down the corridor where the conveyor belt system had been, which led from the cave to the lagering caverns, and looking back into the darkness and mist behind us. I am not sure what I expected to see or hear ---- the sound of other, more ethereal explorers following behind or perhaps the specters of the Lemp's themselves still trudging to the brewery after all of these years? I don't know for sure, but I know that I expected something.

I wish that I could tell you that I had had some ghostly experience while exploring these haunted caverns but unfortunately, I cannot. The ghosts were certainly there though, at least in a figurative sense, because no one can come here and not feel the very tangible spirit of the past. It was a night that I may never be able to experience again ---- and one that I will certainly never forget.

My next overnight stay at the Lemp Mansion was arranged on February 13, 2004 --- the 100th anniversary of the suicide of William Lemp. This momentous occasion was attended by a number of customers and investigators and we gathered at the house in preparation for what we believed would be an active night. A number of us who were present that night, including several investigators from the American Ghost Society, had stayed at the house before and nearly all of us had previously experienced unexplained activity while there. But the "activity" that we would experience that night had nothing to do with ghosts!

After dinner that evening, the group met at the house and established a "base of operations" in one of the rooms on the second floor. We were anticipating a great night because I knew there had been strange happenings in the house in recent months. I heard from several people who stayed in the house during the fall months and they all spoke of the usual phantom footsteps, disembodied voices and items that disappeared and moved about but there was one strange incident that I knew about that I could actually vouch for.

In August 2003, I had invited my friend Leslie Rule, a fellow ghost writer and daughter of crime author Ann Rule, to come to Alton and speak at an event for the History & Hauntings Book Co. She had wanted to stay somewhere haunted while in the area and I helped her to make arrangements to stay at the Lemp Mansion for several nights. She was very excited at the prospect until she called to make reservations and was told by co-owner Patty Pointer that she would have the mansion all to herself during her stay. Leslie was not enthused about sleeping in the haunted house alone and she asked me if I might know of anyone who would consider staying with her. I suggested that she contact my friend, and American Ghost Society member, Anita Dytuco and between the two of them, they planned an overnight at the mansion.

Anita and her 22 year-old daughter, Amy, picked up Leslie at the airport and all of us met for dinner. Anita and Amy had stopped by the mansion before dinner, picked up the keys and had turned on the lights in their rooms "as a test", Amy explained. Since the lights in the empty house had a reputation for turning themselves off and on, she wanted to see what would happen. When we all went back to the house after dinner and found that some of the lights were no longer on though, she nervously dismissed this as someone playing a joke on them.

I wouldn't find out how scared Amy was about staying in the house until after I talked to her and Anita a few days later. Leslie later told me that she was very tentative about exploring the house with her and that it took some urging to get her into some of the creepier parts of the house, like the dark and ominous attic. To make matters worse, their flashlight batteries unexpectedly went out while they were in the attic, unsettling Amy even further.

But perhaps Amy had a good reason to be unsettled. A number of women who have worked and have stayed the night in the house have had encounters with a female spirit or have heard someone calling to them in the darkness. Some believe this spirit may be that of Elsa Lemp, who, while she did not die in the house, spent a large amount of her life here. They were her happiest times and perhaps she has returned here seeking peace after her death. Regardless of who this lovely spirit may be, many women have encountered her --- including Amy.

A few days after her nerve-wracking stay, Amy told me that she had been trying to go to sleep next to her mother in the Lavender Suite on the second floor and was having trouble dozing off. After tossing and turning for awhile, she turned over and was terrified to see a woman in a long dress standing next to the bed. The woman looked very real but there was no way that she could have gotten into the room through the locked door. Before Amy could do or say anything, the woman leaned toward her, placed a finger to her lips and made a "shushing" motion, as if to tell Amy to be quiet and go to sleep. The woman then simply vanished! Needless to say, Amy did not sleep for the rest of the night.

I recalled this incident while unpacking my things for our "anniversary" overnight at the mansion. Since the house had been so active in the preceding months, it seemed even more likely that we were going to be in for an exciting night. What better time to be at the house than on the night when the first Lemp suicide occurred?

We spent the first few hours of the night exploring the house while I recounted the history of the brewery and told of the series of tragic events that had befallen the family. After a time, we split up into groups and began investigating and photographing the house. I wandered between the floors, checking in with the various groups and had just gone down into the basement when I heard a loud gasp from one of the rooms to the back of the house. I went back to see what was going on and I was told by one of the investigators that they had heard someone walking around. They were startled by the footsteps, which explained the loud gasp, and went to find the source of the sounds. We were standing there talking when suddenly, a dark shadow loomed up against the window!

As it turned out, what we thought might be a ghost was actually just a late arrival to the house. The "shadow" was my friend Dave Goodwin, an author and police officer who had been working a late shift and was just then arriving for the anniversary overnight. I let Dave into the house and the night continued with more photos and experimentation with equipment.

The evening took a bad turn when the night's only "activity" began at about 1:30 a.m. One of the investigators happened to glance out the window of one of the downstairs dining rooms and noticed that the trunk of a car in the parking lot was standing open. It turned out to be their car! After alerting everyone, Dave and I went straight outside and saw someone running away from the lot. We soon learned that several of the cars parked in the lot had been broken into and bags, purses and personal items had been stolen. One of the cars belonged to two young men who brought dozens of different pieces of paranormal investigation equipment with them to the overnight. They had so much stuff that they left several cases in their car. They also had a laptop computer and several other expensive items. The laptop was left untouched but the thieves had made off with the cases of ghost detection devices. One can only imagine what went through the minds of the thieves when they opened those cases and saw the bizarre --- and largely useless to most people ---- items inside!

After calling the police and sorting out what had happened, along with what was missing, the evening was largely a bust. With only a couple of hours left to investigate, we made the most of it by either continuing with the investigations or catching a short nap. As it ended up, some of the stolen items were later recovered and everyone breathed a sigh of relief that nothing more valuable had been taken.

It made for a memorable night, but it was definitely not what we had in mind!

The next overnight that I hosted to the Lemp Mansion was in May of that same year. It was a few days after the May 10 anniversary of Charles Lemp's suicide but based on the way that the last "anniversary overnight" had turned out, I decided not to mention it to anyone. I was once again joined at the house by a number of investigators, as well as my friends Darren Deist, his fiancée Laura, Rex Murray and Amanda Schmitt. We all enjoyed the tour and history of the house and working with the various groups as they began their investigations. At one point, a strange event occurred that I was lucky enough to actually witness for myself.

One of the standard things that we do at the Lemp Mansion is bring along a Ouija board and give people a chance to work with it in the house.

The attic of the Lemp Mansion, which was once used as the servant's quarters. This has long been regarded as an area where a lot of strange activity takes place.

Without passing judgment on whether to use a Ouija board or not, the reader may have noticed from earlier in the chapter that such devices have been involved with investigations at the house since the "Haunt Hunters" days of the 1970's. I always bring along the board and make it available for people to use, or not use ---- the choice is up to them. Just to make it interesting though, I tracked down and purchased an antique board that was made in 1915. I figured that if we were going to use one in the house, we might as well use one that came from the era when the place was in its heyday.

On this night, I placed the Ouija board on a small table in the unfinished portion of the attic (which is no longer accessible to the public) and placed some chairs around it to make it easier to use. The attic was quite a mess at that time. There were pieces of wood stacked around, old doors and years of dust and grime. Previous visitors to the attic had left behind garbage in some places, including a number of small candles that had apparently been set up for a séance of some sort. The candles had burned down to the wick, leaving only small foil holders scattered all over the attic's main room.

Throughout the evening, the separate groups took turns using the board during the time they were assigned to that section of the house. Nothing out of the ordinary took place as the evening went by but people were intrigued with the idea of experimenting with the Ouija board.

At some point, just after midnight, I went up to the attic where Rex, Amanda, Darren and Laura were trying out the board. I went up and sat down in one of the chairs and watched as Darren and Laura tried to coax messages from it using the planchette. For the next 20 minutes or so, they had absolutely no luck. Their fingers were placed lightly on it and they asked question after question, waiting to see if the planchette moved. Nothing happened ---- at all.

Finally, after another five minutes or so of frustration, Darren let out a sigh and suggested that someone else might want to give the board a try. Almost as soon as he spoke, all of us present heard the sound of something sliding across the floor. No one had been standing near it but somehow, one of the little candle holders had moved across the floor under its own power. The candle holder slid about 10 feet, from one side of the room to the other, passing directly beneath Darren's chair! The room was now so quiet that you could have heard a pin drop...

"What was that?" someone asked and we quickly deduced that it had been one of the candle holders but we were unable to figure out just how it had moved.

We spent the next hour or so waiting to see if anything else would happen but nothing else occurred. I have never been able to come up with an explanation for how the candle holder moved, other than to say that perhaps it was one of the spirits in the house. Were they trying to make themselves known to us and couldn't do it in any other way?

Since that time, I have visited and stayed the night at the Lemp Mansion on many other occasions. As Paul Pointer once said, those who come to this house are rarely ever disappointed and I would have to agree. While not all of my stays at this old house have been eventful ones, at least when it comes to ghosts, I have to admit that the vivid history that I feel I have experienced when I'm here more than makes up for anything supernatural that I may have missed out on. If you're a ghost hunter, or even an enthusiast of history, then I encourage you to visit the mansion of the once-mighty Lemp family. Their empire may have crumbled many years ago but there is much here to see among the ruins of yesterday.

6. HUNTING FOR THE BELL WITCH

Investigating the Bell Witch Cave with Troy Taylor

There is no greater ghost story in the history of America than that of the Bell Witch of Tennessee. I became so fascinated with this case that I eventually wrote an entire book about it called *Season of the Witch*. Since it would take me far too long to recount the entire history of the witch within these pages, I'll suggest that you pick up a copy of that book to learn more. In short though, the family of a Tennessee farmer named John Bell was plagued by a mysterious and violent spirit for nearly four years. The haunting involved spectral creatures, disembodied voices, unbelievable violence and even resulted in the death of John Bell ---- all at the hands of the infamous Bell Witch.

The haunting began in 1817 when the Bell family began experiencing strange phenomena in their home. First, the house was plagued with knocking and rapping noises and scratching sounds. Blankets were pulled from beds, family members were kicked and scratched and their hair pulled. Particularly tormented was young Elizabeth Bell, who was slapped, pinched, bruised and stuck with pins. At first, John Bell was determined to keep the events a secret, but soon confided in a friend, who

then formed an investigative committee. John Bell's friends soon learned that the strange force in the house had an eerie intelligence. It soon found a voice and from that day on was seldom silent.

The spirit identified itself as the "witch" of Kate Batts, a neighbor of the Bell's, with whom John had experienced bad business dealings over some purchased slaves. "Kate", as the local people began calling the spirit, made daily appearances in the Bell home, wreaking havoc on everyone there. People all over the area of soon learned of the witch and she made appearances, in sounds and voices, all over Robertson County. The ghost became so famous that even General Andrew Jackson decided to visit. He also experienced the antics of the witch and his carriage wheels refused to turn until the witch decided to let them.

During the haunting infestation, Bell fell victim to bouts of strange illness, for which Kate claimed responsibility. While he was sick in bed, the spirit cursed and prodded him, never allowing him to rest. One day, he went to bed and never recovered. He was found senseless in his bed one morning and a strange bottle was found nearby. Bell's breath smelled of the black liquid in the bottle, so a drop of it was placed on the tongue of a cat and the animal dropped dead. John Bell soon followed suit and Kate screamed in triumph. She even made her presence known at his funeral, laughing, cursing and singing as the poor man was buried.

Kate didn't vanish immediately after the death of her proclaimed enemy though. She stayed around, threatening Betsy Bell to not marry the man that she truly loved, Joshua Gardner. The witch would never say why, but she did allow the girl to later marry the local schoolteacher, Richard Powell. Kate soon left the family but promised to return in seven years. She did come back and plagued the family again for two weeks. She soon departed but many believe that she may not have gone far.

Who was the Bell Witch? Was she really a ghost, who claimed to be connected to a living person? Or did the resentment and the hatred of the real Kate Batts create an entity all its own? Or could the haunting have been poltergeist activity linked to Betsy Bell? No one will ever know for sure ---- but whoever, or whatever, the Bell Witch was, many believe that she has never left Adams, Tennessee at all.

Near the Red River, on the former Bell farm, is a cave that has been called the "Bell Witch Cave". Thanks to local legend and lore, many people have come to believe that when the spirit of the witch departed after tormenting the Bell family, she went into this cave. Others (myself included) believe that the cave marks the entrance to a doorway through which Kate came into the world, departed, and perhaps even returns today. Who knows? But I can tell you that with the large number of bizarre incidents reported in and around the cave in modern times, notions of the witch returning may not be as odd as you might think.

While the cave has become quite famous in recent years, there is little mention of it in contemporary accounts of the haunting. It is believed that the cave might have been used for the cool storage of food in those days, thanks to the fact that it remains a constant 56 degrees. It was also mentioned in some accounts that Kate's voice was often heard nearby and one day, Betsy Bell and several of her friends had a close encounter with the witch inside of the cave.

The cave itself is located in the center of a large bluff that overlooks the river. The mouth of the cave opens widely but entrance to the cavern itself must be gained through a fairly long tunnel. The cave is not large compared to most commercial caves, however its true length is unknown because of narrow passages that go beyond the 500 or so feet accessible to visitors. In wet weather, a stream gushes

The interior entrance to the Bell Witch Cave. Does the heavy, locked gate keep people out --- or something else in?

from the mouth of the cavern and tumbles over a cliff into the river below. This makes the cave dangerous and nearly impossible to navigate during wet weather. Those who venture inside are unable to communicate with one another as even shouted conversations become inaudible over the roar of the water.

In dry times though, the cave has proven to be quite an attraction to curiosity-seekers and ghost hunters. Once you pass through the entrance passage, the visitor enters a large room that opens into yet another tunnel and an overhead passageway. Another large room can be found at the rear of the explored portion of the cave, where the few formations can be found, but from that point on the tunnels become smaller, narrower and much more dangerous.

The Bell Witch Cave became an attraction thanks largely to a man named Bill Eden, who owned the property for a number of years. Eden was a wealth of information about the cave and about the fact that strange occurrences were continuing to take place on the land that once belonged to John Bell. Although he was mainly a farmer, Eden did make some early improvements to the cave by adding electrical lights, but that was about all.

Despite being undeveloped though, the cave managed to attract hundreds of visitors every year. Bill always obliged them with a tour although he was always puzzled about how they found the place. There were no signs to point the way at that time but somehow people tracked down directions to the site and they always asked to hear the stories of the witch, and the stories that Eden spun from his own weird experiences at the place. If it was not the witch who lingered here, he maintained, then it was haunted for another reason entirely. Regardless, the place was haunted!

Many of the strange experiences actually happened to Bill Eden himself, while others involved visitors to the cave. For instance, a woman came to visit one day and asked to go down and see the cave. She had brought a group of friends along and in all, about 15 people followed Eden down the rather treacherous path to the cave's entrance. All at once, the woman in charge of the group abruptly sat down in the middle of the path. One of the people with her asked why she was sitting there, and she answered that she wasn't doing it on purpose! She claimed that a heavy weight, which felt like a ton of lead, was pressing her down to the ground and she couldn't get up. Several members of the group managed to get the lady to her feet and half carried her back up the hill to her car.

Bill Eden could also recount a number of encounters he had on his own in the cave. "You can hear footsteps in there all the time and I saw one thing," he once said in an interview. "Lots of people come out here expecting to see a ghost or a witch of whatever you want to call it. I just call it a spirit ---- and it looked like a person with its back turned to you. Looked like it was built out of real white-looking heavy fog or snow, or something real solid white. But you couldn't see through it. It had the complete figure of a person till it got down to about its ankles. It wasn't touching the floor at all. It was just drifting ---- bouncing along."

As Eden mentioned, a lot of people came to the cave hoping to see, or experience, a ghost. While many of them went away disappointed, some got a little more than they bargained for.

Eden had taken a group of young people into the cave one evening for a tour. They had been inside for about an hour and had stopped in the back room where they talked for awhile and Bill told of his experiences in the area. As they were starting to leave, one of the girls in the group started to make some remarks about the authenticity of the place, whether or not it was really haunted, and about how disappointed she was that nothing had appeared or had happened. She continued this monologue into the passage connecting the two rooms, which is quite narrow. Everyone else in the group seemed to be having a good time and Eden was used to the squeals, giggles and laughter that often accompanied young people on tours of the cave. The girl who was complaining was walking directly in front of Eden at this point.

She was walking along and then all of the sudden, stumbled backwards as if she had been pushed. She took a couple of steps back and then sat down hard on the floor of the cave. "Somebody slapped me!" the girl yelled.

Eden shook his head. "You must have bumped your head," he told her and explained that the ceiling is pretty low in spots and sometimes people had to duck down to avoid being injured.

"No," the girl insisted. "I didn't bump my head; whatever it was hit me on the jaw."

Eden helped the girl to her feet, still skeptical, and they all moved to the front room of the cave. Once there, he shined his light on her face to see how badly she had been hurt. He looked at her cheek and was surprised to see a red welt ---- and the prints of fingers that were still visible where she had been struck. He certainly had no explanation for how bumping her head on a low ceiling could have accomplished that.

In the early summer of 1977, several soldiers from Fort Campbell, Kentucky came over to visit the cave. Eden took the young men on a tour and ended up in the back room, where all of them sat around talking and Eden told his stories of the odd events on the farm.

One of the men politely expressed some doubts about the validity of the story. He had been to many places that were supposedly haunted and nothing out of the ordinary had ever occurred to him. Eden laughed and shrugged his shoulders. The man could believe whatever he wanted to, but as for Bill, well, he had seen enough things on the farm to know that something unexplainable was going on. "If something happened, you probably wouldn't ever come back here again," Bill added with a grin.

The group sat and talked for a short while longer and then they all got up to leave -- all except for the young man who had spoke up about his disbelief in ghosts. "Mr. Eden! Come here and help me," the soldier said. "I can't get up."

Eden and the man's friends all assumed that he was joking and they all began to laugh. It wasn't until Bill took a good look at the man that he realized that something really was wrong. The young man was now begging for help and his face was drenched so badly with sweat that it looked like someone had poured a bucket of water over him. When Eden took hold of his hand to help him up, he could feel the man's hand was cold and clammy as if he were going into shock.

The man continued to call for help and claimed that he could feel strong arms wrapped around his chest. They were squeezing him tightly, he said, and he was unable to breathe. Eden and the other men helped their friend to his feet and while the soldiers supported him, Bill wiped his face off with some run-off water from the cave. When the soldier started feeling better, they took him outside of the cave. By the time they were ready to leave, the young man had completely recovered and was suffering no ill effects from his harrowing experience.

As he was heading to his car, he stopped and shook Bill Eden's hand. "Well, you were right about one thing, Mr. Eden," the young soldier said. "I won't ever be back here again."

The winter rains in Tennessee wreak havoc on the Bell Witch Cave, which is why Bill Eden (and the current owners) usually only opened the cave during the summer and early autumn months. Each spring, Bill always had a lot of work to do on the floor of the cave where the rushing water had carved out small holes and ditches.

One Sunday morning, Eden had taken his shovel and rake and was working back some distance in the cave, trying to level out the more damaged portions of the floor. He was chopping at and smoothing over the gravel when he heard a noise that he was not making himself. He spun around because he realized that it was coming from behind him, from the further recesses of the cave. In the darkness, he could hear the distinct sound of someone walking down the passage, their feet crunching in the gravel on the floor. The sounds kept coming, moving toward him, until they stopped a few feet away. Eden strained his eyes to peer into the shadows, but he could see no one there.

"Something I can do for you?" he called out, but he got no answer. He called again, but still no answer came. A little unnerved, he picked up his tools and decided to work near the entrance to the cave ---- where it was much lighter --- for a little while. He walked up front and as he passed through the first room, he noticed his dog sleeping on the little ledge over on the left side of the room.

For the next 30 minutes or so, Eden worked on the floor between the iron gate at the mouth of the cave and the first room. He had just stopped for a moment to rest when he heard the familiar footsteps, tracking through the gravel once more. They were once again coming from the back of the cave and quickly approached the first room, where Bill's dog was sleeping.

Suddenly, the animal's ears pricked up and he jumped to his feet. The hackles rose on the back of his neck and Bill saw his lips curl back to reveal the dog's rather intimidating set of teeth. The animal didn't move though. He just stood there, looking directly at the spot where the footsteps had last been heard. The gravel began crunching again and moved in the direction where Bill was standing. As the sounds moved past the dog, he stared ahead, as though watching someone that Eden was unable to see. The footsteps came directly toward Bill, passed by him, and then continued to the outside of the cave.

Immediately after, both Bill and the dog hurried outside into the sunlight. He admitted later that he did not have the nerve to go back inside right away, nor for several days afterward. From that time on, that particular dog never entered the main part of the cave again. He would follow people to the steel gate but then he would either wait there or return outside. Whatever he had seen that day had frightened him away for good.

Just about anyone who visits the Bell Witch Cave, and who brings along a camera, wants to snap a photograph of the entrance to the cave. This is a shadowy and forbidding spot, but on the other hand, quite beautiful. As you walk down the gravel path from the top of the bluff and cross the last wooden walkway, you find yourself standing just outside of the gaping mouth of the cave itself. The overhanging rock succeeds in cutting off a great portion of the overhead sky and a damp chill filters out from the cave, provoking goose pimples on your exposed skin. Behind you, over the edge of the bluff, you can hear the dull roar of the Red River and you can't help but ponder the distance to the water below.

If you have brought a camera along, this would be the perfect opportunity to use it. By standing back toward the spot where the bluff comes to a sudden end, you should be able to take a photo of the cave entrance and the rocks overhead.

The reader may have noticed that I have written that you should be able to take such a photograph ---- the problem is that many people are never able to do so! Hundreds of visitors have tried and failed. For some reason, there is a spot outside of the cave where not only cameras fail, but sometimes flashlights and batteries refuse to work. In 1997, I was present at the cave when an entire computer system that had been set up to monitor activity in the area refused to work properly. Thanks to whatever anomaly exists here, there are very few photographs in existence of the entrance to the cave.

Even in Bill Eden's time, the cave entrance was hard to photograph. One day, after finishing a tour of the cave, a man was standing and talking to Bill and he asked one of his sons to pose for a picture in front of the cave. The boy took his dog and stood near a large rock in front of the cave. It would be a perfect shot. The man was using a brand new Polaroid camera and he had taken a number of very nice photos inside of the cave. He asked Bill to hold onto the developed shots while he took another one. The man then aimed the camera at the boy and snapped the photo. After the photo developed, the gentleman noticed something strange about the picture ---- something that he had not noticed when the photo was being taken. It showed the dog and the lower part of the boy's body, but the boy's head and shoulders were missing. It looked as though someone had stretched a white, cloudy sheet from one side of the cave to the other, completely covering the boy's face.

A young woman named Leslie Seay had a similar experience at the entrance to the cave in 1989. A friend of hers was visiting from up north and wanted to see the sights of middle Tennessee. Since Leslie lived in Clarksville at the time, she decided to take her to the Bell Witch Cave. As this was between the time when Bill Eden owned the cave and before the current owners had taken over the property, no tours were being offered of the place. However, Leslie and her friend did convince the caretakers to allow them to go down and take a look at the cave, but they promised not to go inside. They hiked down the trail and ended up in front of the cave entrance.

There is a large rock that rests directly in front of the entrance and Leslie's friend decided that she wanted her photo taken while sitting on it. Leslie obliged and snapped the picture, and then the two of them walked back up the bluff and let the owners know that they had returned safely.

"About two weeks later, I sent the film to be developed," Leslie told me. "When I picked up the pictures, the girl told me that one of the photos did not process correctly and that I did not have to pay for it. I didn't look at the pictures until I got to my mother's house and as we were going through them, my mother said that the one in her hand looked rather odd."

She handed the photograph to her daughter and Leslie felt a chill go down her spine. The photo that her mother handed her was the one that she had taken of her friend on the rock outside of the Bell Witch Cave. The photograph was perfectly ordinary --- except for the fact that a large white mist was looming over her friend's head!

"It looked almost like a death shroud", Leslie remembered. "Growing up, I had always heard stories about Kate, but we always considered them to be ghost stories to be told while roasting marshmallows around the campfire. Not until that photo was taken did I ever believe them!"

The current owners have a scrapbook of strange photos that they have taken, along with photos that are sent to them in the mail by people who have visited the cave. They receive dozens of them every year, some showing strange balls of light, misty shapes and fogs and then there are the really weird photos -- photos that simply have no explanation at all! Many of these have been taken outside the entrance to the cave.

One such photo shows a girl seated outside of the cave on a large rock. The photo also shows the apparition of a boy who seems to be looming directly behind her. Despite the odd configuration of the images in the photo, it does not appear to be a double-exposure.

Another photo was taken of two Girl Scouts during a trip to the cave. In the photo, one of the girls is visible, but the other is only partially present and she appears in the photo turned at an impossible angle! Worse yet, is the completely unexplainable image of a two-headed snake that is slithering up the leg of the first girl! Obviously, this was not there when the photo was taken and how it could have appeared in the photograph is totally without explanation.

Other photos, including the one that I believe is the strangest of all the ones that I have seen here, are taken elsewhere on the property. This leads me to believe that perhaps the odd "aura" of the cave permeates the entire farm --- or perhaps whatever is here affects the farm and the cave as well. Whatever the answer may be, one particular photo was taken on the bluff above the cave, where the current owners have a small gift shop and picnic pavilion. One fall afternoon, a party of sixth graders visited the cave from one of the schools in the area. After touring the cave, the students paused for a group photo at the gift shop. One of the chaperones snapped a photo with the teacher's camera and the group departed. The teacher didn't plan to contact the owners of the cave again, except to perhaps schedule another class trip someday --- but then she developed her film from that afternoon.

When she flipped through the packet of photographs, she spotted the group photo that had been taken but thought nothing of it. Then, something odd caught her eye and she looked again. The class, teacher and chaperones had lined up in a couple of rows across the picnic pavilion as they posed for the photo. At first glance, there was nothing wrong with the photo until she realized that one of the children in the front row was missing. He had definitely been there when the photo was taken but in the developed print, there was simply nothing --- and no one --- in his spot. The child who had been sitting next to him even had an outstretched arm around the boy's shoulder ---- or would have if the boy had been there! Instead, the arm was simply suspended in the air, holding on to absolutely nothing. The teacher, and the cave's owner who had been present at the time, have no explanation for what happened. The teacher has sworn that this is no practical joke. She is as befuddled by the photograph as those of us who have studied it are. The only explanation is that this is just one more anomaly of the Bell Witch Cave.

The present-day owners of the Bell Witch Cave, and the piece of the old Bell farm made so famous by Bill Eden, are Chris and Walter Kirby. The Kirby's started out as tobacco farmers and found out that running the cave is a full-time job during the summer months. They not only offer tours of the cave, with their daughter Candy and other local girls helping out as guides, but they also offer a reproduction of the Bell cabin and canoe trips on the Red River. We have been hosting trips to the Bell Witch Cave through the Bump in the Night Tour Co. for a couple of years (as of this writing) and we have never been disappointed.

The Kirby's purchased their section of the old Bell farm in April 1993. The place had been empty for several years after the death of Bill Eden, but by that summer, the cave was open again for business. Over the course of the next year or so, they made a number of improvements to the cave, which included new lights, a new electrical system, an improved path to the cave, wooden walkways to cross the most treacherous areas of the trail, and a number of other things. These improvements continue today.

It wasn't long after the Kirby's moved to the farm, and began conducting tours in the cave, that they realized things were not quite right on the property. They first began to notice that there were strange noises that didn't have an easy explanation. "We've heard them in the cave and we've heard them in the house," Chris has said on occasion. "I feel like if there's any place that could be haunted, it's this place here. First of all, it's got the legend of being haunted. There's an Indian burial mound right above the mouth of the cave on the bluff. And the previous owner of the cave died in our bedroom."

Shortly after moving to the farm, Chris was photographing parts of the property and one of the photos on the developed roll of film managed to capture something pretty amazing. She saw nothing when she took the photo and yet, on the developed print, was a misty shape that hovered above a sinkhole leading down into the cave. The photo continues to defy explanation and was even submitted to Kodak in 1997 for analysis. They stated that there appeared to be nothing wrong with the film or with the developing of the photograph. They also added that there appeared to have been no manipulation with the print and that it was not a double exposure. In short, none of the technicians who examined the film had any explanation for what they saw in the photograph. These were almost identical replies to queries that I would make a year later concerning photos that I had taken myself at the cave.

I first met Chris Kirby in the spring of 1997. I had long been interested in the Bell Witch case and knew that there was a cave located on the property that was purported to be haunted. I was on a trip down south at the time and decided to take a side trip over to Adams. After seeing the Bellwood Cemetery and the old Bell School, I headed for the cave. The cave is a short drive outside of Adams and after rounding a couple of curves on the gravel drive, I found myself parked in the grassy lot at the top of the bluff. In those days, the gift shop did not yet exist and so visitors simply parked outside of the Kirby home and waited until someone came out to greet them.

Over to the right of the parking lot is a large, wooded area that contains the sinkhole near where Chris took the photograph of the strange mist that was mentioned earlier. Behind the house is the trail that leads down to the cave and Chris took me back in that direction after we had chatted for a few minutes. As we walked along that way, we crossed an abandoned road that is really not much more than a depression in the earth now. Later, I would have the chance to walk some distance on this old road and I would learn more about the historical footsteps that I was following. It had been this road that Andrew Jackson had traveled on when he came to visit the Bell farm. It once linked up with an old trace, a last remaining piece of the old Nashville to Clarksville road, but now serves as nothing more than a lane for farm equipment. It was along this stretch of road that Jackson's wagon became mysteriously stuck on his way to the Bell farm and where he had his first encounter with the witch.

A few months later, I returned to the farm for the first investigation that I was ever involved with at this site. I was able to make a journey back along this road and see the original site of the Bell home and the cemetery where the bones of John Bell, several family members and some 30 slaves were laid to rest. The old roadway is quite eerie in some places, even on a bright and sunny afternoon, and it's easy to understand why some of the locals refer to these woods as being "haunted". I found one of the most unnerving places on the old Bell property to be the family cemetery. I can't really explain what bothered me about it so much --- other than that it's a creepy old cemetery, that is. There is just something about the forest on that part of the old farm that will leave you with little doubt that the stories of the Bell Witch are true. I was not surprised to learn that others who have come to this place have felt much the same that I did and still others claim to have encountered ghostly apparitions, cold chills and have heard voices and sounds that cannot be explained.

After walking past the house and across the old stagecoach road, we started down the gloomy pathway that would take us to the Bell Witch Cave. As mentioned earlier, the entrance to the cave is closed off by a locked, heavy steel gate. It is supposed to stop unauthorized visitors from entering the cave, which can be very dangerous, especially in the darkness. There are many sections of the cave that remain unexplored and this fact, along with the ghost stories, proves to be a real magnet for teenagers and curiosity seekers. Chris stated that they always worry that someone will be hurt in there because the gate does not always stop the trespassers. They even had two break-ins within a few weeks of buying the property. In fact, the trespassing becomes so bad at certain times of year that the Kirby's have been forced to prosecute anyone caught inside of the cave at night.

And, as it has been suggested --- perhaps the gate is not always there to keep people out, but to keep something else inside? One afternoon in the late fall of 1977 (during Bill Eden's ownership of the cave), a group of people drove up from Nashville, hoping to take a tour of the place. When they arrived on the property, they found that Eden was not home. Disappointed after having driven so far to get there, they decided that they would at least go down the bluff to have a look at the cave entrance before going home. The visitors hiked down the trail and then entered the mouth of the cave, walking back just far enough to peer into the shadows beyond the gate. As they stood there, one of the members of the group commented that he could almost feel someone watching them from the darkness. Perhaps he was right, for a few moments later, the clear sound of a woman singing could be heard from inside of the cave! They later described it as a high pitched keening noise that was certainly an attempt at singing, although they could not distinguish the words. The group ran from the cave in a panic and climbed to the top of the bluff, where they ran into Bill Eden, who had just arrived home, and told him what had happened.

Although I have since traveled the path a number of times over the years, I still remember my first descent down the bluff and my first look at the cave entrance that I had heard so much about. I could imagine Betsy Bell and her friends having their picnics on the spot where I was now standing and I hoped that if I listened closely, I might hear a voice, as the trespassers of 1977 so eerily did. While I heard no supernatural sounds emanating from the cave that day, I was introduced to the strange incidents that Chris Kirby and her family had experienced since purchasing the property a few years before. The oddities had been weird and frightening enough that Chris told me that she never comes into the cave by herself unless she absolutely has to.

One day, Chris and her dog were leading a tour of the cave for a group of visitors. She was just opening the steel gate that leads inside when she heard a strange sound that was definitely not a natural sound of the cave. "It sounded like real raspy breathing sounds," she said, "like someone couldn't get their breath. It only lasted for a minute and then it was gone." Chris looked back to her tour group, but they were quietly talking amongst themselves and hadn't heard a thing.

The tour continued through the first room, down the narrow passage and into the second room. Here, as is the tradition in Bell Witch Cave Tours, Chris began telling stories of the witch, the haunting and strange incidents on the farm. As she was talking, the dog suddenly reacted to something that no one else could see. The hair on the animal's back stood up and she began showing her teeth and growling. The tour group asked what was wrong with the dog, but Chris had no idea. She was finally able to calm the dog down, but then the animal began whining and tucked her tail between her legs. She cowered back against Chris and at that same moment, the flashlight in Chris' hand suddenly went out! "I guessed that it was just the battery at first," Chris remembered, "but then a lady's video camera stopped working too. We were all standing there in the dark and I'll tell you, I was ready to get out of there and everyone else was too!"

Chris also told us about the strange apparitions that she and visitors to the cave have reported. Some of these shapes are misty and fog-like, sometimes appearing in different parts of the cave, only to vanish when approached. She also recalled another type of image they had seen. "It looked like heat waves that come up over the highway in the summer time," she explained. "You can see them out of the corner of your eye and then they're gone."

One of the ongoing traditions of the Bell Witch Cave involves the removal of any sort of artifact from the premises, be it rocks or anything else found inside of the cave. Some believe that perhaps the energy of the area is imbedded in some way within the actual makeup of the place and by removing a portion of the cave, you are inviting the phenomena that occurs here to travel with you. Others are not so scientific ---- they believe that the spirit of the witch will follow anyone who removes something from the cave.

It's likely that this tradition got started a number of years ago when the remains of a young Native American woman were discovered by men doing construction work on one of the local roads. Because it is well-known that the former Bell farm contains a burial mound, it was requested that the bones of the Indian woman be entombed within the Bell Witch Cave. The remains were laid out in the first room of the cave in a shallow indention that was then lined with limestone slabs. Unfortunately, they did not remain there for long.

A short time later, trespassers made off with the bones, but according to local lore --- not without a price. Gossip in the community has it that each of the persons who removed one of the relics suffered a series of misfortunes, accidents and injuries within days of the theft. For this reason, it has come to be believed that it is bad luck to remove anything at all from the cave. Over the last several years, I have received a number of accounts from people who claim to have taken away stones from the Bell Witch Cave, only to then experience not only bad luck, but strange happenings in their previous un-haunted homes! Chris Kirby has assured me that she has received a number of packages in the mail over the years that have contained rocks and stones that were removed from the cave. After getting them home, the folks who removed them began to suffer all sorts of problems and weird events.

They believe that by mailing them back to the cave, they might alleviate their problems.

Even the Kirby's themselves have not been immune to the strange happenings! Candy Kirby recalled the time that she was exploring the cave and found a small and unusual looking rock, which she proceeded to slip into her pocket and take home. She knew there was a story about bad luck occurring to anyone who removed something from the cave, but she didn't take it seriously. Just one week later though, the family's tobacco barn collapsed without warning, ruining a portion of their crop and doing extensive damage. Just a coincidence? Candy didn't think so and has taken no further chances by removing anything else from the cave.

Nights at the Bell Witch Cave

Since the late 1970's, the Bell Witch Cave has been a destination point for ghost hunters, curiosity seekers and paranormal enthusiasts. A number of television programs have also been filmed here and I have been involved with several of the shows. In most cases though, the "investigations" connected to these programs have been for entertainment only. None of them have approached the location with the same enthusiasm, or with the same chilling results, as Bob Schott. In 1997, Schott, a film and television producer with a company called Global Media Productions, became interested in the story of the Bell Witch and the hauntings at the old Bell farm. He contacted me about the stories and wanted to know if I was interested in perhaps working with him on a (now sadly defunct) series called *Adventures Beyond*, which specialized in intense paranormal phenomena. As it turned out, the Bell Witch Cave was featured on one of the only installments of the series, an episode called *America's Most Haunted.*

The format of Schott's series was different than most seen on television in that it was not a documentary with historical re-enactments but rather about paranormal investigations using the most advanced types of equipment and techniques available. This was likely why the show was never successful for general audiences, despite the fact that paranormal enthusiasts really enjoyed the hard-core, technical aspects of the show. What made it more "interesting" though was Bob Schott himself, an over-the-top, former arm wrestling champion who had made a living working as a film actor in the early 1990's. Thanks to Bob's wild enthusiasm for the subject, combined with his colorful personality, *Adventures Beyond* became a mixture of *Ghostbusters* and professional wrestling. I have been teased relentlessly over the years about the "uniform" that we had to wear to be part of the *Adventures Beyond* investigation team, which included a blue urban camouflage jacket and hat but all that I can say is that we managed to stand out --- and make such an impression that no one who saw the show ever forgot about it!

After the show was filmed, Bob had a hard time getting anyone to take a look at it and eventually put the program out on videotape for a brief time. Disappointed that it was unsuccessful, he eventually sold the rights to the show and got away from film and television production. As of this writing, Bob is now involved with a new company that sells parcels of land on the ocean floor. He is currently billed as "Captain Bob: The Robin Hood of the Seas".

Honestly though, as much as people chuckle about Bob's fervor for the subject matter in *America's Most Haunted*, there is no denying that he knew his stuff. He was well-versed on all of the technical aspects of the equipment and brought many things to the paranormal investigation field that were ahead of their time in those days. On a personal note, Bob was, and is, a great guy and is a rare breed among "Hollywood" producers and television people. He is a generous and well-meaning person who deserved a better shot than he got. I'll always be grateful to him for getting me involved in the most organized and comprehensive investigation that has ever been done at the Bell Witch Cave.

When we came to the cave in the summer of 1997, our investigative team was equipped with high-tech temperature monitoring equipment, electro-magnetic field fluctuation detectors, military quality night-vision equipment, infrared cameras, and, thanks to Tim Harte and the earlier version of the MESA software, a computer system that was capable of detecting any type of change in several different energy fields. As mentioned earlier, the computer system failed completely while it was set up at the mouth of the cave --- something that had never happened before and has not happened since.

"I was looking for a place that was really haunted, really active," Schott reported. "I was familiar, of course, with the story of the Bell Witch and when Troy told me about the phenomena still encountered on the property today -- I knew this was the place."

During the investigation, we spent several days on the Kirby farm, exploring the cave, the sinkhole where Chris had photographed the strange energy, and even the cemetery where John Bell is buried. Our best results came during our late-night forays into the cave but some of the strange events witnessed on the farm came during "down times" on the property. This included a sighting of some of the farm's famous ghost lights.

There had been reports of strange lights on the old Bell property for many years. Many of these stories recount mysterious balls of light that are sometimes seen in the fields, woods and along the roadways of the area. These glowing lights have been responsible for scaring many people, intriguing others and it is suggested that they have even been the cause of many close-call auto accidents over the years.

One story of the "ghost lights" is dated back to around the turn of the last century and told of a group of young boys who journeyed out to the Bell farm at a time when portions of the family's house were still standing. The boys arrived around midnight and went inside of the ramshackle old place. Finding nothing of interest, they walked back out into the field. Just then, a glowing ball of blue and white-colored light emerged from the woods where the Bell cemetery is located. The light began moving across the field toward the boys and they froze in their tracks. It bounced along the hills, dipping down now and then as the terrain raised and lowered and then stopped a short distance from where the young men were standing. The boys quickly ran away!

Other stories say that some people attempt to chase the lights as they travel across the open fields. Whatever the source of these bright orbs, they somehow manage to stay just out of reach of those who try and pursue them. The lights will often vanish when approached, only to appear again in another location.

One of the strangest stories of the unexplained lights was recalled by a man who once lived on the property near the old Bell place. One evening, he saw an unusually bright light appear at the edge of the field next to the homestead. The light seemed to hover in place for a moment, shining and quivering around the tops of the trees by the field, and then it began to circle in the air near the woods. The light drifted for 15 or 20 minutes and then floated over to the top of a nearby barn. He reported that the object stayed there for some time, giving off a tremendous

This photo shows two strange balls of light that were observed moving through the woods on the property. The match the descriptions of the lights reported by Bill Eden and many others.

amount of light. The glow from it was so bright that it lit up a nearby pasture, illuminating all of the cows that had been huddled there in the darkness.

After a few moments, the behavior of the light grew even stranger. While it was suspended at the end of the barn, the glow began to grow. A long crooked tail (about four to five feet long) emerged from the ball and trailed along behind it. The light began to move in a circle once more and started to dip and rise as it went around. It began to drift back in the direction that it had come from and when it reached the graveyard again, it slowly began to move in a circle once more, like some sort of weird bird of prey. Eventually, it vanished.

Our sighting of lights on the farm was not nearly as dramatic as that of the man who once lived on the property. It occurred as we were standing at the edge of the yard, talking for a little while and waiting for Bob to finish with some telephone calls so that we could return to the cave. Just beyond the yard is the sinkhole that drops down into the cave and the spot where Chris took the weird misty photo that has never been explained. It was from this low area that two glowing lights appeared and began moving between the trees, heading in our general direction. We watched, and photographed, the lights for several minutes before they blinked out ---- vanishing as mysteriously as they had appeared.

Things got even weirder though while we were inside of the cave itself. At one point, using two different infrared temperature probes, we picked up a sudden drop in the temperature of the cave. It was as if something very cold moved past us and then continued on through the cave passage. A photograph taken at that same moment was developed and revealed a glowing ball of light. The energy inside of the globe is so intense that it appears to be giving off light. Examinations by independent photography labs, including Kodak, revealed that the image in the photo was not a reflection, nor was it any artificial or natural part of the cave. They could offer no explanation for what it might have been.

In addition, we also had some interesting (and rather chilling) results using a video camera that had been fitted with a Generation III Night Vision lens, which was reportedly 5 times more sensitive than the equipment used by the U.S. Military during the 1991 Gulf War. The lens was so advanced that it had not been available on the civilian market until a short time before the investigation. It had been loaned to Schott by the manufacturer, a company that dealt specifically with sensitive government and military contracts.

During the investigation, the camera and lens picked up what can only be described as a "doorway effect" that appeared in the long passage between

The ball of light captured on film during an investigation of the cave. The light was photographed just after a sudden temperature drop. The photo was analyzed by Kodak and other independent labs and it was reported not to be "lens flare" or anything wrong with the film.

the first room and the second room in the cave. This "doorway" appeared to be an array of light that crossed from one side of the passage to the other, lasting only a few seconds, and then vanished. The effect is very eerie when the film is watched frame by frame. As the light moved across, and then back again, two very distinct faces emerged from the "doorway", remained for a second or two, and then retreated back into the light array again. The faces were horrific-looking and appeared only vaguely human.

I have never been able to explain what this "doorway" could be, nor what the images were in the light ---- other than faces of unknown origin. Not only have I been stumped, but so were the manufacturers of the night vision equipment that had been loaned to Bob for the filming, as well as independent labs and analysts who also studied the footage.

One of Bob Schott's aggressive investigative techniques was to present whatever evidence he obtained to a skeptical, but fair, laboratory for analysis. "We knew that we had good evidence," Bob said, "but it really proves nothing unless we can stump the experts with it."

This is what he managed to do with the film footage from the passageway. Analysts from the company that made the equipment took a look at a copy of the film and were puzzled by what they saw. They, along with other film experts, ran the clip over and over and put it through all sorts of tests to determine if it had been hoaxed, or whether it was merely an accident of light that had created the "doorway effect" and the faces. In their final report on the footage, they stated that they had no explanation for the strange anomalies and that these images could only be paranormal in origin.

"This is some of the best evidence ever obtained for the existence of the supernatural," stated Schott. "We came to the Bell Witch Cave because we heard that it was haunted ---- I think that after this investigation, I can say with a lot of certainty that it is!"

7. A WALES OF A GOOD TIME

Hunting for Ghosts at the Craig-Y-Nos Castle with Len Adams

In June of 2004, Kim and I, along with our good friend Jenifer Elias, went to England on a ghost tour. From the start, it was a disaster in the making. The tour company we went through was a joke. They were very eager to take our money, but not too concerned about customer service for their clients.

The person who saved the day was Kriss Stephens. Kriss was the paranormal expert for MTV's *Fear* program from a few years ago. She was our guest paranormal guide and our "savior". As location after location that we visited in England had no knowledge of our tour (thanks to the ball being dropped by the company), it was Kriss who would hammer the tour company on the phone and force them to make things right.

On the third day of our tour, we finally left London. Our destination was Craig-Y-Nos castle in Wales. Craig-Y-Nos sits alongside the Tarve, in the Upper Swansea Valley of South Wales. It was built in 1840 by Captain Rice Davies Powell. In 1878, opera diva, Adelina Patti purchased the property, turning it into her own private estate. She started major renovations and development to the site after her second marriage to Ernesto Nicolini, using the Theatre Royal, in London's Drury Lane, as the model for her own private theater. It is still used today for operatic performances.

Adelina hosted many heads of state at the castle, going so far as to have a private road built from the castle to the railway station at Penwyllt, with a furnished private waiting room for her guests. The city of Swansea made Adelina Patti its first "free-woman" and they re-erected her winter garden, a gift from Adelina, close to city hall, naming it the "Patti Pavilion".

Think back to all the ghost stories you've read growing up. How many of them started with, "It was a dark and stormy night"? Well, when we arrived at 9:00 p.m. at Craig-Y-Nos, it was a dark and stormy night. The last hour of our journey was spent winding along the narrow, mountainous roads, through a torrent of rain. As the van turned into the courtyard, the lights of the castle were a welcome sight to behold. Within 45 minutes, we had checked into our rooms and were dining on baked chicken with all the fixings. I, of course, eat as if every meal is going to be my last, so it came as no surprise that I was finished ahead of everyone else. Excusing myself, I made my way through the winding corridors of the castle to my room. We had been promised a tour and I needed my video equipment.

Kim, at the end of her meal, assumed I had gone out to the van in the courtyard, not knowing I had put everything in our room. As she stood in the huge covered doorway of the castle, she saw a small girl standing next to the van. Kim said she appeared to be dressed in a nightgown from the early 1900's. She seemed to

be around 12 or 13 years old. The expression on her face was one of fear, as if she was begging to be taken from the place.

On hearing a noise behind her, Kim spun around to see me walking down the hallway. Turning back to the courtyard, she noticed that the little girl had simply vanished. It didn't dawn on her at the time but Kim later realized that even though the girl stood in the pouring rain, she was not getting wet! It seemed the ghost tour of the castle had gotten off to an early start.

Around 11:00 p.m., our group gathered downstairs for our tour of the castle. Leading our expedition was Kelly Burnell, who works for a book publishing company that specializes in dark fiction. She is also the tour coordinator for Craig-Y-Nos castle. She helped Stephen Graham found *The Paranormal World* in 2004.

Kelly was assisted on this night by Glenn Behenna, a tall, soft-spoken man who was our psychic guide for the tour. Most of the people that I've come across who claim to be psychic are nothing more than con artists. I would put him to the test.

For nearly three hours, we wound our way through every nook and cranny of the castle. Through a hole in a wall that I discovered while moving things around, I got some great footage of a couple of orbs moving towards me. They darted up the side of the fireplace, then out of sight.

After making it to the upper reaches of the castle, Kim and I went down a corridor by ourselves as the group went the other way. Because of all of the camera flashes from the group, my video recording was getting screwed up, so I wanted to wander off alone for a bit. I came to a large staircase that I wanted to climb but was stopped by Kim. She had turned pale and was shaking violently. She kept telling me that the old woman at the top of the stairs would hurt me if I went up there. I, of course, saw and felt nothing. Kim went so far as to pull me away from the staircase.

Just then, the rest of our group, led by Kelly and Glenn, made it to our location. I had been impressed throughout the night with Glenn's abilities and demeanor. As he started to ascend the staircase, he suddenly stopped. Like Kim, he turned pale while staring at the top landing area. Glenn turned around, said we would come back later, and then led us down the hall next to the stairs.

After our tour of the next couple of rooms, we returned to the staircase. On gazing up the stairs, Glenn said it was now safe to go up there. I asked him what had been there before. He described the same woman that Kim had seen and also painted her as very angry. Mercifully, she was now gone.

I didn't know about Glenn's abilities before this trip, but I did know about Kim's. Throughout the tour of the castle, Kim would whisper points of interest to me, followed by Glenn telling the group the same thing. Neither one of them had been to the castle before. They certainly had never compared notes either.

Our adventure ended around 2:00 a.m. in the castle's pub. Unfortunately, the bar was closed. If I only knew what was in store for me, I would've needed a couple of pints.

As everyone said their goodnights, I realized that we were scattered throughout the castle. Kim and I, thanks to the wicked humor of Kriss Stephens, were spending the night in the "Bridal Suite".

Kim, exhausted and shaking from our adventures in the castle, soon fell fast asleep. I wanted to make sure that all the equipment was charged and ready to go for our next location, so I decided that I would be up for awhile.

The "Bridal Suite" was a massive 30 foot by 30 foot room with an attached 10 foot by 15 foot bathroom. It sat in the upper reaches of the castle, so window coverings were not needed. Only a mountain goat could look through the windows. We, of course, had electricity in the room, but no television or radio. I was still having difficulty dealing with the time change. Though tired, I couldn't sleep. I soon wished that wasn't the case.

At 3:15 a.m. the voices in the room started.

It was as if two or three people were whispering to each other. I could hear the voices, but not make out what they were saying. Every time I would walk to the part of the room that the voices seemed to come from, they would move. We, the voices and I, did this dance for about 30 minutes before they stopped. I searched the room only to find no cause for the sounds.

By now, the heavy rains of the evening had stopped, revealing a bright and beautiful full moon. With no draperies to block them, the moonbeams illuminated the room.

It was now 4:00 a.m. and time for the next part of the paranormal review. I sat on the side of the bed, praying my video equipment batteries would charge quickly so I could get into bed. However, they weren't charging and I was wondering why when the room turned icy cold. With Kim fast asleep, I wrapped a blanket around me and waited. For what, I didn't know.

Something now caught my eye on the far wall. It was a small, shadowy mass that kept swirling around. The more it moved, the more it grew. I grabbed the camera, but it wouldn't work. When the black shape reached about three feet in diameter it started to move across the wall. It was at the top of the wall, where the ceiling and wall come together. The gyrating shadow made its way completely across the room and then a ball of light, the size of a softball, came out of the floor and shot up, straight into the shadowy mass. In an instant, everything was gone. When the light came out of the floor it was so brilliant that the entire room was aglow. It was much brighter than the moonlight. Just as quickly though, it was gone and the room was plunged into shadow again.

I sprung from the bed and examined the wall. Then I tried pulling on the carpeting and even looked around in the hallway. I was positive that something had been rigged up to scare us. I could find nothing though.

So, there I was.....

Paranormal activity all around me, no functioning video equipment and my only witness sound asleep.

For the next hour I sat bolt upright in the huge four poster bed. In my wildest dreams, I could have never imagined what happened next.

When 5:00 a.m. came, I decided to lay down and see if I could get some sleep. Nothing had happened for an hour by this time. Maybe the show was over for the night, I thought.

I laid down on my right side, pulling the blankets around me, and closed my eyes. It was no more than 10 seconds later that I sensed that things weren't right. The oversized, parade ground of a bed that Kim and I were in was now tilting upwards! The two legs on my side of the bed were lifting off of the floor. On trying to get up to jump out of the bed , I realized, to my horror, that I couldn't move! My head and neck were the only parts of my body that would work. The voices were now back and much louder than before. This time they brought company!

As the bed tilted more and more, it seemed that the wall on the opposite side of the room was starting to spin. I mentioned earlier that the pub was closed at the end of the tour, so it wasn't that kind of spinning. I had the impression that the wall was now like a bank vault. When it reached the proper combination, it would open. I had a very strong feeling that when it opened, I wasn't going to like what came out. I shut my eyes. This had to be a bad dream, but it wasn't. By now, the bed was tilting so much that I was sliding towards the center. The voices in the room were deafening and the spinning wall was starting to slow down.

I closed my eyes and I don't know whether I screamed or just yelled "NO!" in my head. When I opened them, I saw the room was back to normal and I could move again. I jumped, or fell, to the floor. I was now like a madman, crawling under the bed, pounding on the wall, climbing on a chair to examine the ceiling and finally running up and down the hallway. I could find no cause, no set-up for what had just occurred.

At 7:00 in the morning, when the alarm clock went off, I was still sitting up in bed, waiting. Kim awoke bright-eyed and ready for a new day of adventure. I just wanted to yell at her for not waking up and helping me. But, of course, I didn't.

Now that I was officially awake, it was my job to gather up the rest of the party. I had been given the only alarm clock in the castle. My only problem was that I didn't know where everyone was located. I made my way to the front desk. There was no one in sight. I heard noises coming from the kitchen at the end of the hallway.

The hallway was dark and ominous and as I crept along it I saw four glowing eyes at the end, following my every step. I had no choice but to keep walking. I had to go that way. As I got within ten feet of the glowing eyes, I could faintly see that they were attached to two of the castles' cats. They had been watching my every move.

I found the cook in the kitchen and she went off to find the desk clerk, who would give me a map of the castle. With the map I would be able to locate the rest of my party.

As I waited in the hallway, a book on the sideboard caught my eye. After glancing at a few pages, it dawned on me that this was a log of people's experiences while staying at the castle. Room 36, the Bridal Suite, had one entry. Another guest had the same experience in the room that I had, except that he wasn't able to make it stop. According to this fellow, when the wall stopped turning, an old hag floated out and across the floor, disappearing into the wall by the headboard of the bed. As this happened, she left a feeling of death and foreboding in the room. I didn't envy his experience!

I've been told by a couple of my friends, who have real psychic abilities, that I have a very strong presence inside, as well as out. This makes me very attractive to the things that go bump in the night. This strength may have helped me stop the sequence of events from earlier that morning. On further examination, I'm one of only a handful of people who have had that experience in the Bridal Suite. This was the first time that a shiver ran up my spine.

The desk clerk soon returned with a map and I went on my way, exploring the castle in the daylight while waking up the rest of my party.

Over breakfast conversation, it seems that I was the only one to get a show during the night. Needless to say, I was the first one asleep on the bus.

I made some wonderful friends during my short stay. Some of them, such as, Martin Gover (castle owner) and Stephen Graham and Kelly Burnell (*The Paranormal World* founders) came to our American Ghost Society conference in Alton, Illinois in June 2005.

Stephen and Troy and I are currently setting up a paranormal investigator exchange program where our members can spend 6-8 days stationed at the Craig-Y-Nos Castle in Wales. This is an experience that I highly recommend.

And yes, haunted room or not, I'm going back

8. A HAUNTING MYSTERY
Searching for the Ghosts of the Villisca Ax Murder House with Troy Taylor

A Vintage view of the J.B. Moore House

Nearly lost among the rolling hills and fields of southwestern Iowa is the tiny town of Villisca; a quiet, peaceful place of only a few hundred people --- and one tragic and enduring mystery. It was here, in June 1912, that a horrific mass murder took place, wiping out an entire family. The murder was never solved, casting a pall over Villisca that still lingers today. And this dark cloud may not be the only thing still lingering here. There are many who believe that the spirits of the murdered family may still remain here as well, their ghosts haunting the old house where they once lived and tragically died.

I happen to be one of the people who believe that and if you had the chance to experience what I did at this house in May 2005 --- you might be one of the believers too.

Villisca is located in a remote corner of Iowa, far off the modern interstate and a good distance from any town that might have a population of more than a couple of thousand souls. It's an isolated place, accessible by only an old, two-lane highway and, believe it or not, this is in great contrast to how it was back in the early 1900's. In those days, Villisca, which means "pleasant view", was a booming town of more than 2,500 residents. The streets were lined with flourishing businesses and several dozen trains pulled into town everyday. It was a popular spot in Montgomery County in those days, offering not only stores and shops of just about every kind but restaurants and a theater as well.

Villisca was a close-knit community in those days but the peacefulness here was shattered on June 10, 1912 with the discovery of eight bloody corpses in a house along one of the town's tree-lined streets. The J.B. Moore family, respected and well-liked members of the community, along with two overnight guests, were founded murdered in their beds. And now, more than 90 years later, the crimes remain unsolved.

What happened on that dark night in Villisca? And what occurred to cause at least some of the spirits of this terrible crime to stay behind in this world?

Bloody Murder

It was a warm evening in southwestern Iowa and the town of Villisca stirred quietly in the gloom of the setting sun. The dinner hour had long since passed and many residents escaped to the cool of the front porch after the heat of the day started to settle. Stores locked up for the evening and lights began to appear in the windows of homes along the darkening streets. At the Presbyterian Church, music filtered to the street outside, along with laughter and polite applause. The Children's Day Program came to an end around 9:30 p.m. and soon the parishioners began trickling out into the street, heading home for the night.

Sarah Moore, who had coordinated the program, gathered her family around her as they started walking home. She was joined by her husband Josiah, known popularly in town as J.B., and her children, Herman, Catherine, Boyd and Paul. Two young girls, friends of the Moore children who had also been in the evening's program, Lena and Ina Stillinger, came home with the Moore's to spend the night. The children were excited after the evening's festivities and Sarah knew that she would have trouble settling them down for the night. She couldn't help but laugh at their antics and jokes however, especially after J.B. joined in with them. The sound of their laughter could be plainly heard as the small group walked along and they waved happily at the other families and friends they passed.

Everyone liked the Moore's --- and no one who saw them that night could have imagined that this would be the last time the family would be seen alive.

The following morning, June 10, Mary Peckham, the Moore's next door neighbor, stepped out of the back door of her home to hang some laundry on the line. The sun was barely peeking into the sky but it was better to finish the outdoor chores early and avoid the heat that came later in the day. Mary went about her business, wringing water from the wash and hanging the wet clothes on the line that stretched across her backyard. As she worked, she had a clear view of the Moore house next door but thought little about how quiet the place was until she finished with the clothes and realized that the clock in her kitchen now read 7:00 a.m.

She suddenly realized that not only had the Moore's not been outside to start their own chores that morning but that the house itself seemed unusually still. This was very strange as J.B. Moore always left early for work and Sarah was always up at dawn to start breakfast and the day's work. The Moore house was full of young children and so the morning hours were always loud and boisterous. Could the Moore's be sick? Mary waited for a few more minutes and then finally decided to go next door and check on her friend Sarah and the rest of the family. Mary approached the house and knocked on the door. It was still eerily quiet inside. She waited for a few moments and then knocked again. Once more, there was no answer and so she tried to open the door, thinking that she could poke her head inside and call for Sarah. She pulled on the door handle though and found that it was locked from the inside. She found it hard to believe that this was the case but apparently the Moore's had decided to sleep late today.

Mary walked back through the yard, deep in thought. It seemed so unlike the family but who was she to pry? Mary did go out to the small barn behind the Moore house and let the chickens out into the yard. She felt it was the least she could do to help Sarah, who she was convinced must be under the weather. After she let out the chickens, Mary went back into her own house but the more she thought about the silent home next door, the more that she worried. Finally, when she could stand it no more, she placed a telephone call to J.B.'s brother, Ross Moore, and he promised to come over as soon as he could. This was the first step in what would turn out to be one of the most bungled criminal investigations of the era.

When Ross Moore arrived at the home of his brother, he was met by Mary Peckham, who had continued to try and raise someone in the neighboring home. Ross tried the door himself and then leaned up to peer into a bedroom window. It was too dark to see anything, so he returned to the door, banging on it and shouting for his brother and sister-in-law. There was still no answer, so he produced his own set of keys and looked through the ring until he found one that opened the front door. As he pushed open the door, Moore stepped into the parlor with Mary Peckham behind him. She stopped at the entryway however and did not go any farther into the house. Moore looked around, seeing no one in the kitchen. He called out but there was no answer. On the opposite side of the parlor was a doorway that went into one of the children's bedrooms. He carefully opened the door and looked into the room. He nearly cried out when he saw two bloody bodies on the bed and dark stains on the sheets. Moore never even looked to see who was lying there. He ran back to the porch and shouted for Mary Peckham to call the sheriff --- someone had been murdered!

The City Marshall, Hank Horton, arrived a short time later and searched the house. The two bodies in the downstairs bedroom were Lena Stillinger, age 12, and her sister, Ina, age 8. The girls were houseguests of the Moore children. They had come home with them after the church program the night before. The remaining members of the Moore family were found in the upstairs bedrooms. Every person in the house had been brutally murdered, their skulls crushed with an ax. The victims included Josiah Moore, age 43; Sarah Montgomery Moore, age 44; Herman, age 11; Catherine, age 10; Boyd, age 7; Paul, age 5; and the Stillinger sisters.

Almost as soon as the murders were discovered, the news of the massacre traveled quickly throughout Villisca. As friends, neighbors and curiosity seekers descended on the Moore house, the town's small police force quickly lost control of the crime scene. It has been said that literally hundreds of people walked through the house, staring at the bodies, touching everything and even taking souvenirs before the Villisca National Guard unit arrived at noon to close off the scene and secure the home for state police investigators. It's easy for us now to blame this disastrous mismanagement on local police officers but in 1912, such a crime still would have been much more difficult to solve than it would be today. At that time, fingerprinting was still a new idea, crime scene photographs were rarely taken and DNA testing would be unimaginable for decades to come. In short, investigators in rural areas like this simply did not see crimes of this magnitude in 1912. In spite of this, the investigators did manage to make some notes of the scene or all of the clues would have been completely lost. As it was though, any evidence left in the house was likely destroyed.

The detectives did manage to put together a list of clues but at that time, little of it made sense and combined, the clues managed to make the mystery even more perplexing. What was known for a fact was that all eight people in the Moore house had been bludgeoned to death in their sleep, some time between midnight at 5:00 a.m.. A doctor that examined the bodies guessed that the murders had occurred closer to midnight. The murder weapon was presumed to be the bloody ax that had been left behind at the scene. The ax, which belonged to J.B. Moore, was found in the room that had been occupied by the Stillinger girls. The ax was covered with blood but the killer had made an effort to wipe it off.

A kerosene lamp was found sitting on the floor at the foot of J.B. and Sarah's bed. The glass chimney had been removed and placed under the dresser and the wick had been turned down almost all of the way. Another lamp, with the chimney also removed, was found at the foot of the bed where the Stillinger girls had been sleeping. With the wicks turned down the way that they were, the lamps would have provided only a very small amount of light. Perhaps just enough for the killer to carry out the murders?

As mentioned, the Stillinger girls had been murdered downstairs but the bodies of the six members of the Moore family had been found in two bedrooms upstairs. The ceilings in the bedrooms of the parents and the children had gouge marks in them that had apparently been made by the upswing of the ax. This would imply that the killer had used a fairly decent amount of force when striking his victims, which would also suggest that the striking of their skulls, as well as the contact with the ceiling, would have made a fairly loud noise. Strangely though, no one in the family seems to have been awakened during the murders. All of them were slain in their beds, apparently asleep at the time. There is no indication how the killer could have managed this during an obvious "spree" murder but somehow he did.

In each case, he covered the faces of his victims with their bed sheets after he killed them. Modern criminal psychologists would suggest that the killer either knew the victims or that he had a great amount of guilt for what he had done. Some have suggested that this could not have been a stranger, or traveling serial killer, because he covered their faces but this is short-sighted thinking. It's very possible that the murderer may simply have possessed a condition that caused him to immediately regret the murders, even though he was incapable of stopping himself from committing them.

Whatever his state of mind might have been, the killer did not immediately leave the house when he was finished with his work. The first thing that he did was to draw the curtains on all of the windows in the house. Two of the windows did not have curtains on them, so he covered them with clothing that he found in the Moore's closets. This was likely to insure that he could light lamps in the house and not be seen from outside. If lights were seen burning in the house in the very early morning hours, it could have raised suspicion, or attracted attention, from the neighbors. A pan of bloody water was later found in the kitchen, where the killer had attempted to wash up, and it was sitting next to a plate of food that he had prepared but had not eaten. The killer spent quite some time in the house, likely calming down after the murders. But why prepare the food if he did not plan to eat it? It's possible that he may have realized the lateness of the hour, as the sun was starting to lighten the sky, and left the food untouched. The killer also locked all of the doors of the house, something not usually done in this little town at the time, insuring that the bodies would not be discovered until he had plenty of time to escape.

This was the list of information that the investigators compiled but with no fingerprints to match and without technology to look for hair and blood samples, footprints or trace evidence, there was little to go on. The only piece of evidence recovered was a piece of a keychain that was found on the floor in the downstairs bedroom. It did not appear to belong to anyone in the house and the police deduced that it must have been left behind by the killer.

But was it? We may never know for the killer has undoubtedly taken his gruesome secrets with him to the grave --- but this does not keep us from delving deeper into this mystery. Could the answers to the murders lie with the identities of the victims? Or does this even deepen the mystery?

The Villisca Victims

Josiah Moore was one of Villisca's most prominent businessmen. He married Sarah Montgomery in December 1899 and together, the two of them had four children. Moore was a member of the school board and of the Presbyterian Church. He was born in Hanover County, Illinois and came to Iowa with his parents, growing up in Page County. He was one of 16 children, although four of his siblings died as children. Another, Willie, died at age 20 and his sister, Anna, died in November 1910. For a brief time, Anna's husband, Sam Moyer, was considered a suspect in the murders.

At the time of his murder, J.B. had been a resident of Villisca for 13 years and had been employed by Frank Jones at his farm and hardware store for nine of those years. A few years before, he had left his position with Jones, another of the town's most prominent residents, and opened his own implement store. Thanks to his kind manner and generosity, Moore's business became an immediate success. After a short time, his hard work managed to take the John Deere franchise in the area away from Jones. It was an action that, some believed, gave Jones a motive for the killings. Could his animosity towards his former employee have boiled over into murder?

Sarah Montgomery Moore seemed to have even fewer enemies than her well-liked husband. She had been born in Knox County, Illinois in 1873 and had moved to Iowa with her parents and her sister, Mary, in 1894. She was also an active member of the Presbyterian Church in Villisca and was beloved by all of the children that she taught in Sunday School. Sarah was also considered to be a generous and kind-hearted person and her murder was a mystery to everyone who knew her. On the night of the murders, she and J.B. were sleeping in the largest bedroom on the second floor, located at the top of the stairs from the lower level. It is unknown as to whether the adults or the children were murdered first but neither of them stirred while the killer was at work.

Even more tragic, and bewildering, than the slaughter of Sarah and J.B. were the murders of the children in the house. Herman and Catherine were the oldest of J.B and Sarah's children. On the night of the murders, they were sleeping in separate beds in the second upstairs bedroom of the Moore home. The bedroom, located at the front of the house, held three beds. The younger boys, Boyd and Paul, were sleeping in the third bed in this same room. According to testimony given in the Coroner's Inquest by Dr. J. Clark Cooper, the children were also killed in their sleep. "Not a face was exposed." Dr. Cooper testified. "The windows were all down, the curtains were all down and when I went into the south room, I reached up to run the curtain up, and in so doing I knocked that curtain down, I did not put that back up. It seems there was sort of a three window effect, one big window and one little window on each side. I gave it a quick jerk, and I knocked it off, it was so dark in there, and the other in the back room, I ran that up myself." Other witnesses also stated that the bodies were completely covered with sheets or had other clothing draped over them. Strangely, the mirror in this room was also covered.

The bodies of the Stillinger girls were both found in the downstairs bedroom. Lena and Ina were both members of the Presbyterian Church and the Junior Society, which was led by Sarah Moore. They were good friends of Catherine and the other

Moore children and were survived by their parents and seven brothers and sisters.

Joseph Stillinger, the father of the two girls, had come to Villisca when he was only 14 years-old. His father died young and his mother settled a few miles north of Villisca on land that was given to her as the widow of a soldier. His brother, George, bought another farm nearby. When Joseph married Sarah Hastings, he built a large home across the creek from his mother and brother and did so well with his farm that he eventually bought out his brother's land and incorporated it into what came to be known as Doddy Hollow Farm. Joseph became an expert in horticulture and the farm boasted several fine orchards of fruit and nut trees. He also raised cattle and sheep, operated a seed corn business and was involved in a small coal-shipping venture. He received the most acclaim for his orchards however and traveled widely to speak to farmers under the sponsorship of Iowa State College. On a number of occasions, he even appeared before the state legislature to discuss a statewide horticulture program. At one point, he was even nominated as a congressman for the district but refused to take the time to campaign. Even so, he was so well-liked that he only lost to his opponent by two votes.

The murder of the two girls seemed to start a series of tragic events for the Stillinger family in 1912. During the same week that Ina and Lena were murdered, Sarah gave birth to a stillborn child and a few months later, while the family was away, their home burned to the ground, destroying all of their belongings. Sarah Stillinger died in November 1944 and Joseph lived just a few months longer, dying in April 1945. They are both buried in the Villisca Cemetery, next to the graves of their two daughters and stillborn child.

As the reader can see, the lives of the Villisca victims offer no more clues to the murders today than they did to the authorities in 1912. According to contemporary accounts, the Moore's were well-liked, as was Joseph Stillinger. There seems to be no reason why the family would have been killed or why anyone would have been targeting Mr. Stillinger by slaying his daughters. The only person in town who seemed to have a grudge against anyone involved was Frank Jones, the owner of the implement store where Moore had previously worked. But were business problems enough to make someone kill a man and his entire family? Or was there more between the two men than was publicly known? Or could the murders have been the work of a random stranger --- making them even more horrific and more sinister?

Blood On Their Hands?

While no one was ever convicted of the Moore / Stillinger murders, there was never any shortage of suspects in the case. In the days that followed the crime, there were at least four suspects mentioned in every edition of the newspaper. However, leads were quickly exhausted, alibis were established and possibilities began to dwindle. The local police, state investigators, private detectives who were hired, and even amateur detectives looking for the reward that had been offered combed the town and the surrounding region, following every clue that was presented. Dozens of theories were pursued but each time the investigation seemed to be getting close to something, it all fell apart again. As time wore on, the possibility of solving the crime began to fade and eventually, the trail went cold.

Today, historians, and those with an interest in the case, have their own ideas of who committed the murders. There are many who believe the killer was a local man, who was known to the victims, while others believe a deranged preacher, a traveling hobo or dangerous serial killer was responsible for the deaths of the

Moore's and the Stillinger girls.

One of the most popular suspects of the time was Frank F. Jones, the prominent Villisca resident and state Senator. Jones had been born in Bath, New York and he and his family moved from New York to Southern Michigan in 1862, then on to Illinois the following year. In 1875, they relocated and settled in rural Iowa. Jones started out his working life as a schoolteacher but later became a bookkeeper for Baines and Waterman, a farm implement store, in 1882 and moved to Villisca with his wife, Maude. When the Baines and Waterman partnership dissolved, Jones stayed on and worked for J.S. Baines.

In 1886, Jones purchased what was then known as the "Jackson Corner" on 5th Avenue in Villisca and in 1898 began construction on one of the grandest homes in town. In 1890, he took over the Baines implement business with J.L. Smith. The two men remained partners until 1892, when the Waterman Hardware store came up for sale. Smith traded his farm in Nebraska for ownership of the hardware store and Jones took over as the sole owner of what was soon known as "Jones of Villisca". In 1894, he reorganized the business as Jones & Co. after he became a partner in the Farmers Bank, and took on new partners, Henry and Horace Farlin and John Garside. In 1898, the Farlin brothers became the sole owners of Jones & Co. but Jones once again became a partner in 1901 when he bought out Horace Farlin. The store operated as Jones & Farlin until 1902, when Jones took over again as sole proprietor and renamed the place The Jones Store.

In 1903, Jones entered politics and was elected to the Iowa legislature. Around the same time, he also founded the Villisca National Bank, which took over the Farmers Bank, and that put him in control of just about all of the finances in Villisca and the surrounding region. Jones served for a total of three years in the House of Representatives and two years in the Iowa Senate. He and his wife had two children, Albert and Letha, and he also served as a Methodist and Episcopalian Sunday School superintendent for over 30 years.

J.B. Moore worked for Jones for several years until he opened his own implement company in 1908. According to many residents, Jones was extremely upset that Moore left his employ and managed to take the very lucrative John Deere franchise with him. Jones was undoubtedly the most powerful man in town during this era and it's not likely that he would have suffered what he considered a "defeat" lightly. But would this have been enough to murder Moore and his family? Some believe that matters were made even worse by the fact that J.B. Moore was engaged in an affair with Jones' daughter-in-law, Dona. Although no actual evidence of any affair exists, it was a rumor that was going around at the time of the murders. This may have enraged not only Jones but his son, Albert, as well.

After the Burns Detective Agency from Kansas City got involved in the case, their detective in charge, James Newton Wilkerson, became convinced that Jones was involved in the murders. He openly accused Frank and Albert Jones of hiring a man named William Mansfield to carry out the crime. He believed that J.B. Moore was supposed to be the only target but Mansfield had killed everyone in the house instead. Neither of the Jones' was ever arrested and both of them vehemently denied any connection to the killings. Detective Wilkerson was never able to gather enough evidence to get the authorities to charge the men and they were never arrested.

Albert Jones died in 1935 and his father passed away a few years later, in February 1941. The men left this world with a number of mysteries in their wake. When Frank Jones died, the contents of his study were donated to the Villisca Library. A note and some of the Grand Jury statements were found in Jones' home by the

1968 Villisca High School class members that moved the materials to the library. The note read:

> Mr. Jones,
> I made a fool of myself talking about you on the Moore deal. There is only one fool bigger and that is Wilkerson. This is to square with you. Keep it say nothing nobody knows.
> Konshens

What exactly Konshens meant in his note will never be known. In addition, when the current owners of the Jones home purchased the house, they found all of Albert's old diaries and papers in the attic. They destroyed them without ever letting anyone else read them. They simply stated that there was nothing relevant in them. Whether or not they held any answers to the Villisca murders will also remain a mystery. If Frank and Albert Jones were innocent of any involvement in the Moore / Stillinger murders, they also became victims in one of the most horrible crimes in Iowa history.

But were they innocent? Detective Wilkerson didn't think so...

The man accused of carrying out the crime for the Jones' was William Mansfield, who came from Blue Island, Illinois. Wilkerson believed that Mansfield, who was also known under the aliases of George Worley and Jack Turnbaugh, was a cocaine fiend and a killer who was also responsible for other murders. The detective believed that Mansfield murdered his wife, infant child and his wife's parents in Blue Island on July 5, 1914, two years after the Villisca murders, committed murders in Paola, Kansas four days before the Villisca murders and also murdered Jennie Peterson and Jennie Miller in Aurora, Colorado.

Wilkerson's investigation revealed that all of these murders were committed in precisely the same manner, which led him to believe that one man was responsible for all of them. In each case, the detective believed that the evidence showed the killer was either a maniac or a man who was crazed by drugs. In all of the murders, the victims were hacked or bludgeoned to death with an ax and the mirrors in the homes were covered. A burning lamp with a chimney off was left at the foot of the bed and a basin where the killer washed up was found in the kitchen. The killer also avoided leaving fingerprints at all of the crime scenes. Wilkerson believed that this was because Mansfield knew his fingerprints were on file at the federal military prison at Leavenworth. He also stated that he could prove that Mansfield was present in each of these places on the night of the murders.

Wilkerson managed to convince a grand jury to open an investigation in 1916 and Mansfield was arrested and brought to Montgomery County from Kansas City. However, the accused managed to produce payroll records that showed that he was in Illinois at the time of the Villisca murders. Without any other evidence, Mansfield was released. He later won a lawsuit against Wilkerson and was awarded $2,225 in damages. Regardless, Wilkerson always believed that Mansfield, along with Frank and Albert Jones, was responsible for the Villisca murders. He maintained that political pressure from Jones resulted in not only Mansfield's release but also in the subsequent arrest and trial of Reverend George Kelly.

Reverend Kelly, a traveling preacher, became another prime suspect in the Moore / Stillinger murders. Lyn George Jacklin Kelly was born in England in 1878 and came to America with his wife, Laura, around 1904. He desperately wanted to be a minister and soon joined the Presbyterian Church. Kelly was described as a "spidery little man" with protruding ears, a prominent noise, high forehead and a wide mouth with large lips that seemed to turn down at the corners even when he smiled. People recalled his dark eyes and were disconcerted by his mannerisms. He was easily excited and often ranted and spoke so fast that he was sometimes impossible to understand. He was also said to drool excessively and sprayed spit all over those who were close to him when he talked.

Kelly and his wife settled in Macedonia, Iowa in 1912 after several years of preaching throughout the Midwest. He continued as an itinerant preacher and was present at the Children's Day program at the Presbyterian Church on the night of the murders. His presence here, and his departure from town during the early morning hours on June 10, made him a prime suspect in the killings. Kelly had arrived in Villisca and was to attend the program and then stay overnight at the home of Reverend Ewing, pastor of the church, and his wife. When Kelly arrived in Villisca, Seymour Enarson, the son of Henry Enarson, met him at the train depot. He was driven from the depot to the home of Louis Enarson, Seymour's uncle, for supper. After that, Kelly was taken to the Henry Enarson home for the evening.

According to Enarson family accounts, Kelly acted very nervous when he arrived at their farm house, which was located six miles north of Villisca. Almost immediately, he began pacing the living room floor and at one point, told Mrs. Enarson and the children to leave the room because they were too noisy. Kelly spent the night in a small downstairs bedroom and Mrs. Enarson was so alarmed by his strange behavior that she wrapped herself in a blanket and spent a sleepless night on the steps leading to the upstairs bedrooms, listening carefully to any sound the preacher might make.

The next morning, which was the day of the murders, Henry and Seymour Enarson took Kelly to the Pilot Grove Church for a picnic. Prior to lunch, Kelly gave a sermon that Seymour later described as "the strangest he had ever heard". Kelly returned to the Enarson home for supper and then Seymour drove him to Reverend Ewing's home. That was the last time that the Enarson's saw him prior to the murders but they always believed that he had something to do with the killings. They always heard that the minister confessed to the crime on the train going back to Macedonia and that he had committed the murders because he had a vision that told him to "slay and slay utterly", a phrase that allegedly came from the Bible. The Enarson's had no reason to believe that this strange man was not guilty of the crimes that he was accused of.

Before his "confession" though, Kelly wrote a number of letters to the authorities about the Moore / Stillinger deaths. In the letters, Kelly appeared to be obsessed with the murders and supposedly wrote things that only the killer would know. His uttering on the train ("slay and slay utterly") was said to have been overheard by witnesses and he spoke to other passengers about the killings --- before they were even reported, some said. True or not, Kelly did send a bloody shirt to the laundry in Council Bluffs but it was never recovered.

In 1914, Kelly was arrested but not for the murders. He was jailed in South Dakota for sending obscene materials through the mail and was sentenced to prison. Instead, he ended up in a mental hospital in Washington D.C. By 1917 though, suspicions had fallen onto Kelly in Iowa and he was arrested for the Moore / Stillinger murders. Kelly supposedly rambled a nearly incoherent confession and the fact that it was accepted at all had led some to call this a "mockery of law enforcement practices at the time". Kelly withdrew the confession before his trial began. His first trial resulted in a hung jury and he was finally acquitted by the second.

It was said that Kelly returned to England after his release and years later, some of the Enarson children would claim that Kelly wrote to their father and asked him for money to help him return to the United States. The Enarson's ignored the letters but many believe that Kelly managed to return anyway. It's been said that he lived in Kansas City, Connecticut and New York but the remaining years of his life, and final resting place, are a mystery.

Despite what many believed was strong evidence against some of the principals in the case, detectives were unable to ignore other similar murders that occurred in the Midwest around the same time as the Villisca murders. There remains a very strong possibility that a serial killer, before anyone even knew what a "serial killer" was, could have been at work during this time.

Although every hobo, transient and otherwise unaccounted for stranger became a suspect in the Villisca murders at one time or another, there were a few of these travelers who stood out from the others. One of them was a man named Andy Sawyer. Although no real evidence ever linked Sawyer to the crime, his name was often mentioned during the grand jury proceedings.

According to Thomas Dyer of Burlington, Iowa, a bridge foreman and pile driver for the Burlington Railroad, Sawyer approached he and his crew in Creston at 6:00 a.m. on the morning the murders were discovered. Sawyer was clean-shaven and dressed in a brown suit, Dyer recalled in his testimony, but his pants were wet to the knee and his shoes covered in mud. He asked for employment and since Dyer needed another man, he hired him on the spot. It was soon after that Dyer and his men started to notice Sawyer's odd behavior. Was he simply an eccentric and possibly mentally ill hobo --- or something more dangerous?

Dyer stated that when they reached Fontenelle, Iowa, Sawyer purchased a newspaper, which he went off by himself to read. The newspaper had a front page account of the Villisca murders and, according to Dyer, Sawyer "was much interested in it". The crew also began to note Sawyer's peculiarities - he slept with his clothes on, hardly spoke and stayed by himself most of the time. When he did talk, he mostly rambled on about the Moore / Stillinger murders and whether or not the killer had been apprehended. Sawyer told Dyer that he had been in Villisca on the Sunday morning when the murders were discovered but was afraid that he might be considered a suspect and left town before anyone questioned him. One day, as the crew was traveling through Villisca, Sawyer told Dyer's son, J.R., that he could show him how the man who killed the Moore family escaped from town. And while all of this was disturbing, none of it was as disconcerting as the fact that Sawyer slept with an ax at night!

Dyer finally became suspicious enough of Sawyer that he turned him into the police on June 18, 1912. Just before doing so, he testified that he had walked up behind Sawyer and saw the man rubbing his head with both hands and muttering to himself. Suddenly, he jumped up and shouted "I'll cut your god damn heads off!" and began swinging his ax and hitting the ground with it.

Sawyer was arrested and brought in for questioning but was apparently dismissed as a suspect in the case when it was discovered that police records had him in Osceola, Iowa on the night of the murders. He was arrested for vagrancy and the Osceola sheriff recalled putting him on a train out of town at approximately 11:00 p.m. on the night of June 9. Could he have still made it to Villisca to carry out the murders that night? Thomas Dyer, and the nervous men on his crew, believed that he could but his concerns were dismissed and Sawyer vanished into history.

Perhaps the most likely suspect in the "drifter" category was a man named Henry Moore, who was no relation to the murdered family. Although accused of some of the same crimes as William Mansfield, Moore was actually convicted of ax murders a short time after the events in Villisca. Some believe that he was responsible for a bloody spree of murder that wreaked havoc across the Midwest and included the murders of the Moore family and Stillinger girls in Iowa.

An unbalanced man who was prone to violent rages, Moore was prosecuted in December 1912 for the murder of his mother and maternal grandmother in Columbia, Missouri. He had slaughtered both of his victims with an ax and while this was horrific enough, it was just the final act in a bloody rampage that may have spanned 18 months, five states and more than 20 murders. It is thought that the Villisca murders were what finally put federal authorities on Moore's trail.

The discovery of the killing spree might never have been realized if authorities in Villisca had not requested federal assistance in the solution of their local massacre in June 1912. The police had the savaged bodies of the Moore's and the Stillinger girls but had no clues or direction for their investigation. A federal officer, M.W. McClaughry, was assigned to the case and his investigation revealed that the Villisca murders were not unique. Nine months before, in September 1911, a similar massacre had occurred in Colorado Springs, taking the lives of H.C. Wayne, his wife and child, and Mrs. A.J. Burnham and her two children. A month later, in October, another massacre claimed the lives of the Dewson family in Monmouth, Illinois and then a little more than a week later, the five members of the Showman family of Ellsworth, Kansas were also murdered in their beds. In every case, the killer had broken into their homes late at night and had killed everyone with an ax.

On June 5, 1912 --- just days before the carnage in Villisca --- Rollin Hudson and his wife were murdered in Paola, Kansas. The murders were carried out in the same way as the earlier crimes, and just as would occur a short time later in Villisca. Detective James Wilkerson believed that this crime had been carried out by William Mansfield, who he believed had been hired by the Jones' to commit the murders in Villisca. However, McClaughry did not think so. No suspect had ever been identified in any of the cases and rumors of a "romance angle" in the Hudson case produced no leads. McClaughry believed that he was dealing with a transient maniac after the Villisca murders but even so, clues were in short supply.

While McClaughry was a hard working investigator, it would be coincidence and good luck that would point him in the direction of Henry Moore. McClaughry's father was the warden of the federal penitentiary at Leavenworth and was a man with many contacts within the prison system. When he heard about the case of Henry Moore, who was serving a life sentence in Missouri for the December 1912 murders of his mother and grandmother, he informed his son. After comparing the evidence in all of the cases, capped by interviews with Moore, McClaughry announced, on May 9, 1913, that the books had been closed on 23 Midwestern homicides. Unfortunately, no one took his findings seriously and most were happier to believe that the real killer was Reverend George Kelly, who had "confessed" to the Villisca murders.

As readers already know, there were many problems with the minister's confession. On the same day they were publicized, Kelly told his wife that the confession was "pure fabrication". Granted, he had signed the statement but he was not sure why he had done so. He publicly recanted as the trial approached and his ramblings seemed to bolster pleas of mental illness. Kelly was later acquitted after two trials.

During all of the publicity surrounding the trial, the information collected by M.W. McClaughry had been largely forgotten. In spite of this, McClaughry remained convinced of Moore's guilt and always believed that he had solved the Villisca murders.

Officially however, the case remains open to this day.

The Haunting of the Moore House

During the hours before dawn on June 10, 1912, a small frame house in Villisca, Iowa became the site of one of the grisliest massacres in Midwestern history when the family of J.B. Moore and two overnight guests were murdered as they slept. The house earned a place in American crime history that morning and a place in the annals of ghostly legend as well.

The house on Lot 410 in Villisca had originally been built in 1868 by George Loomis. It was purchased by J.B. Moore in 1903 and he and his wife Sarah, along with the children that came along, made their home there until their deaths nine years later. After the massacre, the house remained in estate until 1915, when it was purchased by J.H. Geesman.

Over the course of the next 90 years, the house had seven additional owners, including the Villisca State Savings & Loan, whose name appears on the title from 1963 to 1971. In 1971, the house was sold to Kendrick & Vance and only a month later, was sold again to Darwin Kendrick. He remained as the owner of the house, renting it out to tenants, until it was sold to Rick and Vicki Sprague on January 1, 1994. A few months later, a real estate agent approached Darwin and Martha Linn, local farmers, about the possibility of them purchasing the house. At the time, the Linn's already owned and operated the Olson-Linn Museum located on Villisca's town square and they felt that purchasing the house at Lot 410 would give them the opportunity to preserve more of the area's history. Because of its deteriorating condition, the Moore house was in danger of being razed. If the Linn's had not purchased it, it's likely that it would have been destroyed. They soon set about obtaining the necessary funds to restore the home to its condition at the time of the murders in 1912.

As Darwin and Martha began researching the house, they found that they had a lot of work ahead of them to try and restore the place. Years of renovation would be ahead and some paranormal researchers believe that it was the restorative work that followed which caused the house to become hauntingly "active". In many cases of hauntings, an event may occur that leaves an "impression" on the atmosphere of a place. Such an event may include a traumatic occurrence like a murder, or several murders, as it was at the Moore house. Often this haunting will lay dormant for many years before becoming active again. The activity is usually generated by remodeling or renovation, disturbing the physical presence of the location. This disturbance can often cause effects to occur that are related to the haunting and can include sounds like voices, footsteps and cries, as well as physical effects like doors opening and closing, widows rattling and even knocking and rapping sounds. Is this merely a "recording" of the past that has been activated again or could there be an actual presence that generates the activity? In some locations, like the Villisca Ax Murder House, it may just be both.

As the Linn's attempted to work on the restoration, they found that 13 previous owners were listed on the deed to the Moore house and that it was often used as rental property. At this date, they have started to compile a list of the tenants who lived in the house but progress has been slow and many of the renters stayed for only a short time. They did learn that between 1936 and 1994, the house had undergone extensive changes. The front and back porches were enclosed, plumbing and electricity were added and the outbuildings were either removed or replaced. The house barely resembled the Moore house of 1912 but that was soon to change.

Using old photographs, the Linn's began the renovation work in late 1994. The restoration included the removal of vinyl siding and the repainting of the original wood on the outside, the removal of the enclosures on the front and back porch, the restoration of an outhouse and chicken coop in the backyard and the removal of all of the indoor plumbing and electrical fixtures. The pantry in the original house had been converted to a bathroom years before and this room was now restored to its 1912 condition. Then, using testimony and records from the coroner's inquest and grand jury hearings, the Linn's placed furniture in approximately the same places as it was located at the time of the murders. Unfortunately, the furniture that had belonged to the Moore's had vanished many decades ago but antiques were used to replace what was lost.

The Moore home was added to the National Register of Historic Places in 1998 and remains today as a colorful time capsule of 1912, the ghastly murders that occurred here and the mystery that followed. The walls of the place hide many secrets ---- from the identity of the murderer to just how he managed to carry out his dark deeds without awakening the occupants of the house ---- and these secrets still bring many visitors to the door. Some come looking for the history of the place but most of them come looking for the ghosts.

Ever since the Moore house was opened to overnight visitors several years ago, ghost enthusiasts, curiosity-seekers and diehard paranormal investigators have come here in droves, all seeking the strange, the unusual and the haunted. Some have stayed here alone, like the Des Moines disk jockey who awoke in the night to the sounds of children's voices when no children were present. Others have come in groups and have gone away with mysterious audio, video and photographic evidence that suggests something supernatural lurks within these walls. Tours have been cut short by falling lamps, moving objects, banging sounds and a child's laughter, while psychics who have come here have claimed to communicate with the spirits of the dead.

If even a fraction of the stories circulating about this place were true, I reasoned when I first heard about the so-called "Villisca Ax Murder House", then this would have to be one of the most haunted places in America. The history of the place certainly provided a possibility for the story of the haunting to be true --- but was it? I would find that out for myself in May 2005, when I hosted an overnight stay at this legendary house.

I arrived in Villisca on the evening of our overnight just an hour or so before the sun went down. I met up with the rest of the group at Darwin and Martha Linn's museum, located on the small town's square and just steps away from Villisca's bank and its only restaurants. The museum is located in what was once one of the town's thriving businesses and features a jumbled assortment of old cars, farm equipment, advertising signs and historical records, displays and artifacts from days gone by. A visitor could spend hours in the museum and still not see everything that has been jammed into the two overflowing floors. I met Darwin and Martha for the first time (and have since cultivated a nice friendship with this wonderful couple) and spent a

The J.B. Moore Home --- a.k.a. The "Villisca Ax Murder House"

little while chatting with them before Darwin introduced the group to the bloody history of the Villisca murders through magazine articles and a video that had been produced about the family's last hours in June 1912.

After the introduction, we followed Darwin to the town cemetery, where the Moore's and the Stillinger girls had been buried. The grave markers of the family had been purchased from the sizable reward fund that had been collected in hopes of capturing their killer. Since the reward was never claimed, surviving family members donated the money to be used for the tombstones in Villisca's small cemetery. After leaving the burial ground, Darwin pointed out the once-grand mansion that had belonged to Frank Jones, one of the leading suspects in the murders, and then he led us back to the square and to one of the local restaurants. We fortified ourselves with piles of food --- it would be a long night ahead --- and then we all met back over at the Moore house, where we would spend the rest of our time in town.

As mentioned already, walking into the Moore house is like stepping back in time. There is no electricity in the house, it is only illuminated by candles and kerosene lamps, and no plumbing either. There is now a bathroom in the small barn that has been reconstructed on the property but at the time of my first visit, there was only an old outhouse, which was authentic to 1912. The house is small and we entered through the back door, which let us into the kitchen. The parlor is located at the front of the house, with the bedroom leading off from it where the bodies of the Stillinger girls were found. Also, just off the kitchen, is a small pantry and the staircase that leads to the second floor. At the top of the steps is the bedroom that belonged to J.B. and Sarah Moore and beyond that, at the front of the house, is the children's bedroom, where the blood-soaked bodies of the Moore children were discovered. There is also an unfinished attic room that leads off from the Moore's bedroom.

120

It had been a warm afternoon, fading into evening, when we arrived in Villisca. The heat of the day had generated a line of fierce thunderstorms and soon after arriving at the house, we began to hear rumbles of thunder and see flashes of lightning above the distant, rolling hills. By 11:00 p.m. or so, the rain began to pound on Villisca but it only lasted for a short time. In less than an hour, the storms had moved off, leaving the night warm, still and humid. Our investigations were now set to begin in earnest.

As I may have mentioned earlier, most of the time on these overnight trips, I'm relegated to the proverbial "backseat" and spend the evening observing the investigations and research that the guests are carrying out. I like to allow them to experience the locations for themselves and while I try to help when necessary, I usually stay out of the details of their experiments. In some cases though, as it happened here in Villisca, I can't help but get involved.

Two of the guests, Anney Horn and her daughter, Jada, had been to the Moore house on another occasion and Anney told the group about some rather strange happenings that she had experienced in the children's room on the second floor. She was convinced that one of the Moore children, Paul, remained behind in this room and would interact with visiting researchers in exchange for candy. She had brought along a pocket full of treats and suggested that the group try and make contact with Paul in this room. Everyone agreed and a couple of the other guests, David and Josie Rodriguez, who were part of an investigation team called PRISM from Omaha, Nebraska, set up an array of video equipment in the bedroom to record any strange events that might occur. It would be the camera that was trained on the closet in this room that would capture the most dramatic evidence of the night.

Within a few minutes, a number of the guests assembled in the room. As mentioned, I usually just like to observe whatever is going on and I chose to stay downstairs rather than make the small bedroom any more crowded than it already was. I was in the parlor as the communication attempts began upstairs but David was monitoring what was going on by way of a video feed that he had set up in the kitchen. After 20 minutes or so had passed, he called out and invited me to come in and watch. There was something odd going on, David said, and I should come and take a look.

I went into the kitchen and looked over his shoulder at the monitor. The picture and sound were being fed to a laptop computer and we watched as the guests in the bedroom tried to coax the "ghost boy" into performing on cue for them. They were asking him to close a closet door that they had opened up and as far as we could tell, the door was closing just as they asked it to! This happened several times in a row and after watching it for a little while, I decided that we had to see it for ourselves.

I hurried upstairs and walked into the back room, which was now filled with very excited guests. I squeezed in as they gave me a description of what had been happening. What they told me matched perfectly with what I had been watching on the monitor in the kitchen. I sat down and watched as Anney began to again try and coax "Paul" into closing the closet door that had been opened for him. To be honest, I was very skeptical about what was occurring. I had come upstairs, not because I was excited to see the antics of the alleged ghost, but to find a logical explanation for what was going on. There had to be a reasonable answer for the closet door and I was determined to see what that could be.

Anney called to Paul a few times and promised that she would leave some candy for him if he would make the closet door close for her. We all watched in silence as the door remained standing open at a distance of about eight inches. Nothing happened for several minutes and then all of the sudden, for no apparent reason, the door slowly swung closed. It did not slam closed but rather seemed to just gently close, as though someone was pushing it. There was absolutely no one near it at the time.

I'm not sure how I managed to do it but I convinced the guests to take a break from the investigation and to go downstairs for a few minutes. I wanted to check out the room and the closet. I was dubious about the "ghost boy" and I was sure that there had to be a reason as to why the closet door seemed to be performing on command. I looked at everything ---- I looked for wires, for slopes in the floor, for loose hinges and even tried opening the door and pushing it closed several times. Could it be a draft? I went through the entire upstairs and closed all of the doors and windows so that I could be sure that there was no air current coming in. Could it have been the distance that the door stood open that allowed it to swing closed? I made a note to try coaxing the door closed from other distances. Was it just a coincidence? If the door was left open long enough would it just close anyway? I tried leaving the door standing open for minutes at a time, much longer than it had been left with the room full of people, but it simply refused to close.

Finally, after 20 minutes or so, I was ready for them to try again. I invited the guests back into the bedroom and instructed them to try and get the door to close now that we had sealed off the windows from any outside air. Everyone sat down again and Anney went to work, once again calling out to Paul and asking him to close the door. A minute or two passed and the door swung shut again ---- something that I had been unable to duplicate a short time before. There was no way that I could say that this was caused by air currents or drafts from the windows. The door was opened back up again and she asked Paul to close it again --- and again.

This happened several more times before we stopped and decided to try something else. If the door was not closing because of an air current, could it close on its own anyway, if we waited long enough? I had tried waiting several minutes but what if we waited for an hour or so? Would the door eventually just swing closed? And if so, was it because the doorframe was slanted in some way, which would explain why the door was closing, seemingly "on its own"?

I wanted to see what would happen if we did not ask Paul to close the door. We made an agreement to leave the door standing open and for all of us to leave the room. Anyone who wanted to watch it could do so from the monitor downstairs in the kitchen. With that, we all went downstairs or outside to have a midnight snack and to wait around and see what might happen in the bedroom.

We waited for nearly two hours and did not go back into the room during that time. Through most of that, someone was watching the door from the monitor, or at least checking in periodically to see what was happening. During that entire time, the door never moved. Nothing had changed with it ---- except that no one was asking Paul to close it. It never budged though. It just stood there, open about eight inches, apparently just waiting for us to return.

Finally, at about 2:00 a.m., several of us filed back into the room. The door was standing open, just as we had left it, and we sat down with a clear view of it. It had now been standing open for almost two hours and Anney spoke out loud, asking Paul to close the door.

"Paul? Are you there?" she queried. "Would you close the door for us again? If you do, I'll leave some more candy inside of the closet."

Seconds ticked by and then, without anyone moving, speaking or coming close to the door, the wooden panel slowly swung shut and latched with a click. It had never moved --- until someone asked for it to and then suddenly, the door had closed. I would love to provide one but I have no rational explanation for how this could have happened without some element of the unexplained being involved.

Is the Moore house in Villisca really haunted? There are many who maintain that it's not. They say that many people lived in the house over the years and none of them ever mentioned ghosts or mysterious activity. It was not until the renovations began that visitors began to say that strange events were occurring within the walls of the "Ax Murder House". Are these events merely the products of overactive imaginations or wishful thinking? That's what some would like you to believe but don't be fooled --- and don't take my word for it either.

I have come to believe that this house is haunted because of my own experiences here. I hope the reader will reserve his own judgment until the time comes when he can spend his own night inside of this house. It's not a place for the faint of heart but if you are looking for a place where you might be able to experience paranormal phenomena on your own, then search for Villisca, Iowa on the map and make your own plans to step back in time to this historic ---- and haunted --- place.

9. HUNTING FOR HOAXES

Looking Behind the Legends of Some of America's Greatest Hauntings with Troy Taylor

My first real introduction to "ghost writing" came about when I was about 13 years-old. I was already well aware of the fact that truth was often stranger than fiction and was also already a veteran of the realm of ghosts and the supernatural. I was one of those kids who was always scribbling stories in a battered notebook that I carried around and who could usually be found with his nose buried in a book. I would read just about anything, as long as it allowed me to escape to somewhere else and preferably, gave me a good scare along the way. As early as my grade school years, I can recall reading books with titles like "True Ghost Stories" but no book made an impression on me like the one that I discovered when I was 13.

I was in a local bookstore one day and ran across a paperback book called *Haunted Houses* by Richard Winer and Nancy Osborn. The back cover text was catchy but what really got my attention was that all of it was purported to be true and that everything in the book was "based on documented investigation". It was no recounting of legends and ghost stories --- this was the real thing! I bought the book and quickly devoured page after page, over and over again. In the following weeks, I read the book several times, unable to get enough of it. None of the horror novels that I had read could compare to the real-life exploits of genuine ghost hunters. These people were not just talking about, or writing about, ghosts ---- they were going out and finding them.

The cover of "Haunted Houses", the book that changed my life

I can't remember how many times I read that book, but it literally changed my life. I was determined to become not only a writer, but a writer who sought out ghosts. I wanted to seek out hauntings and ghostly spots and because of the inspiration that I received from *Haunted Houses*, I wanted to see for myself some of the places that Richard Winer and Nancy Osborn had visited and had written about. A couple of years later, they even offered a sequel to the original book called *More Haunted Houses*. It revealed even more haunted places and strange tales and I was as hooked on this one as I was on the first book. Years later, after I became an adult, I started traveling around the county, marking off locations from the book that I had on my list.

In almost every case, I wrote about these locations, sometimes extensively, and tried to discover the "behind the scenes" aspects of the tales. Some of these places included the Bell Witch Farm and Cave, the Winchester Mystery House, the Whaley House, Alcatraz, the city of New Orleans and many others.

I remember that there were two locations, or stories, in these two books that intrigued me perhaps more than any other. One of them, the story of what was originally known as "America's Most Haunted House", was one of the most chilling tales that I had ever heard. The other story was that of the famous Myrtles Plantation in Louisiana, which had to be, based on the stories that I heard, one of the most spirit-infested places in the country.

Or at least this is how it seemed.

I was soon to find however, that not everything was quite the way that it appeared. I was soon to learn an important lesson about ghost research --- no dedicated ghost hunter should be afraid to look for the truth, even if you don't like it after you find it!

The House on Ridge Avenue

The story of the infamous "House on Ridge Avenue" has always been one of my favorite tales of ghosts, horror and the supernatural. I ran across this story for the first time back in 1979 and never forgot it. It chilled me to the bone and perhaps because I was at such an impressionable age then, I never doubted that the story was true. In the years that followed, my interest in the story never faded and as time passed, I should have realized that something was not quite right about it, but I never did. Or perhaps I never wanted to realize it or to doubt that the tale was not an authentic one. I refused to see that the story of the "Original Most Haunted House in America" seemed almost too good to be true.

It seemed too good to be true ----- simply because it was.

I can't help but be embarrassed now as I look back and wonder how I didn't miss the signs in the first place. The story of the House on Ridge Avenue appeared in at least one of my books on ghosts and I had done magazine articles about it as well. By late 2003, my faith in the story had wavered though and I became determined to try and track down the details of the story. It can sometimes be difficult to trace a story that occurred quite some distance away from you (which is my only excuse for being hoodwinked by the tale for as long as I was) but I decided not to let the miles between Illinois and Pittsburgh stand in the way. If someone knew the facts behind this story, I wanted to find them.

As I began contacting people who should have been aware of the salient facts behind the story of the Ridge Avenue house, I realized that those who claimed knowledge were simply repeating back to me the same account that I had already heard. They cited the same sources and as far as I can tell, this "local legend" first appeared in the book *Haunted Houses* by Richard Winer and Nancy Osborn. As this had long been one of my favorite books, I was dismayed when I discovered that Mr. Winer was as fooled by the story as the rest of us were. I have been unable to discover where the authors may have first heard the story themselves.

As I continued my search, I found the same story regurgitated back to me over and over again. People who claimed to recall the details behind the events suddenly forgot them and witnesses who stated that they had information that went beyond the standard accounts became bewildered when the story did not match the historical details of the case.

All I can say is that I hope you enjoy the recounting ---- and the debunking ---- of the legend that follows. This was not a story that I wanted to tell but, as stated before, we cannot be afraid of the truth. If stories that are shown to be fraudulent are reported as real, then how can we expect the real stories to be taken seriously?

The Legend: Part 1

According to the stories, the House on Ridge Avenue was located in a quiet residential neighborhood in Manchester, on the north edge of Pittsburgh. A man named Charles Wright Congelier built it in the 1860's. He had made a fortune for himself in Texas following the Civil War and such men were commonly referred to in the south as "Carpetbaggers". They made a lot of money preying on the broken economy in the former Confederacy. Congelier left Texas by river steamer, taking with him his Mexican wife, Lyda, and a servant girl named Essie. When the steamer docked in Pittsburgh for coal, Congelier decided that the Pennsylvania town looked like a good place to settle. The three of them left the ship and Congelier purchased a lot and began construction of the house.

A few months later, the new brick and mortar mansion was completed. It was located at 1129 Ridge Avenue and was considered one of the finest houses in the area. From the expansive lawn, Congelier could look out and see where the Allegheny and Monongahela Rivers met to form the Ohio, offering a breathtaking view. The former Carpetbagger soon became a respected member of the local business community and his new home became a frequent site for parties and social gatherings. Then, during the winter of 1871, an event took place that would bloody the location for decades to come.

That winter, as cold and snow settled over the region, Congelier became embroiled in an affair with his servant girl, Essie. Whether she was a willing participant or not, Essie soon became a constant bed partner for her employer. For several months, Lyda Congelier was unaware of the affair, but when three people reside in the same house, it's only a matter of time before secrets are revealed.

One afternoon, Lyda returned from a shopping trip and needed the girl to help her with her packages. She came into the house but Essie was nowhere to be found. When Essie did not respond to her call, Lyda went to the girl's room looking for her. As she came down the hallway, she could hear heavy breathing and moaning coming from behind the door. Knowing that her husband was the only man in the house, Lyda became enraged. She hurried to the kitchen and snatched up both a butcher knife and a meat cleaver. As she began climbing the stairs back to the servant's room, Lyda began screaming with rage, which naturally provoked a panic inside of Essie's bedroom. Before Congelier and the girl could dress themselves and exit the room, Lyda had already taken up a post outside. When the door opened, she brought the meat cleaver down on the head of the first person to open it. Charles Congelier fell to the floor, a cry on his lips and blood streaming from the wound on his head. As Essie reared back, bellowing in terror, Lyda proceeded to stab her husband 30 times. Then, she turned toward Essie....

Several days later, a family friend called at the house and when no one responded to his knock, he opened the door and peered inside. He called out, but there was no answer in the darkened house. However, as he entered the foyer, he could hear a faint creaking noise in the parlor. He called out again, but as there was still no answer, he walked further into the house. Following the odd sound, he entered the parlor and saw Lyda Congelier rocking back and forth in front of a large bay window.

The wooden chair that she rested in creaked with each backward and forward motion that she made.

"Lyda? Is everything all right?" he spoke to her.

There was no reply. Lyda continued to rock back and forth in the chair. As her friend drew closer, he could hear her softly crooning a lullaby under her breath. It was a child's nursery song, he realized, and he saw a bundle that was wrapped in a blanket in Lyda's arms. She held it close, as she would hold a baby, rocking it gently. The man felt a sudden chill course through him. He knew that the Congelier's had no children.

He spoke to her once again, but there was still no answer. Lyda stared straight ahead at the snow outside, her eyes glazed and unfocused. He gently leaned over and eased the bundle out of her hands. He carefully opened the pink blanket and then recoiled with horror, dropping the bloody bundle onto the floor! It landed on the wooden floorboards with a solid thud and the contents of the blanket rolled away. The friend fell backwards on the couch as Essie's bloody head came to a halt a short distance away from his feet!

For more than two decades after, the house on Ridge Avenue remained empty. Local folks considered the place "tainted" and avoided it at all costs. Few dared to even trespass on the grounds, although sometimes small children threw stones at the windows and sang about the "old battle-ax and her meat-ax".

The Real Story: Part 1

Like most legends, the story of the house is a clever blending of fact and fiction, although in this case, there is much more fiction than fact. To start with, no one named Charles Wright Congelier ever existed and neither did his wife, Lyda. There is no record of any dealings in Texas and no record of his ever living in Pittsburgh. In addition, there are no police or criminal records that state that Lyda murdered her husband and the servant girl in 1871. The use of a date here adds solidity to the story but it also makes it easier to check the validity of the tale and there is none.

Secondly, the house that is described in the story was not a mansion. There really was a house located at 1129 Ridge Avenue but it was built in the late 1880's, not in the 1860's. It was a standard Manchester row house, commonly owned by working class people of the day. It must be mentioned however that the house was later owned by members of the Congelier family, even though Charles Wright Congelier, and the murderous Lyda, were figments of a creative imagination. This is a further blending of the truth, which will be discussed later.

The Legend: Part 2

In 1892, the house was renovated into an apartment building to house railroad workers. Most refused to stay in the place for long. They constantly complained of hearing screams and the sobbing of a woman that came from empty rooms. Others spoke of the ominous sounds of a rocking chair and of a woman mumbling old nursery rhymes and lullabies. Within two years, the house was abandoned once again.

It remained vacant until 1901, when Dr. Adolph C. Brunrichter purchased the house. The doctor became something of an enigma in the neighborhood. Although he had been warned of the past history of the house, he chose to purchase it anyway and after moving in, had little to do with the nearby residents. He kept to himself and was rarely seen by those who lived close to him. Everyone in the neighborhood watched and held their breath, waiting for something terrible to happen. They didn't have to wait very long.

On August 12, 1901, the family who lived next door to the Brunrichter mansion heard a terrified scream coming from the house. When they ran outside to see what was going on, they saw a bright red flash illuminate the interior of the mansion. The windows of the house shattered and glass shot out onto the lawn. The air was filled with the smell of ozone and the earth under the neighborhood trembled, cracking the sidewalks and knocking over furniture in the surrounding homes.

By the time the police and the fire department arrived, a crowd had gathered outside of Brunrichter's house. It was assumed that the doctor was still inside as no one had seen him leave, but none of the neighbors were brave enough to go in and check. Finally, a contingent of firefighters entered the house in search of Brunrichter. They were unable to find him, but what they did discover was enough to send even the bravest among them running for the street outside!

In one of the upstairs bedrooms, a gut-wrenching scene awaited police investigators. Lying spread-eagled on the blood-soaked bed was the decomposing, naked body of a young woman. Her head was missing and was later found in a makeshift laboratory that the doctor had set up in another room. From what the detectives could determine, Brunrichter had apparently been experimenting with severed heads. Using electrical equipment, he had been trying to keep the heads alive after decapitation. A fault in his equipment had evidently caused the explosion. The young girl's head was found with several others and the graves of five women were discovered in the cellar. Each of the bodies could be matched with one of the heads from the laboratory.

As for Dr. Brunrichter, there was no sign of him. He had apparently escaped during the confusion following the explosion and had vanished. A manhunt produced no clues. He had disappeared without leaving a trace.

In September 1927, an old man was arrested in New York's Bowery district. He was found wandering in a drunken stupor, living among the homeless and the street people. He was arrested and booked for public drunkenness and was taken to the local police station. Standing in line with the other dirty and disheveled men, this particular vagrant seemed to give off what the officers would later recall as a "bad feeling". As the drunks shuffled along, the policemen entered their names into record one at a time. When the old man reached the head of the line, the officer asked him his name.

He replied in a harsh voice, slightly slurred with a foreign accent. "My name is Adolph Brunrichter," the man said. And soon, he began to tell stories of his life to the officers at the police station and they were tales even the most hardened cops would not soon forget.

Brunrichter began by explaining to the officers that he was once an eminent doctor, a physician who worked diligently to prolong life. Unfortunately, he could only succeed with his experiments by ending the lives of certain test subjects. He told of how many years earlier, he had bought a house in Pittsburgh to which he enticed young women as guests. Anticipating romance, the women were instead beheaded and then used in experiments to keep their severed heads alive. Brunrichter told of sex orgies, torture and murder and then gave the locations of graves for other women who were not discovered in the cellar of the house. Authorities later checked the sites, but no bodies were ever found.

Brunrichter was kept behind bars for one month at Blackwell's Island. Despite newspaper stories that called him the "Pittsburgh Spook Man", the mad doctor was deemed "harmless" and was released. On the wall of his cell, scrawled in his own blood, were the words "What Satan hath wrought, let man beware." After those fateful words, nothing was ever heard from the man who claimed to be Dr. Adolph Brunrichter again.

The Real Story: Part 2

The house was built in the late 1880's and while a working-class home, was not used to house railroad workers. During this time, it was owned by Marie Congelier (who would go on to become the only recorded death associated with the house) and it was never purchased by anyone named Dr. Adolph Brunrichter. Like Charles and Lyda Congelier, he never actually existed. The only mention of Brunrichter that I have ever been able to find in my own extensive files and books about American crime is in connection to this house. This seemed rather odd to me since his crimes would have obviously have been gruesome and lurid enough to garner the attention of reporters and crime writers. However, there are no listings for him in any books that I could find.

Not content to let it go at that, I also contacted several noted crime researchers and asked them to check their own files for mentions or records of Brunrichter. None of them could find anything. Another check of newspaper and library archives for New York, where papers had allegedly written of the "Pittsburgh Spook Man", also failed to reveal any listings. The same problem occurred while trying to search for reports of the crimes in Pittsburgh as well. There is no mention of the "explosion" or the discovery of the bodies in the house in the Pittsburgh newspapers. In addition, there is not a single death record, real estate record or police record involving anyone named Brunrichter in connection with the house on Ridge Avenue. The mysterious Dr. Brunrichter vanished without a trace because he never really existed in the first place!

The Legend: Part 3

After the horrific discoveries in the basement of the house, the Ridge Avenue mansion was abandoned. It stood empty again for many years, gaining an even more fearsome reputation. Those with an interest in psychic phenomena made occasional visits to the place and came to believe that the house was inhabited by a "fearsome presence". One medium who probed the house, Julia Murray, detected a horrible spirit there and witnesses who accompanied her to the mansion stated that "objects hurled by unseen hands barely missed striking her". Murray predicted that the entity would kill and would eventually extend out beyond the confines of the house.

In 1920, the stories about the mansion caught the attention of another man, one of the greatest inventors that America has ever known. His name was Thomas Alva Edison and in addition to creating the light bulb, he went to his grave in search of a device that would be able to communicate with the dead.

Edison was a self-taught genius who began experimenting with scientific theories as a child. Throughout his life, he maintained that it was possible to build anything if the right components were available. This would later include the already mentioned machine. Edison was not a believer in the supernatural however, nor a proponent of the popular Spiritualist movement. He had always been an agnostic and although he did not dispute the philosophies of religion, he didn't necessarily believe in their truth either. He believed that when a person died, the body decayed but the intelligence the man possessed lived on. He thought that the so-called "spirit world" was simply a limbo where disembodied intelligence waited to move on. He took these paranormal theories one step further by announcing that he intended to devise a machine that could communicate with this "limbo". Edison's announcement appeared in newspapers after his visit to the house on Ridge Avenue. What happened during his visit to the house is unknown, but whatever it was, it certainly inspired him to go to great lengths to create the machine.

According to journals and papers, Edison began working on the apparatus. The famous magician and friend of Edison's, Joseph Dunninger, claimed that he was shown a prototype of the machine but few others ever say they saw it. Edison reportedly continued working on the machine until his death in October 1931. Did Edison's machine actually exist? And, if so, would it have worked? In the years following his death, curators at both of the Edison museums in Florida and New Jersey have searched extensively for the components, the prototype or even the plans for the machine to communicate with the dead. So far, they have found nothing, making Edison's device the greatest mystery of his complex and intriguing life.

The Real Story: Part 3

In the best hoaxes, fact and fiction is blended using real dates and real people to create a convincing story. In the case of the House on Ridge Avenue, the names of people like Julia Murray and Thomas Edison have been used to make the story seem more real. As everyone knows, Edison really did exist and he did attempt to create a machine to communicate with the dead but unfortunately, no records exist of any spirit medium named Julia Murray. I will not state definitively that she is a fictional character but so far, I have seen nothing that says that she really existed.

Edison, on the other hand, was very real but there is absolutely no record to say that he ever set foot in the house on Ridge Avenue. If he had, he would not have found an empty "haunted" house, but the home of Marie Congelier and her family and would certainly have a memory of a visit by the famous inventor. According to Mrs. Congelier's descendants, no such visit ever took place.

The Legend: Part 4

In the middle 1920's, Julia Murray's premonitions of "evil" connected to the house on Ridge Avenue remained in the back of many minds. During this period, the Equitable Gas Company, which was located just a few blocks away, was nearing the completion of a huge natural gas storage complex. To cut costs, many of the regular workers were laid off and were replaced by Italian immigrants, who would work for a much lower wage. A number of vacant buildings in the neighborhood were converted into apartments, including the house at 1129 Ridge Avenue.

The Italian workers who took up residence in the house quickly realized that something was not right in the old mansion. Their complaints and reports were met with quick explanations from the supervisors at the gas company. They told the immigrants that the strange occurrences were the work of the American workers who had been replaced. The former employees were playing tricks on the new workers, hoping they would abandon their jobs. The men soon dismissed the strange sounds and ghostly footsteps as practical jokes until an incident occurred a few months after they moved in.

One evening, 14 men were seated around the table in the common dining room.

They had just finished consuming large quantities of pasta and were now laughing and talking over glasses of homemade wine. One of the men got up and carried a stack of dirty dishes into the kitchen. He joked to his brother as he left the room, calling out a humorous insult over his shoulder with a smile. The remark was answered with laughter and his brother tossed a crust of bread at his sibling's retreating back. The conversation continued for several minutes before the man realized that his brother had not returned from the kitchen. He got up and walked into the other room to find the door to the basement standing open.

Suddenly, the festive mood in the dining room was shattered by a chilling scream! Rushing into the kitchen, the men saw the basement door as it yawned open. Taking a lantern from atop the icebox, several of the men descended the steps into the cellar. Before they reached the bottom of the steps, they froze, staring at the macabre scene that was illuminated by the glow of the lantern. In the dim light, they saw the man who had left the dining room just moments earlier, now hanging from a floor beam that crossed the ceiling above!

On the floor, directly beneath his feet, was the man's brother. He was lying face down in a spreading pool of blood. A splintered board had been driven through his chest and now exited out through his back.

The leader of the group on the steps crossed himself religiously and a gasp escaped from his lips. His friends repeated the gesture before all of them found themselves slammed backward by a force that they could not see! The feeling of a cold wind pushed against them and then rushed past and up the stairs. The men later said that they could hear the pounding of footsteps on the wooden treads, but could see nothing at all. The door at the top of the stairs slammed shut, startling the men in the kitchen, who didn't hear anything. However, they did report other doors mysteriously slamming throughout the house.

When the police arrived, they attributed both deaths to a bizarre accident. The first man, the detectives stated, tripped on a loose step and fell down, impaling himself on the propped-up board. The other brother's death was the result of the same loose stair step. When he fell though, his head was somehow tangled on an electric wire that was hanging down above the staircase. Accident or not, the other men quickly moved out of the house, wanting nothing more to do with the place.

The Real Story: Part 4

Once again, real-life events blend into the story to make it more compelling. In the 1920's, the nearby Equitable Gas Company did lay off many of their workers and replaced them with Italian immigrants. As many of the houses in the neighborhood were worker's homes anyway, several of them were converted into housing for the replacement employees. However, there were no records of any accidental deaths that took place at 1129 Ridge Avenue that were associated with these workers. One accident did take place however, on the same day that another accident destroyed a gas storage tank nearby.

On the morning of the explosion, November 14, Marie Congelier died from a laceration caused by a piece of glass. The glass had severed her artery and she bled to death on the way to the hospital. She did not die in the house but her death came about because of it --- with nothing supernatural involved. She would become the only death that can truly be connected to the House on Ridge Avenue.

On Monday, November 14, 1927, a crew of sixteen workers climbed to the top of the Equitable Gas Company's huge, 5,000,000-cubic-foot natural gas storage tank to find and repair a leak.

At 8:43 that morning, a great sheet of flame erupted from the tank and the huge container shot impossibly upwards into the air. Steel, stone and human bodies were sent hurling into the sky. Two of the men who had been working on top of the tank were thrown against a brick building more than one hundred feet away and their silhouettes were outlined there in blood. Seconds later, another tank exploded, creating another gigantic ball of fire. Then a third tank, this one only partially full, was wrenched apart and added to the inferno. Smoke and flames were visible for miles. The force was so awesome that it blew out windows and shook buildings for a twenty-mile radius. Locomotives were knocked over and homes and structures damaged as far away as East Liberty.

Across the street, the Union Paint Company was flattened and dozens of workers were buried under the rubble of the building. Bloody men, women and children ran frantically about in the streets.

The Battalion Chief of Engine Company No. 47, Dan Jones, was part of the first fire unit to arrive on the scene. He described the holocaust saying "great waves of black smoke swept through the streets and there was a whining noise in the air." According to a book compiled by the Writer's Project of America, the destruction stunned the city. "As houses collapsed and chimneys toppled," they wrote, "brick, broken glass, twisted pieces of steel and other debris rained on the heads of the dazed and shaken residents who had rushed into the streets from their wrecked homes, believing that an earthquake had visited the city."

Even the rescue workers and firefighters who arrived on the scene were injured and killed when weakened structures collapsed on top of them. Entire neighborhoods were flooded by broken water mains while huge sections of the city lay in ruins. Sections of the giant gas storage tanks were later found more than a thousand feet away. Rough estimates from the following day listed at least 28 killed and more than 600 people injured from the explosion. Rescue crews dynamited the ruins in a search for the bodies of the dozens of others who were still missing. Thousands were left homeless by the destruction.

Mounds of rubble and debris marked the spots where buildings had once stood. At one place though, not even bricks and stone remained. At 1129 Ridge Avenue, just two blocks away from the blast site, there was nothing left but a smoldering crater. Although homes on both sides of, and across the street from, where the Congelier mansion had stood were heavily damaged, they were still standing. Yet where the "most haunted house in America" had stood, and where Julia Murray's proclaimed "evil presence" had lingered, there was nothing. A hole nearly 85 feet deep was all that remained. It was the only house in the vicinity of which no trace could be found.

Today, the Carnegie Science Center occupies the site of the Equitable Gas Company tanks and the terrible explosion is only a faint memory from the past. The house on Ridge Avenue is all but forgotten. Its location is the present-day site of the Route 65 and Interstate 279 interchange. Nothing from the days of Dr. Brunrichter, the Congelier's, or the luckless Italian immigrants still lingers, or does it? If it is possible for the spirits of the past to still wander restlessly along a busy highway, then it would be at this place where such spirits would dwell --- the place where one of the most evil houses in the country could be found.

The Real Story: Part 5

Spooky ending, huh?

Unfortunately, it's not accurate either. The gas storage tank at the Equitable Gas Company did explode on November 14, 1927 and killed 24 people in the surrounding area. The concussion and subsequent fire did wreak havoc in this part of the city and it destroyed many houses and buildings, leaving hundreds of people homeless. The details of the destruction that are recounted in the legend of the house are true and accurate --- for the most part.

Where things veer off course is in regards to the house at 1129 Ridge Avenue. In every version of the story, the house is destroyed by the blast, leaving only an ominous crater behind --- as if it was sucked down into the very pit of hell. While this makes a fitting ending to the dramatic tale of America's "original most haunted house", it's not the way that it happened in real life. In truth, the house only suffered minor damage from the explosion. A number of windows were broken but that was about all. According to a family member, Robert Frederick Congelier, the house stood for several years after the disaster and was only torn down to make way for the freeway and the redevelopment of the area.

There is an old saying that goes "truth is stranger than fiction" and in many ways, I would say that this is the case. However, not with every story. In the tale of the House on Ridge Avenue, fiction was really much stranger than fact ever could be and truth proved to be the undoing of the haunting of "America's original most haunted house."

And that's not the only famous haunting in America that has been "unmasked" by the truth!

THE MYRTLES PLANTATION

Handprints in the mirrors, footsteps on the stairs, mysterious smells, vanishing objects, death by poison, hangings, murder and gunfire -- the Myrtles Plantation in the West Feliciana town of St. Francisville, Louisiana holds the rather dubious record of hosting more ghostly phenomena than just about any other house in the country. But what could be more dubious than the honor itself -- perhaps some of the questionable history that has been presented to "explain" why the house is so haunted in the first place!

Long perceived as one of the most haunted houses in America, the Myrtles attracts an almost endless stream of visitors each year and many of them come in search of ghosts. It is not my purpose to do anything to discourage these visitors from coming --- or even to discourage them from looking for the ghosts that they can almost certainly find here. The purpose behind sharing the truth of the Myrtles is to question the "facts" as they have been presented by several generations of the plantation's owners and guides -- facts and history that many of them know is blatantly false. I have no wish to try and debunk the ghosts, merely the identities that they have been given over the years. The Myrtles, according to hundreds of people who have encountered the unexplained here, is haunted --- but not for the reasons that we have all been told.

But why go to the trouble to debunk the myths that have been created over the last fifty-some-odd years? Surely, they aren't hurting anyone, so why bother to expose them as the creation of rich imaginations? To that, I can only say that no dedicated ghost hunter should

be afraid to seek the truth. As the history of a house is the most important key to discovering just why it might be haunted in the first place, it seems to be imperative to discover the real history of the site. It has often been recommended to sift through the legends and folklore of the place in a search for a kernel of truth. This is exactly what I did when I began researching the history of the Myrtles --- examining the lore in a search for the truth. After a lot of hard work, I believe that I have found it. It might not be as glamorous as the legends of the Myrtles Plantation that we have all heard about but it is certainly strange. The real history of the plantation is filled with death, tragedy and despair, leading us to wonder why a fanciful history was created in its place. That question will likely never be answered but many others will.

The History of the Myrtles Plantation: Truth & Legends

The Myrtles Plantation was constructed by David Bradford in 1794 and since that time, has allegedly been the scene of at least 10 murders. In truth, only one person was ever murdered here but, as has been stated already, some of the people who have owned the house have never let the truth stand in the way of a good story. But as the reader will soon discover, the plantation has an unusual history that genuinely did occur --- and one that may, and likely has, left its own real ghosts behind.

David Bradford was born in America to Irish immigrants and was one of five children. In 1777, he purchased a tract of land and a small stone house near Washington County, Pennsylvania. He became a successful attorney, businessman and Deputy Attorney General for the county. His first attempt to marry ended only days before his wedding (nothing is known about this) but he later met and married Elizabeth Porter in 1785 and started a family.

As his family and business grew, Bradford needed a larger home and built a new one in the town of Washington. The house became well known in the region for its size and remarkable craftsmanship, with a mahogany staircase and woodwork imported from England. Many of the items had to be transported from the east coast and over the Pennsylvania mountains at great expense. Bradford would use the parlor of the house as an office, where he would meet with his clients.

Unfortunately, he was not able to enjoy the house for long. In October 1794, he was forced to flee, leaving his family behind. Bradford became involved in the infamous Whiskey Rebellion and legend has it that President George Washington placed a price on the man's head for his role in the affair. The Whiskey Rebellion took place in western Pennsylvania and began as a series of grievances over high prices and taxes forced on those living along the frontier at that time. The complaints eventually erupted into violence when a mob attacked and burned down the home of a local tax collector. In the months that followed, residents resisted a tax that had been placed on whiskey and while most of the protests were nonviolent, Washington mobilized a militia and sent it in to suppress the rebellion. Once the protests were brought under control, Bradford left the region on the advice of some of the other principals in the affair.

After leaving Washington, Bradford first went to Pittsburgh. Leaving his family in safety, he traveled down the Ohio River to the Mississippi. He eventually settled at Bayou Sara, near what is now St. Francisville, Louisiana. Bradford was no stranger to this area. He had originally traveled here in 1792 to try and obtain a land grant from Spain. When he returned in 1796, he purchased 600 acres of land and a year later, built a modest, eight-room home that he named "Laurel Grove". He lived here alone until 1799, when he received a pardon for his role in the Whiskey Rebellion from newly elected President John Adams. He was given the pardon for his assistance in establishing a boundary line, known historically as "Ellicott's Line", between Spain and the United States.

After receiving the pardon, Bradford returned to Pennsylvania to bring his wife and five children back to Louisiana. He brought them to live at Bayou Sarah and they settled into a comfortable life here. Bradford occasionally took in students who wanted to study the law. One of them, Clark Woodrooff, not only earned a law degree but also married his teacher's daughter, Sarah Mathilda.

Clark Woodrooff was born in Litchfield County, Connecticut in August 1791. Having no desire to follow in his father's footsteps as a farmer, he left Connecticut at the age of 19 and sought his fortune on the Mississippi River, ending up in Bayou Sarah. He arrived in 1810, the same year that citizens of the Feliciana parish rose up in revolt against the Spanish garrison at Baton Rouge. They overthrew the Spanish and then set up a new territory with its capital being St. Francisville. The territory extended from the Mississippi River to as far east as the Perdido River near Mobile.

Still seeking to make his fortune, Woodrooff placed an advertisement in the new St. Francisville newspaper, the *Time Piece* , in the summer of 1811. He informed the public that "an academy would be opening on the first Monday in September for the reception of students". He planned to offer English, grammar, astronomy, geography, elocution, composition, penmanship and Greek and Latin languages. The academy was apparently short-lived for in 1814, he joined Colonel Hide's cavalry regiment from the Feliciana parish to fight alongside Andrew Jackson at the Battle of New Orleans. When the smoke cleared and the War of 1812 had ended, Woodrooff returned to St. Francisville with the intention of studying law.

He began his studies with Judge David Bradford and soon earned his degree. He also succumbed to the charms of the Bradford daughter, the lovely Sarah Mathilda. Their romance blossomed under the shade of the crape myrtle trees that reportedly gave the home its lasting name. The young couple was married on November 19, 1817 and for their honeymoon, Woodrooff took his new bride to the Hermitage, the Tennessee home of his friend, Andrew Jackson.

After the death of David Bradford, Woodrooff managed Laurel Grove for his mother-in-law, Elizabeth. He expanded the holdings of the plantation and planted about 650 acres of indigo and cotton. Together, he and Sarah Mathilda had three children, Cornelia Gale, James, and Mary Octavia. Tragically though, their happiness would not last.

On July 21, 1823, Sarah Mathilda died after contacting yellow fever. The disease was spread through a number of epidemics that swept through Louisiana in those days. Hardly a family in the region went untouched by tragedy and despair. Although heartbroken, Woodrooff continued to manage the plantation and to care for his children with help from Elizabeth. But the dark days were not yet over... On July 15, 1824, his only son James, also died from yellow fever and two months later, in September, Cornelia Gale was also felled by the dreaded disease.

Woodrooff's life would never be the same but he managed to purchase the farm outright from his mother-in-law. She was quite elderly by this time and was happy to see the place in good hands. She continued to live at Laurel Grove with her son-in-law and granddaughter, Mary Octavia, until her death in 1830.

After Elizabeth died, Woodrooff turned his attentions away from farming to the practice of law. He and Mary Octavia moved away from Laurel Grove and he left the plantation under the management of a caretaker. He was appointed to a judge's position over District D in Covington, Louisiana and he served in this capacity until April 1835. On January 1, 1834, he sold Laurel Grove to Ruffin Grey Stirling.

By this time, Woodrooff was living on Rampart Street in New Orleans and had changed the spelling of his last name to "Woodruff". He had also been elected as the president of public works for the city. During this period, Mary Octavia was sent to a finishing school in New Haven, Connecticut but she returned home to live with her father in 1836. Two years later, she married Colonel Lorenzo Augustus Besancon and moved to his plantation, Oaklawn, five miles north of New Orleans.

In 1840, the Louisiana governor, Isaac Johnson, appointed Woodruff to the newly created office of Auditor of Public Works and he served for one term. Then, at 60 years of age, he retired and moved to Oaklawn to live with Mary Octavia and her husband. He devoted the remainder of his life to the study of chemistry and physics and died on November 25, 1851. He was buried in the Girod Street Cemetery in New Orleans.

In 1834, Laurel Grove was purchased by Ruffin Grey Stirling. The Stirling's were a very wealthy family who owned several plantations on both sides of the Mississippi River. On January 1, Ruffin Grey Stirling and his wife, Mary Catherine Cobb, took over the house, land, buildings and all of the slaves that had been bought from Elizabeth Bradford by her son-in-law.

Since the Stirling's were so well thought of in the community, they needed a house that was befitting their social status. They decided to remodel Laurel Grove. Stirling added the broad central hallway of the house and the entire southern section. The walls of the original house were removed and repositioned to create four large rooms that were used as identical ladies and gentlemen's parlors, a formal dining room and a game room. Year-long trips to Europe to purchase fine furnishings resulted in the importation of skilled craftsmen as well. Elaborate plaster cornices were created for many of the rooms, made from a mixture of clay, Spanish moss and cattle hair. On the outside of the house, Stirling added a 107-foot long front gallery that was supported by cast-iron support posts and railings. The original roof of the house was extended to encompass the new addition, copying the existing dormers to maintain a smooth line. The addition had higher ceilings than the original house so the second story floor was raised one foot. The completed project nearby doubled the size of David Bradford's house and in keeping with the renovations, the name of the plantation was officially changed to the "Myrtles".

Four years after the completion of the project, Stirling died of consumption on July 17, 1854. He left his vast holdings in the care of his wife, Mary Cobb, who most referred to as a remarkable woman. Many other plantation owners stated that she "had the business acumen of a man", which was high praise for a woman in those days, and she managed to run all of her and her husband's farms almost single-handedly, for many years.

In spite of this, the family was often visited by tragedy. Of nine children, only four of them lived to be old enough to marry. The oldest son, Lewis, died in the same year as his father and daughter Sarah Mulford's husband was actually murdered on the front porch of the house after the Civil War. The war itself wreaked havoc on the Myrtles and the Stirling family. Many of the family's personal belongings were looted and destroyed by Federal soldiers and the wealth that they had accumulated was ultimately in worthless Confederate currency. To make matters worse, Mary Cobb had invested heavily in sugar plantations that had been ravaged by the war. She eventually lost all of her property. She never let the tragedies of the war, and others that followed after, overcome her however and she held onto the Myrtles until her death in August 1880. She is buried next to her husband in a family plot at Grace Church in St. Francisville.

On December 5, 1865, Mary Cobb hired William Drew Winter, the husband of her daughter, Sarah Mulford, to act as her agent and attorney and to help her manage the plantation lands. As part of the deal, she gave Sarah and William the Myrtles as their home.

William Winter had been born to Captain Samuel Winter and Sarah Bowman on October 28, 1820 in Bath, Maine. Little is known about his life or how he managed to meet Sarah Mulford Stirling. However, they were married on June 3, 1852 at the Myrtles and together, they had six children, Mary, Sarah, Kate, Ruffin, William and Francis. Kate died from typhoid at the age of three. The Winter's first lived at Gantmore plantation, near Clinton, Louisiana and then bought a plantation on the west side of the Mississippi known as Arbroath.

Twelve years after the death of Ruffin Stirling, and after the Civil War, William was named as agent and attorney by Mary Stirling to help her with the remaining lands, including Ingleside, Crescent Park, Botany Bay and the Myrtles. In return, Mary gave William the use of the Myrtles as his home. Times were terrible though and Winter was unable to hold onto it. By December 1867, he was completely bankrupt and the Myrtles was sold by the U.S. Marshal to the New York Warehouse & Security Company on April 15, 1868. Two years later however, on April 23, the property was sold back to Mrs. Sarah M. Winter as the heir of her late father, Ruffin G. Stirling. It is unknown just what occurred to cause this reversal of fortune but it seemed as though things were improving for the family once again.

But soon after, tragedy struck the Myrtles once more. According to the January 1871 issue of the Point Coupee *Democrat* newspaper, Winter was teaching a Sunday School lesson in the gentlemen's parlor of the house when he heard someone approach the house on horseback. After the stranger called out to him and told him that he had some business with him, Winter went out onto the side gallery of the house and was shot. He collapsed onto the porch and died. Those inside of the house, stunned by the sound of gunfire and the retreating horse, hurried outside to find the fallen man. Winter died on January 26, 1871 and was buried the following day at Grace Church. The newspaper reported that a man named E.S. Webber was to stand trial for Winter's murder but no outcome of the case was ever recorded. As far as is known, Winter's killer remains unidentified and unpunished.

Sarah was devastated by the incident and never remarried. She remained at the Myrtles with her mother and brothers until her death in April 1878 at the age of only 44.

After the death of Mary Cobb Stirling in 1880, the Myrtles was purchased by Stephen Stirling, one of her sons. He bought out his brothers but only maintained ownership of the house until March 1886. There are some who say that he squandered what was left of his fortune and lost the plantation in a game of chance but most likely, the place was just too deep in debt for him to hold onto. He sold the Myrtles to Oran D. Brooks, ending his family's ownership. Brooks kept it until January 1889 when, after a series of transfers, it was purchased by Harrison Milton Williams, a Mississippi widower who brought his young son and second wife, Fannie Lintot Haralson, to the house in 1891.

Injured during the Civil War, in which he began service as a 15 year-old Confederate cavalry courier, Williams planted cotton and gained a reputation as a hard-working and industrious man. He and his family, which grew to include his wife and seven children, kept the Myrtles going during the hard times of the post-war South. But tragedy was soon to strike the Myrtles again.

During a storm, the Williams' oldest son, Harry, was trying to gather up some stray cattle and fell into the Mississippi and drowned. Shattered with grief, Harrison and Fannie turned over management of the property to their son, Surget Minor Williams. He later married a local girl named Jessie Folkes and provided a home at the Myrtles for his spinster sister and maiden aunt, Katie. Secretly called "the colonel" behind her back, Katie was a true Southern character. Eccentric and kind, but with a gruff exterior, she kept life interesting at the house for years.

By the 1950's, the property surrounding the house had been divided among the Williams heirs and the house itself was sold to Marjorie Munson, an Oklahoma widow who had been made wealthy by chicken farms. It was at this point, they say, that the ghost stories of the house began. They started innocently enough but soon, what may have been real-life ghostly occurrences soon took on a "life" of their own.

Ghost Stories of the Myrtles
Separating Fact From Fiction

There is no question that the most famous ghostly tale of the Myrtles is that of Chloe, the vengeful slave who murdered the wife and two daughters of Clark Woodruff in a fit of jealously and anger. Those who have been reading the article so far have already guessed that there are some serious flaws in this story but for the sake of being complete, we have include the story here as it has long been told by owners and guides at the house.

According to the story, the troubles that led to the haunting at the Myrtles began in 1817 when Sarah Mathilda married Clark Woodruff. Sara Matilda had given birth to two daughters and was carrying a third child, when an event took place that still haunts the Myrtles today.

Woodruff, had a reputation in the region for integrity with men and with the law, but was also known for being promiscuous. While his wife was pregnant with their third child, he started an intimate relationship with one of his slaves. This particular girl, whose name was Chloe, was a household servant who, while she hated being forced to give in to Woodruff's sexual demands, realized that if she didn't, could be sent to work in the fields, which was the most brutal of the slave's work.

Eventually, Woodruff tired of Chloe and chose another girl with whom to carry on. Chloe feared the worst, sure that she was going to be sent to the fields, and she began eavesdropping on the Woodruff family's private conversations, dreading the mention of her name. One day, the Judge caught her at this and ordered that one of her ears be cut off to teach her a lesson and to put her in her place. After that time, she always wore a green turban around her head to hide the ugly scar that the knife had left behind.

What actually happened next is still unclear. Some claim that what occurred was done so that the family would just get sick and then Chloe could nurse them back to health and earn the Judge's gratitude. In this way, she would be safe from ever being returned to the fields. Others say that her motives were not so pure though and that what she did was for one reason only ---- revenge!

For whatever reason, Chloe put a small amount of poison into a birthday cake that was made in honor of the Woodruff's oldest daughter. Mixed in with the flour and sugar was a handful of crushed oleander flowers. The two children, and Sarah Mathilda, each had slices of the poisoned cake but Woodruff didn't eat any of it. Before the end of the day, all of them were very sick. Chloe patiently attended to their needs, never realizing (if it was an accident) that she had given them too much poison. In a matter of hours, all three of them were dead.

The other slaves, perhaps afraid that their owner would punish them also, dragged Chloe from her room and hanged her from a nearby tree. Her body was later cut down, weighted with rocks and thrown into the river. Woodruff closed off the children's dining room, where the party was held, and never allowed it to be used again as long as he lived. Tragically, his life was cut short a few years later by a murderer. To this day, the room where the children were poisoned has never again been used for dining. It is called the game room today.

Since her death, the ghost of Chloe has often been reported at the Myrtles. The former slave is thought to be the most frequently encountered ghost at the Myrtles. She has often been seen in her green turban, wandering the place at night. Sometimes the cries of little children accompany her appearances and at other times, those who are sleeping are startled awake by her face, peering at them from the side of the bed.

I am sure that after reading this story, even the most non-discerning readers have discovered a number of errors and problems with the tale. In fact, there are so many errors that it's difficult to know where to begin. However, to start, it's a shame that the character of Clark Woodruff has been so thoroughly damaged over the years with stories about his adulterous affairs with his slaves and claims that he had the ear cut off of one of his lovers. Sadly, these stories have been accepted as fact, even though no evidence whatsoever exists to say that they are true. In fact, history seems to show that Woodruff was very devoted to his wife and in fact, was so distraught over her death that he never remarried.

Before we get to the problem of Chloe's existence, we should also examine the alleged murders of Sarah Mathilda and her two daughters. In this case, the legend has twisted the truth so far that it is unrecognizable. Sarah Mathilda was not murdered. She died tragically from yellow fever (according to historical record) in 1823. Her children, a son and a daughter ---- not both daughters ----- died more than a year after she did. They certainly did not die from the result of a poisoned birthday cake. Also, with this legend, Mary Octavia would not have existed at all (her mother was supposed to have been pregnant when murdered) but we know that she lived with her father, got married and lived to a ripe old age. In addition, Woodruff was not killed either. He died peacefully at his daughter and son-in-law's plantation in 1851.

The key to the legend of course, is Chloe, the murderous slave. The problem with this is that as far as we can tell, Chloe never existed at all. Not only did she not murder members of the Woodruff family but it's unlikely that the family ever even had a slave by this name. Countless hours have been spent looking through the property records of the Woodruff family (which are still available and on file as public record in St. Francisville) searching for any evidence that Chloe existed. It was a great disappointment to learn that the Woodruff's had never owned a slave owned, or had any record of, a slave named Chloe, or Cleo, as she appears in some versions of the story. The records list all of the other slaves owned by the Woodruff family but Chloe simply did not exist.

So how did such a story get started?

In the 1950's, the Myrtles was owned by wealthy widow Marjorie Munson, who began to notice that odd things were occurring in the house, according to local stories. Wondering if perhaps the old mansion might be haunted, she asked around and that's when the legend of "Chloe" got its start. According to the granddaughter of Harrison and Fannie Williams, Lucile Lawrason, her aunts used to talk about the ghost of an old woman who haunted the Myrtles and who wore a green bonnet. They often laughed about it and it became a family story. She was never given a name and in fact, the "ghost" with the green bonnet from the story was described as an older woman, never as a young slave who might have been involved in an affair with the owner of the house. Regardless, someone repeated this story of the Williams' family ghost to Marjorie Munson and she soon penned a song about the ghost of the Myrtles, a woman in a green beret.

As time wore on, the story grew and changed. The Myrtles changed hands several more times and in the 1970's, it was restored again under the ownership of Arlin Dease and Mr. and Mrs. Robert F. Ward. During this period, the story grew even larger and was greatly embellished to include the poison murders and the severed ear. Up until this point though, it was largely just a story that was passed on by word of mouth and it received little attention outside of the area. All of that changed though when James and Frances Kermeen Myers passed through on a riverboat and decided to purchase the Myrtles. The house came furnished with period antiques and enough ghost stories to attract people from all over the country.

Soon, the story of the Myrtles was appearing in magazines and books and receiving a warm reception from ghost enthusiasts, who had no idea that what they were hearing was a badly skewed version of the truth. The house appeared in a November 1980 issue of *LIFE* magazine but the first book mention that I have been able to find about the house was in a book by author Richard Winer. Both the magazine article and the Winer book mentioned the poison deaths of Sarah Mathilda and her daughters.

As time went on and more books and television shows came calling at the Myrtles, the story changed again and this time, took on even more murders. In addition to the deaths of Sarah Mathilda, her daughters and Chloe, it was alleged that as many as six other people had also been killed in the house. One of them, Lewis Stirling, the oldest son of Ruffin Grey Stirling, was claimed to have been stabbed to death in the house over a gambling debt. However, burial records in St. Francisville state that he died in October 1854 from yellow fever.

According to legend, three Union soldiers were killed in the house after they broke in and attempted to loot the place. They were allegedly shot to death in the gentlemen's parlor, leaving bloodstains on the floor that refused to be wiped away. One fanciful account has it that years later, after the Myrtles was opened as an inn, a maid was mopping the floor and came to a spot that, no matter how hard she pushed, she was unable to reach. Supposedly, the spot was the same size as a human body and this was said to have been where one of the Union soldiers fell. The strange phenomenon was said to have lasted for a month and has not occurred since. The only problem with this story is that no soldiers were ever killed in the house. There are no records or evidence to say that there were and in fact, surviving family members denied the story was true. If the ghostly incident occurred, then it must have been caused by something else.

Another murder allegedly occurred in 1927, when a caretaker at the house was killed during a robbery. Once again, no record exists of this crime and something as recent as this would have been widely reported. The only event even close to this, which may have spawned this part of the story, occurred when the brother of Fannie Williams, Eddie Haralson, was living in a small house on the property. He was killed while being robbed but this did not occur in the main house, as the story states.

The only verifiable murder to occur at the Myrtles was that of William Drew Winter and it differs wildly from the legends that have been told. As described previously, Winter was lured out of the house by a rider, who shot him to death on the side porch. It is here where the stories take a turn for the worse. In the legend, Winter was shot and then mortally wounded, staggered back into the house, passed through the gentlemen's parlor and the ladies parlor and onto the staircase that rises from the central hallway. He then managed to climb just high enough to die in his beloved's arms on exactly the 17th step. It has since been claimed that ghostly footsteps have been heard coming into the house, walking to the stairs and then climbing to the 17th step where they, of course, come to an end.

While dramatic, this event never happened either. Winter was indeed murdered on the front porch by an unknown assailant but after being shot, he immediately fell down and died. His bloody trip through the house never took place --- information that was easily found in historical records.

So, is the Myrtles really haunted?

The purpose of exposing the truth behind the legends of the Myrtles has never been to say that the Myrtles Plantation is not haunted. In fact, there is no denying that the sheer number of accounts that have been reported and collected here would cause the house to qualify as one of the most haunted sites in the country. However, as you can see from the preceding pages, the house may be haunted ---- but not for the reasons that have been claimed for so many years.

In all likelihood, the infamous Chloe never existed and even if she did, historical records prove that Sarah Mathilda and her children were never murdered but died from a terrible disease instead. Instead of 10 murders in the house, only one occurred and when William Winter died, he certainly did not stagger up the staircase to die on the 17th step, as the stories of his phantom footsteps allegedly bear out. Such tales belong in the realm of fiction and ghostlore --- stories that were created to explain the weird goings-on that were really taking place at the Myrtles.

The house may really be haunted by the ghost of a woman in a green turban or bonnet. The Williams family had an ongoing tale of her and while it may have been a story that was never meant to be told outside of the family, the story was told regardless. They admit that while she did exist, no identity was ever given to her. It's also very likely that something unusual was going on at the Myrtles when Marjorie Munson lived there, which led to her seeking answers and to her first introduction to the ghost in the green headdress. Did she see the ghost? Who knows --- but many others have claimed that they have.

Frances Myers claimed that she encountered the ghost in the green turban in 1987. She was asleep in one of the downstairs bedrooms when she was awakened suddenly by a black woman wearing a green turban and a long dress. She was standing silently beside the bed, holding a metal candlestick in her hand. She was so real that the candle even gave off a soft glow. Knowing nothing about ghosts, she was terrified and pulled the covers over her head and started screaming! Then she slowly looked out and reached out a hand to touch the woman, who had never moved, and to her amazement, the apparition vanished.

Others claim that they have also seen the ghost and in fact, she was purportedly photographed a number of years ago. The resulting image seems to show a woman that does not fit the description of a young woman like Chloe would have been. In fact, it looks more like the older woman that was described by the Williams family. Could this be the real ghost of the Myrtles?

Even after leaving out the ridiculous stories of the poisonings and Winter's dramatic death on the staircase, the history of the Myrtles is still filled with more than enough trauma and tragedy to cause the place to become haunted. There were a number of deaths in the house, from yellow fever alone, and it's certainly possible that any of the deceased might have stayed behind after death. If ghosts stay behind in this world because of unfinished business, there are a number of candidates to be the restless ghosts of the plantation's stories.

And, if we believe the stories, the place truly is infested by spirits from different periods in the history of the house. There have been many reports of children who are seen playing on the wide verandah of the house, in the hallways and in the rooms. The small boy and girl may be the Woodruff children who, while not poisoned, died within months of each other during one of the many yellow fever epidemics that brought tragedy to the Myrtles. A young girl, with long curly hair and wearing an ankle-length dress, has been seen floating outside the window of the game room, cupping her hands and trying to peer inside through the glass. Is she Cornelia Gale Woodruff or perhaps one of the Stirling children who did not survive until adulthood?

The grand piano on the first floor plays by itself, usually repeating the same chord over and over again. Sometimes it continues on through the night. When someone comes into the room to check on the sound, the music stops and will only start again when they leave.

Scores of people have filed strange reports about the house. In recent times, various owners have taken advantage of the Myrtles' infamous reputation and the place is now open to guests for tours and as a haunted bed and breakfast. Rooms are rented in the house and in cottages on the grounds. The plantation has played host to a wide variety of guests from curiosity-seekers to historians to ghost hunters. Over the years, a number of films and documentaries have been shot on the grounds and many of them have been paranormal in nature.

One film, which was decidedly not paranormal, was a television mini-series remake of *The Long Hot Summer*, starring Don Johnson, Cybill Shepherd, Ava Gardner and Jason Robards. A portion of the show was shot at the Myrtles and it was not an experience that the cast and crew would soon forget. One day, the crew moved the furniture in the game room and the dining room for filming and then left the room. When they returned, they reported that the furniture had been moved back to its original position. No one was inside of either room while the crew was absent! This happened several times, to the dismay of the crew, although they did manage to get the shots they needed. They added that the cast was happy to move on to another set once the filming at the Myrtles was completed.

The employees at the house often get the worst of the events that happen here. They are often exposed, first-hand, to happenings that would have weaker folks running from the place in terror. And some of them do! One employee, a gateman, was hired to greet guests at the front gate each day. One day while he was at work, a woman in a white, old-fashioned dress walked through the gate without speaking to him. She walked up to the house and vanished through the front door without ever opening it. The gateman quit his job and never returned to the house.

As you can see, the Myrtles can be a perplexing place. History has shown that many of the stories that have been told about the place, mostly to explain the hauntings, never actually occurred. In spite of this, the house seems to be haunted anyway. The truth seems to be an elusive thing at this grand old plantation house but there seems to be no question for those who have stayed or visited here that it is a spirited place. At the Myrtles, the ghosts of the past are never very far away from the present --whether we know their identities or not.

1o. IN SEARCH OF THE HORNET SPOOK LIGHT

Hunting for One of America's Great Mysteries with Troy Taylor

Spook lights, or ghost lights as they are often called, have long been a part of anomalous history in America. Such a light is best defined as being a luminous phenomena that, because of the way that it behaves, its location and regular manifestation, is put into a separate category from ball lightning or from such supernatural phenomena as ghosts. However, most spook lights, especially those that appear regularly over a period of time and in one location tend to take on a supernatural air. Legends tend to grow around them concerning strange deaths and most often, a beheading for which a ghost returns looking for the severed head. The spook light is most often said to be the light of a lantern that the spirit carries to assist him in the search.

According to stories, there have long been such lights in America. A book written in 1685 by a Nathaniel Crouch called *The English Empire in America* makes note of a remarkable flame "that appears before the death of an Indian or English upon their wigwams in the dead of night." Native American tales and early settler stories often told of such light appearing as a forewarning of death, perhaps hearkening back to similar tales from the Old World. Those stories told of "corpse candles" that would signify the presence of a spirit left behind by a death.

In February 1909, newspaper accounts told of strange happenings in Stockton, Pennsylvania concerning the nighttime appearance of an "arrow of flame" that would hover over a spot on the mountain where the body of a murdered woman had been found two years before. The locals insisted that the light was the avenging spirit of the dead woman who kept coming back to the spot on a nightly basis to insure that the history of the crime was kept alive. In that way, the legend went, she could try and make sure that her killer was someday apprehended.

Spook lights appear in hundreds of places around the country and while most of them have an eerie legend or two attached to their appearance, few explanations can be reached as to why they appear. In the instances when the lights have been thoroughly investigated, the results have been inconclusive at best and at the worst, disappointing. In some cases, the mysterious lights turn out to be nothing more than the headlights of cars on distant highways or reflections of stars and lights that refract though layers of different air temperatures. But that's not always the case...

There are a number of locations where spook lights appear that manage to escape such explanations. These are locations where reports of the lights date back to well before the advent of the automobile and where claims of artificial lights in the distance just don't hold up. These are lights that serious researchers have been unable to debunk. And while it is the opinion of many with an interest in such things that spook lights are a natural part of our world for which we do not yet have an explanation, the most compelling ones still remain unsolved.

I have always been interested in spook lights and in fact, grew up with stories of such lights in my family. Some readers may remember in my previous book, *Confessions of a Ghost Hunter,* that I wrote about spotting the "Greenwood Ghost Lights" that appear among the hills of a old cemetery in Decatur, Illinois. Those particular lights had been around for so long that older members of my family used to go out looking for the lights when they were teenagers. In addition to these lights, I also heard about the "phantom brakeman" light that "haunted" the railroad yard near the Wabash train station in Decatur.

According to the legend, a train stopped in Decatur one night in the late 1890's. The steam engines had to be filled on a regular basis and on the Wabash line, there was a water tower just east of the train station. The train pulled to a stop and the brakeman climbed down from the rear platform of the caboose to begin his usual system of checking the cars with his lantern. He had only gone a short distance when he spotted trouble. He leaned into the space between two freight cars and looked down. The couplings between the two cars were open and the cars were only connected by the safety chain. Unfortunately, he was performing this check just as the engineer was positioning the engine to fill the tanks with water. The train lurched forward and the safety chain between the two loose cars snapped upwards and the brakeman was knocked off his feet. He stumbled and fell, and as he did, his head fell between the couplings on the two cars just as they slammed closed.

The fireman saw the brakeman's lantern fall and he ran to help. A crowd of men quickly gathered around the brakeman's body and they quickly took the fallen man into the train station. In all of the excitement, no one thought to look for what was left of his head. To this day, the ghost of the brakeman is said to still walk the tracks just past the old railroad station. On certain nights, the bobbing light of a railroad lantern can be seen tracing the line of a long forgotten freight train ---- as a phantom brakeman searches in vain for his missing head.

Needless to say, stories like this can be found all over the country and most of us don't take them too seriously. But what about the stories that actually can be taken seriously? What about the locations where spook lights appear that have no logical explanation at all?

The Mysterious History of the Hornet Spook Light

Located about 20 miles or so southwest of Joplin, Missouri is a roughly paved road where my favorite American spook light puts in a regular appearance. This old and otherwise forgotten track runs across the Oklahoma border but is only about four miles long. Nearby is the border village of Hornet and close to that is the site of what once was a spook light museum. The place is remote and far from civilization, so why do so many people come here?

They are searching for an unexplained enigma ---- a puzzle that many of them find. It has been seen along this road since 1866 and has created such a mystery that even the Army Corps of Engineers officially concluded that it was a "mysterious light of unknown origin". It has been called by many names since it started appearing here, near what is called the Devil's Promenade, but it's most commonly known as the Hornet Spook Light.

"Spook Light Road", where the Hornet light puts in its appearances

This light has appeared, looking like a ball of fire, for nearly a century and a half, varying in size from a softball to larger. It spins down the center of this gravel road at great speed, rises up high, bobs and weaves to the right and left. It appears to be a large lantern, but there is never anyone carrying it. The light has appeared inside of vehicles, seems to retreat when it is pursued and never allows anyone to get to close to it. Does the light have some sort of intelligence? This remains just one of the many mysteries connected to this light.

No one has ever been injured by the light but many claim to have been frightened by it while walking and driving down this road at night. Sometimes it seems to come from nowhere and a few witnesses claim they have felt the heat from it as it passed close to them. Occasionally, some observer will even take a shot or two at the light, like Franklin Rossman, who lived near the Devil's Promenade for years. He twice attempted to shoot the light with a hunting rifle but the shots had no effect on it whatsoever. He told a spook light investigator that he was unable to judge the distance to the light because it had such an odd look to it. When asked what he meant by this, Rossman was unable to explain. It just looked "sort of blurry", he said.

There have been many theories that have attempted to explain why this mysterious light appears here. Originally, a number of legends sprung up around the place. One of them claimed the light was connected to the spirit of two young Quapaw Indians who died in the area many years ago. Another claimed the light was the spirit of an Osage Indian chief who had been beheaded on the Devil's Promenade and the light was said to be his torch as he searched for his missing head. Another legend tells of a miner whose children were kidnapped by Indians and he set off looking for them with only a lantern to light his way. The light is said to be that very lantern as the farmer's ghost continues looking for the children that he will never find.

Locals claim that the stories of the Hornet Light originated back in the 1800's but most printed accounts are of a much more recent vintage. As far as is known, the first account of it appeared in the *Kansas City Star* in 1936 and then in the 1947 book *Ozark Superstitions* by Vance Randolph, the famed Missouri folklorist. Randolph was the first to put into print the oral legends of the light's origins, from beheaded Indians to lost children.

In 1958, a writer for the *Ford Times* investigated the light and described it as a diffused, orange glow that floated and weaved along the roadway. He also noted that it seemed to change size as he watched it, varying between the size of apple to that of a bushel basket. While present, he also saw the light split off into three different lights and then as a single light, it settled down upon the branch of a tree and changed colors from orange to blue.

Over the years, the light has been studied, researched, chased, photographed and shot at ---- but what is it? While legends give one reason for the light, its genuine origins seem to present a formidable problem. Many suggestions have been offered as to what could cause the light to appear and for many years the most popular theory was that it was merely will-o'-the-wisp, the name given to a biological phenomenon that is caused by the decay of wood and organic materials. The emission of light that comes from the decay often glows brightly and can be seen on occasion in wooded areas and damp regions. As fascinating as this is, it really doesn't explain the Hornet Light. Instances of will-o'-the-wisp simply do not give off the intensity of light that has been reported along the Devil's Promenade.

Another suggestion has been the ever-popular "marsh gas". Unfortunately, while an abundance of marsh gas in a marsh or swamp would certainly be flammable, it cannot spontaneously light itself. Even if it did, wind and rain would soon extinguish any flame that appeared. Strong winds that have been reported during sightings of the Hornet Light do not seem to disturb it and they don't keep it from moving in whatever direction it pleases.

There have also been suggestions that the light might be a glow coming from minerals in the area. This seems doubtful though, as the light does not always appear in the same place. One plausible suggestion theorizes that the light might be formed by electrical fields in areas where earthquakes and ground shifts take place. This is a possibility since there are fault lines in the region. Four earthquakes took place here in the early 1800's that had a devastating effect on this part of the state. It is possible that the lights started appearing around the time of the earthquakes but were not reported until the population in the area started to grow around the time of the Civil War.

Other "experts" claim they have the mystery solved and that it's not unexplainable at all. They claim the light is caused by automobiles driving on the highway about five miles east of what's known as "Spook Light Road". They say the highway is on a direct line with it but at a slightly lower elevation. When it is pointed out that a high ridge separates the area from the highway, the experts explain how refraction causes light to bend and creates the eerie effect that so many people have reported as the spook light.

Believe it or not, several investigations that have been conducted at the site have shown that some of the sightings here may be attributed to this. Dr. George W. Ward, formerly of the Bureau of Standards in Washington and later with the Midwest Research Institute, investigated the light in 1945. He said that shortly after arriving at the site, he saw a diffused glow appear over some low hills. A few moments later, a sphere of light appeared that looked to be four to six feet in diameter. Ward humorously added that the Publicity Director of the Midwest Institute remarked to the others assembled that he had seen all that he cared to and as the light approached the group, he quickly locked himself inside of their automobile.

But Ward was critical about the source of the light. During his study, he decided that the light must originate to the west of the viewing site and over the range of hills in the distance. He surmised that the refraction of auto headlights from a road that was in line with the country lane could create an illusion of a traveling light. Dr. Ward checked his maps and found that such a road did exist, a section of highway that ran east and west between Commerce and Quapaw, Oklahoma. He suggested that an airplane might be used to spot cars on the highway and relay the information to observers at the Spook Light site. If the lights could be shown to correspond with the Hornet light, the mystery would be solved.

Captain Bob E. Loftin followed these speculations with his own experiments a few years later. He discovered that colored test lights that were placed on the suspected areas of Route 66 could be seen from Spook Light Road. He further reasoned that the presence of moving cars along the highway would appear as spheres of light, closely grouped together. He also added that changing humidity and temperature would cause the lights that were created to behave strangely. This, they reasoned, would explain the number of unusual stories told about the way the light acted.

And while this would admittedly explain some of the sightings of the Hornet Light, it is impossible that it could explain them all. The most important point to remember is that the light was being seen before the invention of automobiles!

These were far from the only investigations conducted at the site. Author Raymond Bayless embarked on an extensive study of the spook light in October 1963. Around dusk on the evening of October 17, he and several assistants spotted the light for the first time, as it appeared as a bright light some distance along the roadway. He reported that the light fluctuated in intensity and at times became two separate lights, hovering one above the other. The light returned again about an hour later and according to Bayless, was so bright that it caused a reflection on the dirt surface of the road. A few minutes after the light appeared, the investigation group began moving westward along the road in pursuit of it. The light receded backward (or appeared to) as they got closer to it. The group began navigating the hills and ravines of the road and the light vanished. It did not reappear until they reached a point near the old spook light museum, which was still in operation at that time.

The "Spooksville Museum", operated then by Leslie W. Robertson, offered not only photographs and a collection of accounts about the light but also a viewing platform for people to observe the light with the naked eye or through telescopes and cameras. A member of Bayless' group set up a small refracting telescope on the platform and they were able to learn that what appeared to be a single light was actually composed of a number of smaller lights. Bayless stated that they moved very close together, weaving slightly, expanding and contracting back and forth. It was amber and gold in color and sometimes gained a reddish tint for a few moments at a time. Through the telescope, the edges of the light were observed to be like a "flame" in that they were not uniform and constantly changed.

Bayless was fascinated with the many explanations of the light and was able to rule out almost all of the ones that had been proposed, including the theory that all of the sightings could be explained away as the refraction of auto headlights. In fact, Mr. Arthur Holbrook, a resident of the area and a man who had investigated the light many times, told Bayless that he had first seen the light in 1905. At that time, Holbrook explained, there were only about a dozen automobiles in Joplin, the closest large town. He also added that there had been no highways at that period and because of this, headlights could not have explained his sightings of the light. The few cars that were in existence in the area at that time did not travel about on remote, dirt lanes that were best suited for horses and any autos that would have traveled around the region were only fitted with oil and carbide lamps, which would not have been capable of creating the long, intense beams of modern headlights. To add even more credibility to his account, Holbrook was in the automotive profession and would have been very aware of the number of autos in the region in those days and the state of the roads and highways.

But did the light actually exist before automobiles came to southwest Missouri or was this merely a part of the local legend? Many skeptics claimed that the enigma's longevity was merely a part of the light's folklore but Bayless did not agree. After conducting a number of interviews in the area, he began to believe that it had been seen in the 1800's. He did not feel that his own sighting of the light was comparable to auto headlights but as it had been shown that some lights would appear on the road as refraction from the highway, he needed to gather as much evidence as possible to show the light pre-dated automobiles. Mr. Holbrook had experienced his first sighting of the light in 1905 and had heard of the light for several years before that. After that first sighting, he rode out in a buggy to see the light many times and told Bayless that the light was the same in the 1960's as it had been in 1905.

Bayless also interviewed Leslie Robertson, the curator of the Spooksville Museum, who first saw the light in 1916. He was only 14 years-old at the time and from childhood to adulthood, he had seen the light literally "thousands of times".

Mr. John Muening of Joplin first saw the light around 1928 and had heard stories about it for a number of years before that. He told Bayless that "we have watched it all night... Highway 66 has nothing to do with the light. It couldn't have, as it didn't exist when the light was first seen, of that I am sure."

Bayless also collected testimony from a Mrs. Rene Waller of Joplin, who also said that she had seen the Hornet Light before Route 66 was put in through Quapaw, Oklahoma. She stated that the original highway was a dirt road and was traveled infrequently. She had first seen the light in the late 1920's, when auto headlights would have been too seldom on the road to have created the effect of the light.

Mr. and Mrs. L.C. Ferguson of Joplin also stated that they had been familiar with the Hornet Light since 1910 and at the time they first saw it, they were told that the light had been seen along the road for many years already.

These claims of the light's longevity were substantiated by Mr. J. Leonard, who was a member of the Miami Indian tribe at the time of his interview in the early 1960's. He told Bayless that his parents had spoken of the light many times when he was a boy. He could personally remember seeing it for as long as he had been alive (he had been born in 1896) and according to stories, the light had been in existence for several generations or at least 100 years. Another Native American from the area, Guy Jennison, recalled hearing about the light when he was a boy attending the Quapaw Mission School in 1892. By that time, it was a local topic of conversation, implying that reports of the light had been around for at least a few years. Jennison believed that, like Mr. Leonard, the light might have appeared several generations before, based on the Indian legends that had been suggested to explain its origin. Unfortunately, during the time of the Bayless investigation, there were few Native Americans left who had knowledge of when the stories originated.

Even without the earlier dates though, Bayless was able to show that the Hornet Light existed prior to the use of automobiles in the area. He did not dispute the idea that some sightings could be caused by headlights, but he did debunk the idea that headlights could be the only cause. Others have suggested that perhaps lights from Quapaw or from mining camps in the area could have caused a refraction of light, thus creating the Spook Light, but there is little evidence to suggest this or to suggest that these stationary lights could manage to create a light that moves about and comes and goes as the Hornet Light does.

With that in mind, Raymond Bayless' investigations of the light should be considered groundbreaking. Although he certainly did not solve the mystery of the

Hornet Light, he did manage to present some compelling evidence for its early existence. The only problem to come out of his investigations was that he managed, by showing how long the light had been around and by showing that not all of the sightings could be dismissed, to make the mystery even more perplexing.

Photographer Marta Churchwell captured the Hornet Light on film for a Joplin newspaper in the 1960's

The Hunt for the Hornet Spook Light

Bayless was not the first, nor would he be the last, to investigate the Hornet Spook Light. Literally thousands of curiosity-seekers visit the Devil's Promenade each year and many of those are serious researchers of the unknown. The old "Spook Light Museum" is gone now but long after Leslie Robertson, came Garland "Spooky" Middleton, who also operated the place for a time. Along with the photographs and newspaper articles, Middleton sold soda to tourists and entertained them with his own encounters with the mysterious light, like the time he saw it in a field near the museum. He said that the light appeared one night on the road, just after sunset, and began to roll like a ball, giving off sparks as it traveled along the gravel road. It entered a field where several cattle grazed and managed to move among the animals, not disturbing them at all.

On three different occasions, starting in the late 1990's, I visited Spook Light Road, each time hoping to get a glimpse of the elusive light. My diligence was never rewarded but I didn't give up on the idea that I might be at the right place at the right time at some point. Eventually, my persistence paid off! In December 2005, I took a group of American Hauntings tour guests in search of the light and in addition to a near case of frostbite, several of us got a look at this mysterious wonder as well.

We traveled by van to the far southwest corner of Missouri on a cold day in early December. After visiting the nearby Bluff Dweller's Cave, followed by a hearty dinner, we set out for Spook Light Road using several different sets of directions. Prior to this, I had always visited the site as a passenger, riding along with someone else who knew the way. With this in mind, friends who accompanied me on the trip, Rex Murray, Garrett Henson and Bill Alsing, all collected directions to get to Spook Light Road and to the best place to see the light. I had my own directions and when we put them together, we had four different routes to get to the same place. Not surprisingly, we drove around for about an hour before I realized that the road looked familiar. We had somehow crossed into Oklahoma though and were driving along the old road in reverse! Once we figured this out, we found a good spot to stop and set up camp and made preparations to hunt for the light.

The afternoon had been a cold one but it was nothing compared to how cold it got after nightfall. It was a clear, crisp night and temperatures were hovering near 4 degrees (F) by the time we were in position along the road to watch for the light. Even though the clear skies had made it bitterly cold, they treated us to a sky that was unbelievably filled with stars. With no city lights or hazy clouds to interfere with our view, we saw more stars that night than on any occasion I can ever remember. Shooting stars streaked across the sky about every few minutes or so, which made standing in the cold well worth the effort ---- even if we didn't see the Hornet Spook Light.

Luckily though, we didn't have to make that sacrifice. The light put in its brief appearance some time around 2:30 a.m. By then, we had been standing out in the cold for several hours. I don't remember much about this but do recall that I could no longer feel my feet or any of my extremities. This is despite the fact that I was wearing boots, insulated socks, long underwear, jeans, a t-shirt, long-sleeved Henley, a sweatshirt, parka, hat, scarf, gloves and --- eventually I got so cold --- a thick blanket draped over my head. Bill Alsing, who had wrapped a blanket around his head Arab-style because he had forgotten his hat, was so cold that he would occasionally just jump up, mumble something and then start walking up and down the road for awhile. He later told me that it was the only way that he could keep the blood circulating to his feet!

When the spook light finally put in Its appearance, there were perhaps six of us huddled around the van, trying to stay warm. Several of the guests had fallen asleep in the van at this point, wrapped up in sleeping bags and blankets, while others had vanished to other vantage points along the roadway. We had several false alarms during the night, with several of us thinking we saw the light, but each time it turned out to be headlights approaching along this lonely road. When the light did show up --- there was no mistaking it for anything else.

It was Becky Ray, a frequent American Hauntings guest and a representative for the American Ghost Society in Kansas City, who spotted it first. Her quick response got the attention of several of the others who were standing together and we saw the light appear at the crest of a small hill about 50 yards away.

The spook light was directly west of where we had parked the van along Spook Light Road and it did not seem to have come up the hill --- it just appeared there --- and it shot sideways to our right about seven or eight feet. The light was yellowish-orange in color and it left a faint "trail" behind it as it moved. The trail streaked out in a jagged motion, moving slightly up and down, and then blinked out into darkness. It was almost like a firework display on a summer night, shooting outward and then burning itself out as quickly as it had appeared. The sighting lasted no longer than 10 seconds but it's not something that I will soon forget.

What is the Hornet Spook Light? No one knows but I think that it's still described best in the words of the Army Corps of Engineers as a "mysterious light of unknown origin". Regardless of what it may be, one thing is certain ---- it's something that has to be seen if possible. There are those who believe that the Hornet Light is slowly burning itself out; that sightings of the light are going to become more and more infrequent in the years to come. I hope that this is not the case, and not only for my own selfish desire to see the light again, but also for all of those who have not had the chance to experience this wonder firsthand.

The Hornet Spook Light is one of America's greatest unsolved mysteries and since no one has managed to puzzle out the answers to this enigma just yet, we need it to be around for future generations to ponder for themselves.

11. WHO IS THAT IN THE LOOKING GLASS?

Hunting Ghosts in Lebanon, Illinois with Len Adams

The community of Lebanon, Illinois, is about ten miles northeast of Belleville, where I now reside. I have been going to Lebanon since the end of 1997, for one reason --- the theater. The Looking Glass Theater is located at 301 West St. Louis Street in Lebanon and it's housed inside of a venerable old building that used to be the Arcade Movie House. I once found an ad for the movie theater from 1911, calling it the "best ten cent theater around".

The Looking Glass Theater players had been renting the old building until November of 1980, when, in a daring move, they incorporated and bought the place. Over the years the Looking Glass Playhouse has developed into the finest community theater in St. Louis' metro-east area. Thousands of patrons have been entertained by a myriad of performers who have graced the stage. The stage itself, or back third of the building, was added on by volunteer labor. This spirit of volunteerism continues to this day.

Since I joined the theater group in 1997, I'm proud to have been a small part of the theaters' renovations. Though slowed by arthritis, which makes stage appearances few and far between, I've been able to stay active with the theater by being on the Board of Directors. I was elected Board President this past December and took over the position on January 1, 2006. Needless to say, four or five trips a week into Lebanon is not unusual.

One of my favorite projects at the theater was doing "Haunted Happenings", a fundraiser the performers did for one weekend every October to raise money for theater repairs and upgrades. Walkers in Victorian costumes would escort the theater patrons on a journey up and down the main street of Lebanon. During seven or so stops (some inside, some outside) performers would spin classic tales of horror. I was fortunate to have been part of this fundraiser for five years. Now, with the popularity of the Alton tours (real ghosts), I no longer can participate in "Haunted Happenings". My past involvement in the fundraiser did lead to a treasure-trove of ghostly tales in the small community.

In June of 2003, I had to have both of my hands operated on for carpal tunnel syndrome. I spent the entire summer recovering and doing rehab to get back the use of my hands. It must be standard advice for all doctors but I was told not to lay around --- I was to walk, walk and then walk some more. I was fat enough and sitting around all day wasn't going to help me. You can only prowl the streets of your own neighborhood so many times before boredom sets in so to conquer this, I started walking up and down the main streets of Lebanon. These are the same streets that had seen the likes of Charles Dickens and Abraham Lincoln.

Being the social animal I am, I would stop in the shops and visit with the owners. Through doing "Haunted Happenings" for five years, and appearing on stage at the theater on many occasions, many of the shopkeepers knew me and we were now friends. Most of them knew my interest in the telling of ghost stories, but didn't know how serious I was to gather real stories of the paranormal.

By the second week of my treks through Lebanon, owner after owner started telling me about the real happenings in their buildings. Over the next several years I have investigated shop after shop and quite frankly, I believe that Lebanon could give Alton a run for it's money when it comes to being "one of the most haunted small towns in America". I am currently finishing up my research on several locations and hope to have a book on the ghosts of the "Looking Glass Prairie" completed in the near future.

On August 18, 1874, Lebanon, Illinois, was chartered as a city. The area though, had seen the coming of the white man as early as 1800. A stroll down the main street is like stepping back in time. Lebanon's historic flavor has been preserved to this day.

One of the shopkeepers that I met on my travels was Michele Rowe. Michele is the owner of Town N' Country Shop. This antique, collectable and gift shop has been operated by the Rowe family since 1975. A mutual friend had alerted me to a possible ghost story connected with Michele.

In June 2005, during one of my rehab strolls through town (this time for my back), I happened into Town N' Country looking for a candle. Michele was by herself, no customers in the shop. This was a change because the place is usually packed with shoppers. As a conversation with me always does, our little chat soon turned to talk of ghosts and hauntings. Michele said she had wanted to talk to me about a possible haunting, but wasn't sure how to approach me. With no one else around, the time was now right. Michele started to tell me about the house she had grown up in, along with her parents, Althea and Charles Rowe, and her brother, Ed.

Charles and Althea had bought the house in 1963. The two-story brick home, built in the Federal style, was erected around 1847. The longest ownership of the house was by Joseph James McKee and his wife, Lillie, from 1867 to 1920. This was the first home in Lebanon to be presented with a Landmark Plaque by the St. Clair County Historical Society for architectural value.

Michele informed me that the house was going up for sale in four days and she wanted to know if I would take a look at it. She wouldn't say that it was haunted, only that there were strong sensations in the house. Later that day, I met Michele at her childhood home. The house had certainly seen better days. Five years of sitting empty, after a major fire, had done considerable damage to the place. I could see the pain and nostalgia in Michele's eyes as we made our way through the house. This was a place she loved, but could no longer afford to keep.

In December 2000, Michele's mother, Althea, was living alone in the house. Charles had passed away several years before. A strong-willed woman of 71, Althea didn't entertain guests so much as she held court. Seated in her chair by the fireplace in the sitting room, Althea was a commanding presence.

We all have our little vices and Althea had two of them. To say she smoked would be misleading. Althea would light up a cigarette, take a puff, and then let it almost burn itself out before taking one last drag. She also liked to have a cocktail, or two, during the day, but never to excess.

That December, Althea was battling several ailments that caused her to become dizzy. These spells usually didn't last long and would be soon forgotten. No one

The house in Lebanon where Michelle's mother died in a tragic fire

knows for sure if the dizzy spells, the smoking or the cocktails caused the fire that December day. It didn't matter because the result was the same. Althea had perished in a fire in the summer kitchen.

Over the next five years, Michele would battle with the insurance companies, bad contractors, and even her brother over what to do with the house. The house sustained a heavy amount of damage from the fire and from the smoke. The contractors that the insurance companies insisted on using caused more damage. By the time I saw the house, it was a wreck. The wallpaper was gone. Large pieces of plaster had fallen off the ceilings and walls. The summer kitchen had been torn down and rebuilt by people I wouldn't hire to build a tree house. This once proud structure now sat silent and forlorn. Michele's brother was pressing her to just sell the place. She finally gave in and the house and property was going to the auction block in a couple of days.

Memories overwhelmed Michele as we went from room to room. After about an hour, she had to go back to the store. I decided to stay awhile longer.

I always say that you should trust your gut in any situation. That extra little voice has helped me many times. As I walked Michele outside, she said that she always had the feeling that her mother had passed out, due to the dizzy spells, and hit her head on the island in the kitchen. After the fire, Altheas' head had sustained a hard knock from something.

Paranormal investigating has always been fun for me. This was the first time that I had a friend involved. The sadness in her eyes didn't make this any easier.

When Michele left, I re-entered the house. After wandering through the entire location, I decided to spend my time in the sitting room and the kitchen.

Michele never claimed that the house was haunted. I think she just wanted to know if any remnants of her family still existed in the house. Because she was a friend, I said I'd check and see what I could find. Nothing out of the ordinary came up on the Tri-Field Meter. I snapped several photos. Nothing but the dust that I had stirred up appeared on them. The whole time I walked through the house I had been asking questions out loud and was hoping to record answers on my tape recorder. On entering the sitting room, I decided to put the tape recorder on the fireplace mantel and just sit and ask questions.

To my amazement, the tape recorder came alive! It kept stopping and starting on its own. After about 10 minutes, the tape ran out. I decided that this was enough for one day, so I picked up my toys and went out to the car.

The excitement over the tape recorder was too much for me. Instead of listening to the tape when I got home, I rewound it in the driveway. All the answers, which were surely on the tape, might provide Michele with some closure and I would have proof of existence on the other side. My amazement turned to amusement though as nothing but my voice popped up on the tape. On examining the tape recorder, I found that when I placed the recorder on the fireplace mantel, I had accidentally switched it to the voice activated mode. I had been recording myself the entire time!

Not to be deterred, I went back to the house the next day with Bill Alsing. You may remember that Bill owns the History and Hauntings Bookstore in Alton. Bill and I made our way through the entire house and came up with nothing unusual. After relating my adventure with the tape recorder, we decided to try it again. This time we would check all the buttons. I placed the tape recorder and Bill's Tri-Field Meter on the fireplace mantel. At the doorway between the sitting room and the kitchen, we set my Tri-Field Meter. We then asked if anyone was present with us, to give us a sign such as a rap on the wall or something physical that we could see or hear. When nothing happened, we decided to walk around the outside of the house. I've found that sometimes the entities are bashful and don't like an audience.

As Bill and I got back to the summer kitchen, Michele pulled up in the driveway. She was getting ready to leave for a well-deserved vacation. She just wanted to know if we had found anything. The heartache and demands of the past five years, coupled with a bad head cold and frazzled nerves, were taking its toll on her. Michele just needed to get out of town before the house auction. She just needed to get away and bring some closure to this chapter of her life.

With tears in her eyes, Michele entered the new summer kitchen area with us, then followed us into the kitchen. As we stood there, both of our Tri-Field Meters went crazy. The tape recorder was working on its own and it wasn't on the voice activated mode. This went on for 30 minutes. As much as she wanted to stay, Michele had to leave. Her vacation destination was calling. As I walked her out to the car, I promised to let her know what we found when she came back.

As I went back into the sitting room, I saw Bill standing there wide-eyed. He said that as soon as Michele and I went outside, everything stopped. On examining the tape recorder, we found nothing on the tape. The Tri-Field Meters were silent. We made one last sweep of the house and did pick up a few readings on the meters in an upstairs bedroom, but that was all.

As we discussed this case amongst ourselves, and with a few American Ghost Society members who were more qualified than we were, we all came to the same conclusion. We believe that the house held many memories for Michele. They were all good until the last five years. This place of happiness and joy had turned into a nightmare for her. The fighting with insurance people and family members had worn her down. She just wanted closure.

Because the last time she entered the house would be the very last time, I feel that she was overwhelmed with emotions. These emotions, coupled with a bad cold and the need to say goodbye, may have caused the equipment to go crazy. I've always felt that nothing

When Michelle came into the house, the meters on the fireplace began going off with no explanation

is stronger than human emotions. I honestly believe that the emotional energy from Michele made the equipment come to life. When she left the house, everything stopped.

The house has since been sold and the new owners are putting some much needed work into the place. The best part of the investigation for me was being able to help a friend. By finding nothing unusual in the house, we were able to help Michele with her grief and bring closure to a painful chapter of her life.

12. ALBINO CROSSINGS & CRY-BABY BRIDGES

Looking for Some of Illinois' Mystery Spots with Troy Taylor

When I was growing up in Illinois, and developing an interest in strange happenings and paranormal sites, I collected dozens of accounts and legends concerning mystery bridges and railroad tracks where phantoms assist the cars that pass over them. In all of my years of searching for the mysterious in this state, I have heard more stories of this type than just about anything else. I can't remember how many times I have gone off on some wild goose chase, hoping to find that one elusive site where the story about the bridge, or railroad crossing, actually turned out to be true.

Believe it or not, after literally years of searching, I finally found one that defied explanation. But it was not a short trip to get there!

The Bridges ---- Where Babies Cry & Students Die

Hidden among the forests and cornfields of rural Illinois is a lonely old steel bridge that eases a dusty roadway over the swirling of the water below. It was on this rusted bridge in the quiet calm of dusk that an eerie tale unfolded --- a tale that tells of a horror-filled night from many years ago. On this night, a young woman, after engaging in a heated argument with her husband over the incessant crying of their baby, pulled her car to a stop on the bridge and, in one swift, frantic motion, inexplicably threw the baby over the bridge railing and into the river below.

What ever became of the young couple is unknown, but the story goes that on certain nights, perhaps when the moon is full in the sky, the crying of the baby can still be heard by those who stand on this bridge in the darkness.

In another version of the story, a young mother and her baby were traveling along this same road and the woman somehow lost control of her car, plunging it off the bridge into the river below. The infant was thrown clear of the crash but died from exposure soon after. As the years have passed, those who park their own cars on this bridge at midnight are rewarded by the sound of a baby eerily crying in the darkness.

These are the most popular versions of the story known as the "Crybaby Bridge". This popular urban legend is believed to have gotten its start along a spooky, country lane called Lottsford Road, near Mitchellville, Maryland. The story is believed to have spread from an old one-lane bridge along this road to similar bridges all over America. As with almost all urban legends, the supernatural story of the location (in this case, a rural bridge) bears little resemblance to its true history.

I have yet to find one of these locations where an accident, or murder, involving a baby actually occurred and yet the stories of the chilling cries in the night continue to be told.

Another variation of the "Crybaby Bridge" is the accident that involves a group of students. In this version, the terrible auto accident claims the lives of a group of high school students who are out drinking and riding around on country back roads. They also lose control of their car and crash off the bridge into the river. Today, instead of the sounds of crying in the dark, it is said that the ghosts of the students will help drivers who come to the bridge make it safely across. After parking your car at the head of the bridge, and shifting into neutral, a visitor will find that the car moves across the bridge to the other side. In some cases, it's been said that the ghosts will leave their handprints behind on the trunk of the car after it has moved. Again, a check of local records will not find evidence of any such accident and yet the stories are told over and over again, often through several generations of students.

Thanks to the longevity of the stories, and the fact that they simply refuse to die, I have long been fascinated with tales of the Crybaby Bridge and its variations. I have spent dozens of late nights sitting on dark bridges, waiting to see if my car moves or listening closely for the sound of a baby crying in the darkness. It seldom happens and when it does, a solution to the mystery is usually quickly reached.

I was first told about such a bridge in the middle 1990's and immediately made plans to check it out. I was assured that the story was true and that "dozens of people" had actually heard the crying. I drove to a secluded area just west of Monticello, Illinois and tracked down the old steel bridge. On three different nights, I waited there on that narrow expanse for a couple of hours each time, hoping that no car would need to pass by me on the bridge. I listened carefully --- hearing nothing but the ripple of the river below me, birds calling out and the natural sounds of the forest at night. Needless to say, no crying baby! It was an eerie spot but the truthfulness of the tale was definitely called into question.

While nothing occurred that night, I was hooked on tracking down other bridges. I reasoned that if the stories continued to be told then perhaps they had some kernel of truth at the heart of them. Over the next decade, I searched for Crybaby Bridges all over Illinois and while my outings were always an adventure, they were never filled with ghosts.

One Crybaby Bridge that I learned of was located in Loraine, Illinois, about 20 miles or so north of Quincy. This bridge actually pre-dated automobiles and its legend went back to the middle 1800's. A young local woman became pregnant and feared that she would be punished by her parents if they found out about the baby. After giving birth in secret, she drowned the baby in the nearby creek. According to the legend, if you cross the bridge over the creek in your car, you will hear the sound of the baby crying. In addition, if you stop and park, your windows will fog over in a matter of seconds and baby footprints will appear on the windshield.

Needless to say, I was anxious to experience this and made a trip to Loraine one night and found the creek outside of town. I waited until late in the evening and then parked my car on the bridge. It was a cool, damp night in November and I waited on the bridge for about an hour with my car window cracked open, straining to hear the sound of the baby. It took a lot longer than "a matter of seconds" but eventually, my windshield fogged over and I watched for the footprints to appear. But there was no crying that night --- and no "baby footprints" either.

My next expedition took me to the Illinois town of Canton in search of another

Crybaby Bridge. In this case, which occurred in the early 1900's, a young woman threw her newborn baby into a local creek and watched it drown. Those who dare go to the bridge that crosses this creek today will hear the sound of the baby crying in the darkness but the person I heard the story from hinted at darker things that might occur too. "Don't get out of your car if it breaks down on the bridge," she told me. "Bad things happen to those who do. If you should break down, lock the doors, roll up the windows and don't get out of the car. And oh yeah, don't ever go there alone!"

So, one spring evening, I drove to Canton ---- alone --- and followed the directions that I had been given to Blackjack Road, where the bridge was located. I followed 11th Avenue north out of Canton and turned right on Cypress away from town. It eventually turned onto a gravel road, which was Blackjack Road, and I found the bridge. I had been assured, by my witness (and others) that the bridge was legitimately haunted and I could understand her nervousness about the location after I arrived there. The bridge is located in a pretty remote and secluded area and not surprisingly, there were no streetlights anywhere around. I had planned my trip to arrive at just a little before midnight, which was the time when the cries were supposed to be heard. I waited for almost two hours but the mysterious cries never materialized.

A year later, I tracked down another story near Cherry Valley. This one involved the creepily-named Bloods Point Road and a bridge that crossed high over some railroad tracks. According to the story (which had no basis in history), a school bus full of children plunged off the bridge many years ago, killing everyone on board. I was told that if you put your car in neutral, while sitting in the middle of the bridge, your car would roll to safety on the other side of it. I drove out to the bridge with some friends one night and we parked the car in the center and shifted into neutral. We waited for about 20 minutes and then ------ nothing happened. We waited around for another hour or so but this Crybaby Bridge variation also failed to produce anything that could not be explained.

A few years later though, I had much greater success on another bridge --- or at least success of a sort. This particular bridge was located outside of the northern Illinois town of Monmouth and I investigated it with a group of students from Knox College in Galesburg. The students had heard about a rural bridge where a group of teenagers had been killed in an accident many years before. The driver had been drunk and accidentally steered his vehicle, filled with a number of friends, off into the river. All of them had died --- but did not rest in peace. According to the local legends, and to those who had personally experienced it, if you parked your automobile on the bridge and placed it in neutral, the ghosts of the dead teenagers would push you across it to safety.

Enthused by the chance to experience this oddity, the students took me out to the bridge one cold February night when I was at Knox College giving an annual lecture on the paranormal. We arrived that snowy night and traveled down a long and curving hill to the edge of the bridge. I parked my car and when I was sure that we

159

were at a complete stop, I shifted into neutral and waited for the ghostly hands to push us to the other side.

Within a few moments, the car began to move!

I stayed behind the wheel and steered the car as we crossed the bridge and then went down a short hill to the roadway. We were all excited by what had happened and I ran back to take another look at the bridge. It certainly appeared to be level and I couldn't, at first glance, see any reason why the car would have rolled on its own from a complete stop.

That's what I thought at first anyway.... I decided to look a little closer and with help from the students, took some measurements of the bridge and then got out a basic carpenter's level to make sure that the bridge was not angled at all. I was disappointed to learn that the bridge only looked level. Even though a hill led down to the entrance to the bridge, it did not appear, to the naked eye, that the slope continued across the span. According to the carpenter's level though, the bridge actually angled downhill. This would certainly account for the seemingly inexplicable movement of the car. What had seemed like a great story was now just another "wild goose chase".

Haunted Railroad Crossings

I continued to be undeterred by my failures after that cold winter's night and stayed on the look-out for other bridges that seemed to defy the laws of physics. As the search went on, I found other variations on the Crybaby Bridge legend that veered away from bridges and onto railroad tracks and crossings. In this variation, a railroad crossing would be the scene of an accident or murder where children or students were killed. If a visitor parked at the crossing, he would find that his car was pushed through the crossing by invisible means. According to one legend that I tracked down, which took place on Munger Road near Bartlett, visitors were instructed to also dust the back of the car with baby powder. After the car was pushed over the railroad tracks, the handprints of a boy who was killed by a train at the crossing would appear in the powder.

I soon discovered that this was a familiar theme to the "haunted railroad crossing" stories and went in search of other spots where ghostly children were supposed to help drivers over railroad tracks.

The first one that I sought out was in Kankakee in 1999. The legend had it that a train had killed a busload of children one day (it didn't) on the tracks when the bus stalled as it was making the crossing. Witnesses claimed that since that day, when you pass over the train tracks at night, you can hear the sound of children laughing. It's been said that some have stopped their cars on the tracks and listened closely. In addition to the sound of the children, they have also supposedly heard the sound of a phantom train approaching. Within moments, their cars started to move slowly off the tracks, as though it was being pushed to safety. Those who have tried this, I was told, have found small handprints on their car trunks afterward.

A similar story was told in Wayne, west of Chicago, where I carried out an investigation of the railroad crossing in 2001. In this version of the story, a woman was driving over the tracks with a car filled with children. The car stalled just as she was crossing the tracks. She was preoccupied with cranking the engine and didn't realize that a train was coming around the curve. When she finally heard the warning, she tried to get the kids out of the car but it was too late. The engine slammed into the car and killed everyone but the mother, who was miraculously thrown to safety.

160

The legend states that if you park your car over the tracks at night, the children who died in the accident will try and push the car over the tracks. Those who check their trunk afterwards will find that small handprints have somehow appeared on the car.

Fascinated with the story (I knew of a similar one in San Antonio, Texas), I made arrangements with a couple of friends to go with me to Wayne and check out the tracks. By asking at a couple of gas stations and convenience stores in town, we managed to pinpoint the location of the railroad crossing in question and scouted it out before it got dark. The crossing was located in a quiet part of town, where we were pretty sure we wouldn't be bothered, and after making plans, we went to get something to eat. We went back to the crossing after dark and parked the car near-by. We planned to follow the directions as we had been given them but wanted to "dust" my sport utility vehicle with baby powder first. If the ghostly handprints actually appeared, we wanted to be sure they could be clearly seen.

After photographing the clean surface, we covered the back of the car with a light layer of baby powder. One of my friends stayed off to the side of the tracks to take photos and my other assistant and I climbed in and drove onto the tracks. We turned off the engine, shifted it into neutral and then waited for something to happen. The crossing looked level to the naked eye but we had held off on taking measurements until after we saw what would happen. As with many of these locations, the car slowly began to move. It rolled forward, just as it would have if it were pushed, and crossed to the other side of the tracks.

Paranormal? Unfortunately, it wasn't. After checking the crossing with carpenter's levels (as I had done with the bridge near Monmouth), we determined that it was sloped toward the opposite side. The crossing looked level but it wasn't, which was why cars had been reported rolling across it for years. No ghosts here, we decided.

Disappointed, we stood around talking for a few minutes at the back of the car and then suddenly, one of my friends gasped and urged us to come and take a look at something. We hurried over to where he was standing and saw what he was looking at. Scattered across the back of the car, clearly visible in the baby powder that we had spread there, were a number of eerie-looking handprints! Could there be more to this railroad crossing than we thought?

Very excited now, we grabbed our cameras and began snapping photos of the "ghostly" handprints that had mysteriously appeared on the car. We knew that no one had been near the car after we had dusted it with the powder and our friend could vouch for the fact that no one had pushed it through the rail crossing. There was no explanation for how the handprints had appeared on the car --- or was there?

As I looked at the handprints closely, I realized that the size of them seemed familiar. For one thing, they were much too large to be the handprints of children, but what else could they be? Out of reflex, and over the cries of protest from my friends, I reached out and placed my own hand over one of the phantom prints --- it was a perfect match. The handprints were mine! But how did it happen? I knew that I had not touched the car after we had spread the powder over it, so how did my prints manage to wind up on it? I soon came to the realization that the baby powder had only enhanced the prints that were already there. The natural oils of my skin had left prints on the car during normal use. My opening and closing of the rear door of the SUV had naturally left my handprints on it. The prints were largely invisible --- until we had dusted the back with the powder. After that, the prints could suddenly be seen.

The mystery of the "ghostly handprints" had been solved!

Although a lot of people (much smarter ones!) would have given up looking for authentic bridges and railroad crossings by this time, I never stopped looking. This is why I was so excited when I heard about the so-called "Albino Railroad Tracks" that are located between the small Illinois towns of Mascoutah and Belleville.

I was assured by a number of people that these railroad tracks were an authentic anomaly but as the reader can attest, I'd heard that one before. To make matters worse, the legend connected to them did not offer a lot of hope. As with the other bridges and railroad tracks that I had run across, the story behind the railroad crossing involved horrific deaths and helpful spirits that aided motorists in making it across the tracks to the other side. One thing that I had to admit was that this story was a little bit more original than most of the others.

The legend actually had several variations to it but all of them included the story that the railroad tracks were the scene of a terrible accident in the late 1800's. In one of the stories, several small children from a local farm decided to take the family horse and wagon for a drive one afternoon without their parent's permission. They were crossing the railroad tracks as they neared their home but the wagon got stuck on the rails with a train coming a short distance away. No matter how hard they tried to get the wagon to move, they were unable to escape in time and the train killed all of them. There is a small cemetery, a few miles away from the railroad crossing and near the family's farm, that contains only the graves of the children who died in the accident.

Another version of the legend describes how the railroad crossing came to be called the "Albino Tracks". This story also takes place in the late 1800's when a pair of albino twins was born to a local farm family near the small railroad village of Rentchler Station. The birth was an amazing oddity and sparked a lot of gossip in the area. Coincidentally, shortly after the twins were born, an epidemic broke out in the surrounding community and several people died. Some of the more superstitious residents came to believe that the albinos were to blame for the sickness. The infants were taken from their home and then abandoned on the railroad tracks in hopes that a passing train would run them over and free the community from its afflictions. The albinos were killed on the spot and ever since that time, they have haunted the railroad crossing. Of course, it has never been clear as to whether they are trying to help or hinder the cars that cross the tracks. Some believe they are assisting people who cross the tracks, so that they don't get hit by a train, but others insist they are looking for revenge - hoping to push the autos into the path of an oncoming locomotive.

No matter what version of the story that you accept, the common thread of each variation is that spirits lurk here at the tracks, pushing cars from one side of it to the other. Some witnesses have claimed that the sound of gravel crunching under invisible feet can often be heard and that small handprints will sometimes appear in the dust on the back of the car. They are said to be the prints of the children as they push the cars over the tracks.

One witness to the weird happenings at the Albino Tracks had a pretty frightening story to tell. "I went to high school in Mascoutah," he explained, "and my friends and I went to check out the tracks one night for ourselves. We drove out there and did exactly what we had been told. And it did happen! The car was in neutral but it 'rolled' over the 'tracks'. We freaked out! I put the car into drive and took off!"

The teenagers drove quickly away and a short distance down the road came to what looked like an old schoolhouse. In the story they had heard, the schoolhouse had been attended by the children who had been killed in the wagon accident (first version of the story). They stopped at the school house and "just for laughs", the driver turned off the car and they sat there in the dark for a few minutes.

"All of the sudden, we heard laughing, like from a lot of kids, and something banging on the car like it was being hit with fists," he recalled. "Of course, we panicked and I couldn't get the car started right away. Finally, I did and we took off! I was 17 and haven't been back there since. We didn't find any handprints on the car but we couldn't deny the sounds we heard that night when we went out to the old railroad tracks. We just weren't prepared for what else we would find."

The old railroad crossing where the "Albino Tracks" were once located

Perhaps most compelling to me was the fact that the Albino Tracks were no sloping bridge, like the site that I had encountered near Monmouth. According to every witness, automobiles here were somehow pushed uphill to get to the other side of the crossing! I was told that investigations conducted here had involved excavating the site and testing it for magnetic fields to see if this could be the answer as to how it worked. I became determined to see this phenomenon for myself.

The Albino Tracks are located off of Rentchler Road, between Belleville and Mascoutah. This is a rural area of farm roads, field and woods and is too secluded and isolated for the casual tourist. I spent quite a bit of time getting good directions to the site and was finally able to find out where it was. I struck out one afternoon in the company of my daughter, Maggie, who was two years-old that summer, and we tracked down the railroad crossing.

The rail line that once crossed the roadway is gone now. The line had belonged to the Louisville & Southern Railroad but it was taken out years ago. I had been assured though that this does not prevent the mysterious happenings from taking place. I was told to pull over where the tracks used to be and go down the road until I came to a "dead end" sign on the other side of the old crossing. Turn the car around, I was instructed, put it in neutral and then wait as it gets pushed uphill and over the tracks.

I drove along the country back roads until I reached Rentchler Road and then turned past a house that was located at the site of what was once the small town's hotel. I traveled west on the road for a short distance, past an abandoned tavern, and then spotted the weather beaten "dead end" sign that I had been told about. It was over on the far side of the small hill that used to be the railroad tracks. This was the spot where the albinos were said to push cars along the roadway. I didn't waste any time driving my truck across the former tracks and when I got to the other side, I turned around and faced back toward the missing tracks. I pushed the gear shift into the neutral position and waited for the mysterious to occur. The truck paused for a few moments and then amazingly, it started to move! I couldn't believe it but the truck actually rolled forward a few feet, going uphill, and eased over the rail bed to

163

the other side. We picked up speed as the vehicle edged onto the downhill slope and I had to apply the brakes to keep from rolling out into the crossroads.

I couldn't believe what we had experienced! Maggie was not as impressed but was excited when I got her out of the truck after turning the vehicle around and heading it toward the rail crossing again. After pulling my daughter out of her car seat, she patiently watched as I measured the crossing, took photographs and then pulled out my trusty carpenter's level to see if the crossing was merely a trick of the eye. Could the rail crossing look like it was sloped even though it really wasn't? Hard to believe (especially for me) but this was not the case ---- the railroad crossing was a pretty sharp uphill climb and somehow my truck had defied gravity when it went over the tracks.

I was now determined to see this happening from outside of the vehicle and so Maggie and I stood back to watch after I had put the truck in neutral and waited for it to move again. I stood there at the edge of the road, with Maggie on my shoulders, and we waited --- and we waited. The truck sat there, smoothly idling but sitting absolutely still. This time, it didn't move at all. What in the world was happening now?

Puzzled about what to do next, I opened up the driver's side door and plopped Maggie down on the front seat. I wanted to take a look around the truck and couldn't do it with her in my arms. Not surprisingly, she was pleased to be able to play with the wheel for a minute and I closed the door so there would be no chance of her falling out. Then, breaking every rule of parenting, I walked to the back of the truck, curious to see whether it would move if I gave it a little shove to get it started. Before I could lay a finger on it though, the truck slowly began to move, again rolling up the hill and over the rail crossing!

Torn between the fact that I was witnessing another unexplained event and the fact that my two year-old daughter was now steering the truck, I hesitated for only a moment before running up to the driver's door and stopping the truck from going any further. Maggie seemed irritated with my decision.

She quickly warmed up to me though after I let her sit on my lap and navigate the railroad crossing a few more times. Each time we tried, the truck rolled right over the tracks, just as it did the first time.

I can't tell you for sure why it happened. Some have suggested that perhaps the magnetic properties of the site only seem to react when there is a person inside of the vehicle, giving off some sort of energy or electrical field. Others have been a bit more fanciful. They believe that the site may be truly haunted and that the spirits of the children who are present caused the truck to move whenever Maggie was inside of it. Were the ghosts of the children trying to protect another child by making sure the vehicle never stopped on the railroad crossing?

Who knows? I have come to discover that the "truth" in locations like this can sometimes be as elusive as the mystery spots themselves. But no matter what I experienced here, I hope that the adventurous reader will make an effort to discover this unusual spot on his or her own. Ghostly children and spectral albinos or not, the old tracks are a part of the mystery of Illinois that I would hate to see anyone miss out on.

13. GHOSTS!

Chasing Haunts at the Waverly Hills Sanatorium with Troy Taylor & Len Adams

One of the first questions that people ask me when they learn what I write about for a living is whether or not searching for real ghosts ever scares me. For a very long time, I assured them that I was never frightened during these outings to haunted places and for the most part this was true. My reply would have to change though after I not only experienced Waverly Hills Sanatorium for the first time but saw an actual full-figured apparition for the first time as well!

Readers of my book *Confessions of a Ghost Hunter* will recall that I first saw a ghost (after years of researching the paranormal) in July 2001. While visiting a haunted farm in northwest Indiana, another ghost hunter and I experienced something that had never happened to either of us before. After spending several hours at the farm, which had a long history of strange happenings, disappearing objects, unexplained sights and sounds and anomalous photos, the other investigator, Rob Johnson, and I ended up in the barn. The evening had been largely uneventful but we decided to stake out the barn to see if anything strange occurred. Rob, along with my friends Tom and Michelle Bonadurer, had been to the farm before and had already recorded some weird incidents in the old building.

We had been in the building for about 40 minutes when we heard a loud noise that sounded like a "groan". It startled both of us and we had just recovered when, just seconds later, the foyer of the barn was filled with a brilliant white light. As we stood there looking, the area around the locked door filled with light, just as if someone had walked into the barn with a lantern. The light seemed to draw itself through the wall of the foyer and it entered the first horse stall in the barn. As it did so, the foyer grew dark and the stall was filled with light. It was about the same size as a person and roughly the same height. The light was so bright that it cast a glow toward us, lighting up the entire area around it, banishing the notion that it could be a person with a light in his hand. It then shimmered and entered the next stall. It moved at the speed of a fast walk, passing through the wall of each stall, one after another, all of the way along the length of the barn and out the back wall. At that point, the light vanished, plunging the interior of the barn into complete darkness.

We spent hours trying to explain away the weird encounter and after eliminating every possibility, we were left with nothing but to accept the fact that we had come face-to-face with one of the farm's resident ghosts. In all of the years that I had spent writing about ghosts before that, I had experienced many strange things but I had never actually seen a ghost. A couple of years later, I would see another and it would not be until that time that I would ever be as genuinely frightened during an investigation as I was on that night at Waverly Hills.

A DARK NIGHT AT WAVERLY HILLS

During the 1800's and early 1900's, America was ravaged by a deadly disease known by many as the "white death" --- tuberculosis. This terrifying and very contagious plague, for which no cure existed, claimed entire families and sometimes entire towns. In 1900, Louisville, Kentucky had the highest tuberculosis death rate in America. Built on low swampland, the area was the perfect breeding ground for disease and in 1910, a hospital, designed to combat the horrific disease, was constructed on a windswept hill in southern Jefferson County. The hospital quickly became overcrowded though and with donations of money and land, a new hospital was started in 1924.

The new structure, known as Waverly Hills, opened two years later in 1926. It was considered the most advanced tuberculosis sanatorium in the country but even then, most of the patients succumbed to the disease. In those days before medicine was available to treat the disease, it was thought that the best treatment for tuberculosis was fresh air, plenty of nutritious food and lots of rest. Many patients survived their stay at Waverly Hills but, while records have been lost, it is estimated that tens of thousands died here at the height of the epidemic.

In many cases, the treatments for the disease were as bad as the disease itself. Some of the experiments that were conducted in search of a cure seem barbaric by today's standards but others are now common practice. Patient's lungs were exposed to ultraviolet light to try and stop the spread of bacteria. This was done in "sun rooms", using artificial light in place of sunlight, or on the roof or open porches of the hospital. Since fresh air was thought to also be a possible cure, patients were often placed in front of huge windows or on the open porches, no matter what the season. Old photographs show patients lounging in chairs, taking in the fresh air, while literally covered with snow.

Other treatments were less pleasant --- and much bloodier. Balloons would be surgically implanted in the lungs and then filled with air to expand them. Needless

166

to say, this often had disastrous results, as did operations where muscles and ribs were removed from a patient's chest to allow the lungs to expand further and let in more oxygen. This blood-soaked procedure was seen as a "last resort" and few of the patients survived it.

While the patients who survived both the disease and the treatments left Waverly Hills through the front door, the majority of patients left through what came to be known as the "body chute". This enclosed tunnel for the dead led from the hospital to the railroad tracks at the bottom of the hill. Using a motorized rail and cable system, the bodies were lowered in secret to the waiting trains. This was done so that patients would not see how many were leaving the hospital as corpses. Their mental health, the doctors believed, was just as important as their physical health.

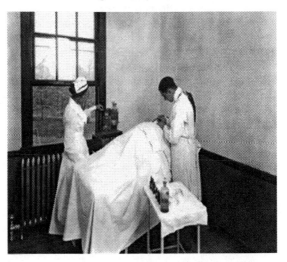

(Above) A staged display of one of the bloody treatments used on tuberculosis patients. (Below) Patients making the best of life at Waverly Hills
(U of L Archive Photos)

By the late 1930's, tuberculosis had begun to decline around the world and by 1943, new medicines had largely eradicated the disease in the United States. In 1961, Waverly Hills was closed down but was re-opened a year later as Woodhaven Geriatrics Sanitarium. There have been many rumors and stories told about patient mistreatment and unusual experiments during the years that the building was used as an old age home. Some of them have been proven to be false but others have unfortunately turned out to be true. Electroshock therapy, which was considered to be highly effective in those days, was widely used for a variety of ail-

ments. Budget cuts in the 1960's and 1970's led to both horrible conditions and patient mistreatments and in 1982, the state closed the facility for good.

Is it any wonder, after all of the death, pain and agony within these walls, that Waverly Hills is considered to be one of the most haunted places in the country?

The buildings and land were auctioned off and changed hands many times over the course of the next two decades. By 2001, the once stately building had been nearly destroyed by time, the elements and the vandals who came here looking for a thrill. Waverly Hills had become the local "haunted house" and it became a magnet for the homeless, looking for shelter, and teenagers, who broke in looking for ghosts. The hospital soon gained a reputation for being haunted and stories began to circulate of resident ghosts like the little girl who was seen running up and down the third floor solarium; the little boy who was spotted with a leather ball; the hearse that appeared in the back of the building dropping off coffins; the woman with the bleeding wrists who cried for help and others. Visitors told of slamming doors, lights in the windows as if power was still running through the building, strange sounds and eerie footsteps in empty rooms.

It was at this time that the hospital came to the attention of my friend, Keith Age, and the Louisville Ghost Hunter's Society. Keith was a long-time friend of mine and a representative for the American Ghost Society in Louisville. It would be his work with a television show that would bring him to Waverly Hills. He had been inside of the place years before but in 2001, he returned to scout the place out and to see what damage had been done during the years it had been empty. In addition to looking at the broken windows and the trash left behind by vandals, he and members of his group also came looking for ghosts.

They decided to explore the morgue wing first. As they walked along an almost pitch dark hallway, the electromagnetic field meter that Keith carried with him began clicking. Moments later, it was jumping off the scale. This type of meter, usually called an EMF meter, is one of the main pieces of equipment used in ghost research. It is believed that ghosts are made up of energy and that when present, they disrupt the electromagnetic fields of a location. EMF meters are used to detect this disturbance and can be a good indicator that something anomalous is present, especially in a building like Waverly Hills, which had no artificial interference from power lines.

The meter that Keith carried pointed to the fact that whatever was causing a disturbance was moving and he followed the signal to a small room that was cut in half by a low cinder-block wall. As he walked into the center of the room, the meter in his hand spiked to the top of the scale and let out a high-pitched squeal. The needle on the meter pegged to the top of the scale and then made a loud cracking noise, stopping the needle at the highest reading. The squealing noise ceased but the meter actually started to get warm in Keith's hand. In fact, it got so hot that the solder actually melted on the circuit board! Keith later gave this meter to me so that I could look it over. I passed it on to a distributor that I purchase this type of equipment from and he had absolutely no explanation for how this could have happened. The only way that it could have melted in this manner, he explained to me, was if the meter had been exposed to incredible heat. However, the casing of the meter was not damaged --- only the inside of the meter, which measured the amount of magnetic energy had melted down.

Moments after the meter heated up in Keith's hands, he and the others suddenly realized that the room around them was getting quite cold. It was a hot summer evening and while the concrete and stone building was a little cooler than outside, the concrete could not explain a temperature drop of more than 20 degrees! The chill soon dissipated, disappearing with as little explanation as it had come, and the investigators left the building to get another EMF meter and to look over the hospital's floor plan. Keith was shocked to discover that the room where the weird incidents had occurred was where electroshock therapy had been carried out during the Woodhaven years.

After going back into the building, the group continued to explore the place and was greeted with other unexplainable encounters. One of the legends told of Waverly Hills involves a man in a white coat who has been seen walking in the kitchen and the smell of cooking food that sometimes wafts through the room. The kitchen was a disaster, a ruin of broken windows, fallen plaster, broken tables and chairs and puddles of water and debris that resulted from a leaking roof. The cafeteria had not fared much better. It was also in ruins and the team quickly retreated. Before they could do so though, several of them reported the sounds of footsteps, a door swinging shut and the smell of fresh baked bread in the air. A quick search revealed that no one else was in the building and there was certainly no one cooking anything in the kitchen. They could come up with no logical explanation for what had occurred.

The exploration continued and the group found themselves on the fifth floor of the building. The fifth floor of the old hospital consisted of two nurses' stations, a pantry, a linen room, medicine room and two medium-sized rooms on both sides of the two nurses' stations. One of these, Room 502, is the subject of many rumors and legends and just about every curiosity-seeker that had broken into Waverly Hills over the years wanted to see it. This is where, according to the stories, people have jumped to their deaths, have seen shapes moving in the windows and have heard disembodied voices that order trespassers to "get out".

There is a lot of speculation as to what went on in this part of the hospital but what is actually known is that mentally insane tuberculosis patients were housed on the fifth floor. This kept them far away from the rest of the patients in the hospital but still in an area where they could benefit from the fresh air and sunshine. This floor is actually centered in the middle of the hospital and the two wards, extending out from the nurses' station, is glassed in on all sides and opens out onto a patio-type roof. The patients were isolated on either side of the nurses' stations and they had to go to a half door at each station to get their food and medicine and to use the restroom, which was located adjacent to the station.

In 1928, the head nurse in Room 502 was found dead in the room. She had committed suicide by hanging herself from the light fixture. She was 29 years-old at the time of her death and according to records, unmarried and pregnant. Her depression over the situation led her to take her own life. It's unknown how long she may have been hanging in this room before her body was discovered. And this would not be the only tragedy to occur in this room.

In 1932, another nurse who worked in Room 502 jumped from the roof patio and plunged several stories to her death. No one seems to know why she would have done this but many have speculated that she may have actually been pushed over the edge. There are no records to indicate this but rumors continue to persist.

When Keith and his group got to the fifth floor that night, they were accompanied by one of the owners of the building. They went into Room 502 and almost immediately, the EMF meter picked up something unusual. Even stranger, the temperature in the room suddenly jumped up from 86 to 98 degrees! It continued to climb so high that the group actually retreated from the room. The owner wanted to see what was going on and so they cautiously went back into the room --- just in time to see the temperature drop down to 68 degrees. Just as strangely, a few moments later, the temperature climbed back up to normal. Keith searched the room to see what could have caused the weird reactions of the meter and what might have made the temperature change so abruptly but there was nothing to explain it.

The group from the Louisville Ghost Hunters Society left the hospital that night intrigued but completely unaware of just how Waverly Hills was going to overwhelm them in the years to come. Over the course of the next few years, they would introduce the sanatorium to a national television audience, hold two ghost conferences here and spend scores of thankless hours taking literally thousands of people through the building on more haunted tours than they could begin to count. They would also, during independent investigations and tours, experience numerous incidents of paranormal activity.

During a less than five year period, Keith Age and other members of the Louisville Ghost Hunters Society experienced ghostly sounds, heard slamming doors, saw lights appear in the building when there should have been none, had objects thrown at them, were struck by unseen hands, saw apparitions in doorways and corridors and more. But none of the stories that I had been told could have prepared me for my first visit to Waverly Hills.

Len's Waverly Hills Account:

Before Troy recounts his first visit to Waverly Hills, I wanted to tell you about my own. In September 2004, I had the opportunity to visit this place, regarded as one of the most haunted sites in America.

The Waverly Hills Sanatorium opened in 1926 in Louisville, Kentucky. A hospital was desperately needed to fight an American plague, tuberculosis. This dreaded disease took the life of thousands of people. In 1943, Albert Schatz of Rutgers University discovered Streptomycin. Finally, a cure was at hand. By 1961, the disease was eradicated and Waverly Hills closed its doors, but, not for long. The massive structure reopened in 1962 as the Woodhouse Geriatrics Sanitarium. The death and disease of the past could not hold a candle to the depravity of this now mental institution. Horrible experiments and patient abuse soon took its toll. Thousands of defenseless patients suffered an agonizing demise. The State of Kentucky shut down the place in 1982.

Several individuals have owned the place since then. One owner wanted to build the world's largest statue of Jesus at the site. He was able to have every building on the property torn down, except the main hospital, before he was stopped. The hospital was on the National Historic Register's "endangered" list. The owner then decided that if he could have the building condemned, he would then be able to tear it down. From a combination of his dream for the site, and vandals, the once majestic building sat in a sad state.

New owners took over the property in 2001. That's when Keith Age and The Louisville Ghost Hunters' Society joined in the effort to save the Waverly. Over the years, they've held conferences and tours of the hospital. Their time and efforts have helped raise many dollars for the restoration of the building and although this has not always been appreciated in the way that it should be, they have been largely responsible for the fact that the old hospital still stands.

In September 2004, Luke, Matt, Bill, Kim and I went to the conference in Louisville. We were planning to meet up with Troy, who was a guest speaker at the event. We were up early the next morning and soon arrived at the place.

The Waverly Hills Sanatorium sits atop a hill, with a long and winding road for access. Our first trip there would take our breath away. We were wondering if we'd even find the place as we drove the long, narrow back road. Suddenly, as we drove through the front gate, we were awestruck by what we saw. In a large clearing, atop the hill, stood Waverly Hills. I can only compare it in scope to seeing a shot of the hotel used for the movie, *The Shining*. The structure was massive!

For all of its former glory though, it was immediately clear to all that this building had seen better days. Doors and windows were missing, debris was piled everywhere, and graffiti was on almost every wall.

By 9:15, we had located Troy and spent the rest of the day helping him with book sales, listening to speakers, and meeting many new people, including the group from the LGHS. Keith and his group were all dressed in black and, quite frankly, could've passed for a motorcycle gang ---- but looks can be deceiving. The Louisville Ghost Hunter's Society, to a person, are some of the nicest people you will ever meet.

By the time that dinner rolled around, we were starving. The huge, outside barbeque took care of that. Just before we started eating, our little group gathered at a picnic table at the end of the grounds. As we were admiring some raccoons who were thinking about joining us, a young man appeared out of nowhere, coming to stand next to Troy.

He asked Troy if he was indeed "the famous Troy Taylor". The young man couldn't have been older that 22 or 23. His clothes were something out of the late 70's. He had black, slicked down hair, thick glasses, a purple shirt with large collar, tight sweater-vest and polyester pants. Troy admitted that he was "Troy Taylor" (leaving off the 'famous' part) and the young man's next series of questions caught us all off guard.

He next wanted to know if Troy was the paranormal investigator from the movie *The St. Francisville Experiment*. Troy said yes and then joked about the guy not being able to get his money back, his usual quip to apologize for the movie being so bad. We all laughed but the kid just stood there, stone-faced. His final question sent chills running up and down our spines. He wanted to know if the psychic girl in the film was okay. When the hand reached out of the mirror for her, was she all right? Did she escape? Evidently, the line between fantasy and reality was totally blurred for him. Troy politely said that she was fine, not bothering to explain that it was just a movie and not real. The guy would not be interested in hearing that. Troy's answer made this guy happy. He trotted off to sit at a table that had an open chair. Eerily though, he spent the rest of the meal not really eating. He just sat and stared our way, apparently fixated on Troy. When I say we're more afraid of the living, than the dead, I'm not kidding!

After dinner, Luke, Matt ,Bill, Kim and I became Troy's "posse", his bodyguards. Whenever the young man tried to approach Troy, we would divert his attention so that Troy could move to another location. We didn't know what the guy was capable of and we didn't want to find out!

Finally, after being at the conference since 9:00 a.m., we were ushered into the building. It was now 11:00 p.m. and we were exhausted. Luke and Matt fell asleep on the floor of the cafeteria as we were given a lecture on spirit photography. Mercifully, at 11:45 p.m., we met our guide and went to our first destination. We were so excited about finally being able to investigate the hospital. But not yet..... Our first area to investigate was outside in the courtyard! It seemed like we were never meant to be in the Waverly.

At 12:30 in the morning, it was finally time to go back inside. As we stumbled along the dark path, I tripped over something in the road. Before I could warn anyone else, Kim tripped and took one heck of a spill. She ended up spraining her ankle and knee on her right leg. We had waited all day to see this place and she tried to grin and bear the pain in her knee. Within an hour though, the pain was too much. So I did what any caring, supportive husband would do ---- I put her in the van and

The door to infamous Room 502 at Waverly Hills

propped her leg up. No reason for me to leave, I was fine. Really, I'm not that bad. Troy was so tired by that time that he decided to call it a night and he dropped Kim off at our hotel. That left Luke, Matt, Bill and I to go it alone.

It turned out to be worth the wait. Every floor, every hallway, every room in the old building seemed to be alive with activity. It was now 4:00 a.m. and I was getting a little frustrated. Even though the numbers in our group kept dwindling, it was still hard for me to film. I was doing video, but kept getting everyone else's flashes from their cameras. By the fourth floor it was impossible to film, so I broke the one rule that we always live by, I left the group and struck out on my own.

I made my way to the fifth floor. It was smaller than the rest, so I couldn't get lost. As I wandered around, I came to room 502. I knew it was a nurse's station and that something was supposed to have happened there. I stepped in the room and started to film. After a couple of minutes, even though it wasn't too cold, I started to shake. I didn't know why, but I couldn't stop. Suddenly, a massive wave of fear struck me. Something was about to happen. I didn't know what and I couldn't stop it! Tears started flowing down my cheeks as the shaking became more violent. Feelings of depression and fear kept getting stronger and stronger. I tried to move but I was paralyzed. I had never been more scared in my life!

Whatever was happening to me was suddenly broken when Luke and Matt entered the room. All I heard was, " Hey, Len's in here. What's going on?" I fell back into the wall as the spell was broken. I rushed out of the room and into the hallway. For the next 10 minutes, I leaned against the wall shaking and crying. On gaining my composure, I re-entered the room, this time with some members of the group. It was now like every other room I had been in that night.

On further investigation, I found out that room 502 had supposedly seen quite a bit of tragedy. In 1928, a nurse was found hanging by the neck in station 502. She was 29 years old, unmarried and pregnant. In 1932, another nurse jumped, or was pushed, out the window and died on the pavement below.

If these stories are true, and they have left an impression at the location, I wondered if we could become part of the action. I don't mean that we could change anything. I just wonder if being in the area where a residual haunting is replaying itself can cause us to relive the feelings and emotions of those involved in that particular episode? If this is so, was I reliving the terror and dread of those that died in that room? During both incarnations of the building, the fifth floor was where the worst of the worst were kept. There had been so many traumas here and so many emotions.

As far as I'm concerned, the most valuable lesson from that night was to never,

ever, go anywhere investigating on your own. It's a rule I've stood by to this day.

See a Ghost --- My First Night at Waverly Hills
With Troy Taylor

As I mentioned previously, I first heard about the old hospital from Keith and he told me about the time that when they first got access to it. In fact, the meter that had been destroyed in the former electroshock therapy room had been purchased from my company and when I heard about what had happened to it, I asked Keith to return it to me. I then sent the meter to my distributor, who has been in business for more than a decade and is an expert on electromagnetic field meters, and asked him to look it over. He had never seen anything like the damage that had been done to the meter before ---- and he had no explanation for what could have caused it.

The first time that I visited the hospital was in September 2002. I was in town for the first Mid-South Paranormal Convention and one of the places that I asked Keith to show me in Louisville was Waverly Hills. I was already interested in the history of the place and had heard about the investigations that had been conducted there. I was anxious to see it and so Keith arranged a tour. It was literally a dark and stormy night when we arrived at the hospital and it had been raining all day. I was looking forward to seeing the place, no matter what the weather, and not because I was convinced that I would meet one of the former patients face to face--- it was simply to experience the place for myself. By this time, I had traveled all over the country and had been to hundreds of places that were alleged to be haunted. I had felt just this same way before exploring all of them, so Waverly Hills was no different. To me, it was just an old, spooky building with a fascinating history. The fact that it was alleged to be haunted simply added to the experience. I had long since abandoned the idea of going in expecting too much.

After meeting with the owners, Keith and I went inside and started our exploration of the building. The place was almost silent. All that I could hear was the sound of our own footsteps, our hushed voices and the drip of rain as it slipped through the cracks in the roof and splashed down onto the floor. Keith led me through the place and pointed out the various rooms, the treatment areas, the kitchen, morgue and on and on. We climbed the stairs to the top floor and I saw legendary Room 502, as well as the lights of Louisville as they reflected off the low and ominous-looking clouds that had gathered above the city.

During our excursion, I mentioned to Keith that there had been one floor that we had missed ---- the fourth floor. He explained that this was the only floor in the building whose entrance was kept locked and he had saved it for last. I remembered then some of the stories that had been passed on to me about this floor. Most of those who had spent much time here regarded the fourth floor as the most active --- and most frightening --- part of Waverly Hills.

The most unusual experience that I had heard about was when Keith was in one of the rooms here. He had been walking along the corridor of the fourth floor with an EMF detector and was followed by two members of his group with a video camera. He started to picking up readings with the meter and he was led into one of the former treatment rooms. The intensity of the magnetic energy in the room continued to increase and the strongest readings seemed to be in the southeast corner of the room. Keith was standing in the corner, looking at the changes on the meter scale, when an empty plastic soda bottle came seemingly out of nowhere and struck him in the back. As he turned to see what had happened, an overhead fluorescent light fixture suddenly came loose from the ceiling with a loud crack. With one end of it still anchored to the ceiling, the other end swung loose and hit Keith in the side of the head! The long burned-out bulb that remained in the fixture shattered when it collided with Keith and showered him with glass. Before he even had time to react, he heard the sound of a brick scrape across the concrete floor. The noise came from the opposite corner of the room and when he looked over, he saw the brick moving across the floor towards him. With a lurch, it shot into the air and directly at him! As he scrambled to get out of the line of fire, it hit him in the small of the back. Needless to say, he quickly retreated from the room. The other investigators had not seen where the brick or the soda bottle had come from, but they had clearly heard the brick move and had seen both objects strike Keith. This is still regarded as one of the most chilling events to occur in the building.

This would not be the only time that Keith would see an object move in the building either. I was present on one other occasion when it happened, along with a tour attendee and authors Alan Brown and Dave Goodwin. In September 2003, I returned to Louisville for another conference and that night, we took a group tour of the old hospital. As we were climbing the stairs and going past the fourth floor landing, the several of us at the front of the line clearly saw a heavy metal door open up a few inches and then slam shut under its own power. Keith was just a few feet away from it at the time and he jumped in surprise. No one had been near the door and at the time, the floor was still locked so there was no way that anyone could have gotten on it to manipulate the door.

A year earlier though, when I entered the fourth floor for the first time, I got the distinct feeling that something strange was in the air. I make absolutely no claims of any psychic ability whatsoever but there was just something about this floor of the hospital that felt different than any of the others. What had been nothing more than just an old ramshackle and broken down building suddenly seemed different. I can't really put into words what felt so strange about it but it almost seemed to be a tangible "presence" that I had not encountered anywhere else in the place. And, right away, eerie things started to happen.

We had entered the floor in what I believe was the center of the building. Behind us was a wing that I was told was not safe to enter. Sections of the floor had fallen in and this area was off-limits to tours and visitors. The strange thing about it was that both Keith and I clearly heard the sounds of doors slamming from this part of the building. I can assure the reader that it was not the wind either. The wind was not strong enough that night to have moved those heavy doors and this clearly sounded as though someone was closing them very hard. When I questioned Keith about who else could be up there with us, he explained to me about how unsafe the floors were in that section. I investigated on my own and determined that he was correct --- there was no one walking around on that part of the fourth floor.

As we started down the hallway, Keith told me about some of the other happenings that had been experienced by investigators on this floor. The experiences involved the strange shapes that had been seen. The sightings had started the previous October when, on consecutive nights, investigators were able to see what looked like human shadows moving up and down the fourth floor hallway. One of the shadows in particular actually appeared to look around corners at them and all of the shapes passed back and forth across the doorways. Keith added that sightings like this had occurred at other times as well and happened most often when no flashlights were used in the corridor.

The dark (and scary) hallway where Keith and I spotted the phantom figure

I switched off my flashlight and we walked down the corridor using only the dim, ambient light from outside. The hallway runs through the center of the building and on either side of it are former patient rooms. Beyond the rooms is the "porch" area that opens to the outside. It was here where the patients were placed to take in the fresh air. There was no glass ever placed in the huge outer windows, which has left the interior of the floor open to the elements ever since. On this night, the windows also illuminated the corridor, thanks to the low-hanging clouds that glowed with the lights of Louisville. We walked down through the dark and murky corridor and I began to see shadows that flickered back and forth. I was sure that this was a trick of the eye though, likely caused by the lights or the wind moving something outside and so I urged Keith on for a closer look. It was where the corridor angled to the right that I got a look at something that was definitely not a trick of the eye!

So that the reader can understand what I saw, I have to explain that the hallway ahead of us continued straight for a short distance and then turned sharply to the right. In the early 1900's, most institutions of this type were designed in this manner. It was what was dubbed the "bat-wing" design, which meant that there was a main center in each building and then the wings extended right and left, then angled again so that they ran slightly backward like a bird, or bat, wings. Directly at the angle ahead of us was a doorway that led into a treatment room. I only noticed the doorway in the darkness because the dim light from the windows beyond it had caused it to glow slightly. This made it impossible to miss since it was straight ahead of us.

We took a few more steps and then, without warning, the clear and distinct silhouette of a man crossed the lighted doorway, passed into the hall and then vanished into a room on the other side of the corridor! I got a distinct look at the figure and I know that it was a man and that he was wearing what appeared to be a long, white drape that could have been a doctor's coat. The sighting only lasted a few seconds but I knew what I had seen.

And for some reason, it shocked and startled me so badly that I let out a yell and grabbed a hold of Keith's jacket. I am not sure why it affected me in that way but perhaps it was the setting, the man's sudden appearance, my own anxiety --- or likely all of these things. Regardless, after my yell, I demanded that Keith turn on the light and that he help me to examine the room the man had vanished into. After my initial fright, I became convinced that someone else was on the floor with us. Keith assured me we were the only ones there but he did help me search for the intruder. There was no one there though. He was right. Whoever the figure had been, he had utterly and completely vanished.

I was not the first person to have seen this mysterious figure on the fourth floor and it's unlikely that I will be the last. However, for me, this put Waverly Hills into a unique category for there are not many places that I will firmly state are genuinely haunted. Before I can do that, I have to have my own unexplainable experience and hopefully, it will be something that goes beyond a mere "bump in the night" or spooky photograph. In this case, it was much more than that because I actually saw a ghost. In all of my years of paranormal research, I can count the times that I have seen ghosts on just two fingers and one of them was at Waverly Hills.

In this case, seeing really was believing.

So, There I Was....

AFTERWORD

BY LEN ADAMS

I hope you've found these few tales of the paranormal as entertaining, funny and scary as we did living them. The funny thing about this field of research is that the deeper you go, the hazier the lines become. Life is definitely gray, not black and white.

All the major religions believe in an afterlife. We won't really know about the other side until we make that journey ourselves. Maybe our endeavors can answer some of the questions. The problem is that the deeper I go into the field of the paranormal, the more questions I come up with.

I have found some things to be helpful in the field:

1. Have fun to help relieve the pressure. Be serious when it's time to be. Hopefully, you'll be as lucky as I've been to make many new friends along the way.

2. Make up your research team with both sexes. We are different and experience things differently. Cover all the bases.

3. Don't take out the human element of observation and feelings by becoming glued to all the cameras, tape recorders and other gadgets. There is so much going on around us that we tend to shut out our observation faculties. With the many tours, overnights and live theater that I do, I return home late on many a night. After making sure that the family's safe and sound, I like to just stand in the yard with the dog and gaze at the stars. It's something I've always done and it is quite relaxing. Remember, the world needs dreamers too!

4. Be respectful. Ghosts are just people without bodies. Most of the stuff you see on the television and at the movies just doesn't happen. 98% of the things you come across will not be demons from hell.

5. Perseverance pays off. Even if others believe you're nuts, hang in there.

6. Most importantly, trust your gut. If you are somewhere and it just doesn't feel right, get out. The voice in the back of your head might just be some psychic ability that I believe we all have. It's always fascinated me why animals and children seem to have many ghostly experiences. Then I realized that the children haven't been taught to put the walls of denial in front of them, like many adults have. Animals just see things the way they really are.

Be careful out there and, of course, happy hauntings.

BIBLIOGRAPHY & RECOMMENDED READING

Adams, Charles J. III - Philadelphia Ghost Stories (1998)
Age, Keith with Jay Gravatte & Troy Taylor - Waverly Hills Sanitorium (2004)
Asfar, Dan - Ghost Stories of Pennsylvania (2002)
Brehm, H.C. - Echoes of the Bell Witch in the Twentieth Century (1979)
Eastern State Penitentiary staff
Graham, Stephen & Kelly Burnell - www.theparanormalworld.net
Johnston, Normal - Eastern State Penitentiary: Crucible of Good Intentions (1994)
Lebanon Centennial Commission - Lebanon Illinois: History in a Nutshell (1974)
Lebanon Chamber of Commerce - A Pictorial View of Lebanon, Illinois
Linn, Darwin & Martha --- VIllisca Ax Murder House website (www.villiscaiowa.com)
Monroe, Dona - A History of the Looking Glass Playhouse, 1972-1990.
Night Visitors (Documentary - Impact TV / 2000)
Perrot, Mark - Hope Abandoned: Eastern State Penitentiary (1992)
Phillips, Ben - Eastern State Penitentiary: 140 Years of Reform (1996)
Roussin, Donald & Kevin Kious- William J. Lemp Brewing Company: A Tale of Triumph & Tragedy in St. Louis, Missouri - American Breweriana Journal (March-April 1999)
Sifakis, Carl - Encyclopedia of American Crime (1982)
Taylor, Troy - Confessions of a Ghost Hunter (2002)
Taylor, Troy - Haunted Alton (2003)
Taylor, Troy - Haunted Chicago (2003)
Taylor, Troy - Haunted St. Louis (2002)
Taylor, Troy - Haunting of America (2001)
Taylor, Troy - No Rest of the Wicked (2001)
Taylor, Troy - Season of the Witch (2003)
Walker, Stephen - Lemp: The Haunting History (1988)
Winer, Richard & Nancy Osborn - Haunted Houses (1979)
Winer, Richard - Houses of Horror (1983)
Winer, Richard & Nancy Osborn Ishmael - More Haunted Houses (1981)

Personal Interviews & Correspondence

SPECIAL THANKS To:

Kim Young (proofreading & editing services)
John Winterbauer
Bill Alsing
Luke Naliborski
Julie Warren
Steve Mangin

Matt & Kelly Blunt

Kim Adams
Megan Stroot
Josh Adams
Andrea Easlick

& Haven Taylor

ABOUT THE AUTHORS:

Troy Taylor is the author of 46 books about history, hauntings and the unexplained in America, including *Haunted Illinois*, *The Ghost Hunter's Guidebook*, *Weird Illinois* and many others. He is the founder and president of the "American Ghost Society", a national network of ghost hunters that collects stories of ghost sightings and haunted houses and uses investigative techniques to track down evidence of the supernatural.

He is the owner of the Illinois Hauntings Tours with ghost tours in Alton, Decatur, Chicago, Springfield, Lebanon & Jacksonville and the American Hauntings Tours, which offers haunted road trips and overnight excursions around the country.

Along with writing about the unusual and hosting tours, Taylor is also a public speaker on the subject of ghosts and hauntings and has spoken to literally hundreds of private and public groups on a variety of paranormal subjects. He has appeared in newspaper and magazine articles about ghosts and has also been fortunate enough to be interviewed hundreds of times for radio and television broadcasts about the supernatural. He has also appeared in a number of documentary films, several television series and in one feature film about the paranormal.

He currently resides in Central Illinois with his wife, Haven, in a decidedly non-haunted house.

Len Adams is the Vice-President, Chief of Operations and Investigation Coordinator of The American Ghost Society and lead guide for Troy Taylor's Alton Hauntings Tours in southwestern Illinois. He has been actively investigating ghosts for many years and currently handles the AGS investigations for most of downstate Illinois. This is his first book.

Adams has been hosting ghost tours in Alton for several years, as well as haunted overnights in Southern Illinois, and has also appeared in a number of newspaper articles about ghosts and hauntings. He has been interviewed numerous times for radio and television broadcasts about the paranormal and has been featured for several local news broadcasts. He has also served as a public speaker for private and public groups in St. Louis and the surrounding area.

Born in St. Louis and raised in southern Illinois, Len now resides in Belleville with his wife, Kim. His current house is "ghost free" but as he says --- "there's always hope".

WHITECHAPEL PRESS

Whitechapel Productions Press is a small publisher, specializing in books about ghosts and hauntings. Since 1993, the company has been one of America's leading publishers of supernatural books and has produced such best-selling titles as "Haunted Illinois", "The Ghost Hunter's Guidebook" and many others. With nearly a dozen different authors producing high quality books on all aspects of ghosts, hauntings and the paranormal, Whitechapel Press has made its mark with America's ghost enthusiasts.

You can visit Whitechapel Productions Press online and browse through our selection of ghostly titles, plus get information on ghosts and hauntings, haunted history, spirit photographs, information on ghost hunting and much more. by visiting the internet website at:

www.prairieghosts.com

Whitechapel Press is the headquarters for the Illinois Hauntings Tour Co, offering the following ghost tours:

Alton Hauntings Ghost Tours / Alton, Illinois
Created by Troy Taylor, these tours are an interactive experience that allow readers to visit the historically haunted locations of the city and can be booked every year from April through October.Hosted by Len Adams, Luke Naliborski & Troy Taylor --- **www.altonhauntings.com**

American Hauntings Tours
These tours offer Haunted Overnight Excursions to ghostly places around the Midwest and throughout the country. Available all year round! **www.illinoishauntings.com**

Weird Chicago Tours / Chicago, Illinois
The Alternative Tour of Chicago's Ghosts, Gangsters & Ghouls! The most authentic tours in the Windy City take visitors to Chicago's weirdest and most haunted sites! Available all year round! Hosted by Ken Berg, Adam Selzer & Troy Taylor **www.weirdchicago.com**

Springfield Hauntings Ghost Tours / Springfield, Illinois
Join us in the Prairie State's haunted Capital City for Springfield's only authentic ghost tours. Experience the hauntings of Abraham Lincoln, the Springfield Theater Center and much more! Available April through October and hosted by John Winterbauer ---- **www.springfieldhauntings.com**

Printed in the United States
77519LV00001B/26